Gerhart von Schulze-Gaevernitz, Oscar Standring Hall

The Cotton Trade in England and on the Continent

A Study in the Field of the Cotton Industry

Gerhart von Schulze-Gaevernitz, Oscar Standring Hall

The Cotton Trade in England and on the Continent
A Study in the Field of the Cotton Industry

ISBN/EAN: 9783337397418

Printed in Europe, USA, Canada, Australia, Japan

Cover: Foto ©ninafisch / pixelio.de

More available books at **www.hansebooks.com**

The Cotton Trade in England and on the Continent.

A STUDY IN THE FIELD OF THE COTTON INDUSTRY.

BY

Dr. G. von SCHULZE-GAEVERNITZ,

FREIBURG I. B.

TRANSLATED FROM THE GERMAN BY

OSCAR S. HALL, M. I. MECH. E., BURY.

LONDON:

SIMPKIN, MARSHALL, HAMILTON, KENT, AND CO., LTD.

MANCHESTER:

MARSDEN AND CO., LTD., CARR STREET.

1895.

CONTENTS.

TRANSLATOR'S PREFACE.

We live in troubled and momentous times. Discordant voices resound on every side. The social aspirations of daily bread toilers seem to many to be in direct antagonism to all existing and peaceful relations, to ultimate economical welfare. The upward striving of the masses appears to many minds to threaten the very core of whole industries, to sap their economical foundations. Capital is jealously and quietly putting on its armour; Labour is eagerly equipping itself for further fray and the defence of its already achieved position. Whatever be the outcome, there seems inevitably close at hand a period of suffering and privation for many—the unavoidable companion of transition from one economical stage to another. And if the result of the agitation should place this country at an economical disadvantage the battle will at no distant period be renewed, probably many steps retraced, and bring further discontent and distress in its train. It therefore behoves all parties to the struggle to study the question minutely, to weigh carefully all that can be said in each other's favour, all that can be brought forward to show lucidly the position which ought to be taken up for the economical welfare of the community in general.

Without committing myself to the whole of the positions taken up by Dr. G. von Schulze-Gaevernitz, I came to the conclusion whilst reading the work that within it lay the elements by which the future position of our whole industries and economical prosperity might be guided to a safe haven. It seemed to me that such an admirable work should be as widely distributed as possible: that many misleading and mischievous ideas—probably none the less due to honest conviction—would be dispersed by a careful perusal of the results of the Professor's patient, industrious inquiry and research. These were the reasons which induced me to undertake the translation. The results of my work—accomplished in leisure moments snatched from an active business life—in translating, I leave to the reader to judge and criticise leniently. I have tried to reproduce as simply as possible the exact meaning intended in the original. A few additions to the original work have been made by the author, and the whole book has undergone careful revision to bring it up to date.

Whatever be the merits or demerits of the translation, I trust it will be favourably received and carefully studied by all those who have the welfare of our industries, and especially the prosperity of the staple trade of Lancashire, at heart.

OSCAR S. HALL.

Bury.

INTRODUCTION.

BY THE EDITOR OF THE "TEXTILE MERCURY."

The student of industrial, political, and social matters, coming to the investigation of the developments of the 19th century, will find in these subjects ample material to engage the services of schoolsful of colleagues. In no preceding period was the ferment of material science, mechanical invention, industrial change, political revolution, and social progress so active as during the century now nearing its close. No time in the past can compare with it, and, so far as we can see, though the future centuries may have much in store, they are not likely to eclipse it in any similar period of time. It seems to us that it will be much more accordant with the natural sequence of events, if the past affords grounds for any safe inferences regarding the future, that a long period of comparative repose should follow one of such unprecedented activity. Such periods succeeded the collapse of the Roman Empire, the Crusades, and the Reformation, and intervened between the English Revolution of 1688 and the French uprising of a century later. In these intervals there was little of intellectual activity, and less of social and industrial progress, whilst science in its best sense had hardly been born. These facts form a basis for the above reasonable and natural conclusion. Should it be realised, the students will be able to work at their investigations of 19th century life and progress undisturbed by the noise of

contemporaneous disputes, the excitements of new scientific dis-
coveries, or the rapid spread of economic and social theories
that may contain within themselves the germs of social salvation
or destruction. We venture to predict that it will be the latter
phases of 19th century development which will excite the most
curious interest in the minds of future students of social progress,
because the factor that has been active amidst the numerous
causes contributing so very largely to the amelioration of the lot
of the human race—and under the influences of which it has
benefited so enormously, and yet is not satisfied—will to a large
degree be hidden from superficial inspection. At no period in
the history of mankind has the task of labour been so light, or
its reward so large and generous. And yet, notwithstanding
this, a wave of dissatisfaction with the new conditions seems,
during the past few years, to have spread over the industrial
world. This has been followed by the development of a feeling
of hostility to every one of the new and beneficent factors of
progress that have come into being during the century, which
threatens their destruction. Is the basis of this movement a
gross mental delusion—a hideous nightmare—which has taken
possession for a time of the intellectual nature of the industrial
classes, and from which we may hope that in an early time they
will shake themselves free? This is our impression. We need
not wonder that the phenomena to which we have referred are
beginning to engage the earnest and careful attention of inquirers
of high culture, independent thought, and philosophic minds,
and that these are making careful inquisition into the facts in
order to discover whether the popular impression is in any sense
justified, or whether it is the delusion we believe it to be. If the
former, it will be incumbent upon those responsible for the con-
duct of our political destinies to so guide the ship of State which
carries our affairs that it shall not run upon breakers whose

presence has thus clearly been pointed out. If the latter, it will be the duty of the investigators to so state the truths and conclusions to which they have been led as to dissipate the causeless fears and misconceptions now so widely entertained amongst our industrial classes, and more or less shared in by others in whom such a degree of intelligence prevails as might have been thought would have safeguarded them from the intrusions of philosophic heresies.

Amongst the foremost of the investigators of the industrial and social problems that confront society to-day is Dr. G. von Schulze-Gaevernitz, of Freiburg i.B., whose recent work on "Social Peace" commanded a great deal of attention in circles capable of appreciating it. It was patent on the face of the problem he set out to solve, if possible, that the industrial world is in a state of transition brought about by the introduction of mechanical appliances for the better performance of labour, and the consequent supersession of the mass of handicraft workers that had previously supplied the world's requirements. It was inevitable that in the reorganisation of the armies of labour on the new lines much friction should occur and much contention arise as to the equitable distribution of the profits of labour, owing to the shifting of the burden of the task from the man to the machine. These points form the crux of the industrial disputes, the frequent occurrence and repetition of which are inflicting such enormous losses upon communities at the present time that they are doing a great deal to destroy all the benefits that the world rationally expects to reap from the progress that has been made. The economic principles upon which profits are distributed have been called in question by the leaders of the workpeople, who are inciting them to repudiate them and to demand the substitution of others that, certainly on a first glance, do not present many commendable features. It is into the working of the existing principles, the equity of the allocation of profits under them, and the merits of the principles proposed to be substituted for them that inquiry must be made. Also to discover whether there is anything necessarily beneficial or the opposite in the organisation of machinery with human supervision, to produce on a large scale what was until the introduction of machinery perforce produced on a small scale by human labour alone. These are some of the phases of the problems which Dr. von Schulze-Gaevernitz has undertaken to investigate. The results of his inquiries in their several aspects he has placed before the world in his recent work on "Social Peace." He was so struck, however, by the phenomena presented in the origin, development, organisation, and social results attending the growth of the modern cotton industry—the parent of all mechanical industries—that he has preferred to treat this subject in a separate work, in order to do full justice to its teachings. This work was issued in Germany in the autumn of 1893, and immediately on its appearance the present writer, the editor of "The Textile Mercury," entered into communication with Dr. Schulze-Gaevernitz, with a view to its translation and reproduction in this country. The author immediately consented, and the work was therefore put in hand. Mr. Oscar S. Hall, M. I. Mech. E., of the old and well-known firm of machinists (Messrs. Robert Hall and Sons, Bury, Limited) of Bury, voluntarily undertook the work. Mr. Hall brought to the task exceptionally high qualifications in a thorough knowledge of German, acquired by residence in the country, and maintained and increased by frequent visits and an extensive commercial intercourse with it. To add to this, he is familiar with the history of the development of machinery in the cotton industry, and is a technical expert in all that relates to its present condition both at home and on the Continent. Few people could bring to the task a more extensive or perfect repertory of knowledge of the subject in these respects than did Mr. Hall. When we add that he possesses literary ability of a high order we have said all that is necessary to justify the statement that the author has been exceptionally fortunate in that the translation of his important work has fallen into such capable hands. We conclude these introductory remarks with one further observation. We have never yet been able to arrive at the conclusion that under any circumstances man could attain infallibility in his researches and conclusions; but even if we could have done so we should lack the infallible perception of discriminating the individual in which it reposed. This being the case, we desire to say that the author alone will be responsible for the opinions expressed. We say this in justice to Dr. Schulze-Gaevernitz and ourselves and the translator, and at the same time beg to express our appreciation of the high privilege he has so freely and fully accorded to " The Textile Mercury" of translating, publishing, and republishing this important contribution to the economic science of modern industry. The translation first appeared in " The Textile Mercury," from the pages of which it is now reproduced, and the editor bespeaks for it the careful perusal of those interested in the cotton trade, in social developments, and the favour of the public generally.

RD. MARSDEN.

CHAPTER I.

INTRODUCTORY.

In what relation does economical progress stand to the advancement of the working classes? What value has a higher or lower standard of living for the economical power development of a nation? These questions have long been subjects of controversy. There is certainly a development noticeable in the arguing of different opinions. One view was originally only opposed by few; as time went on this was universally vetoed by science, and the opposite opinion almost generally accepted, whilst the former view was still adhered to and defended only by a minority, especially by practical men in countries and in industries which have lagged behind in economics.

The discussion takes different phases at different periods. So long as wages maintained a normal fixed position the variation in the price of wheat was the deciding element for the standard of living of the working classes. It was therefore asked whether high or low prices of food were essential for the economical development of a nation. To which in England was added the further query, whether the State by means of legislative measures, and especially by bounties on the export of wheat, should or should not keep the prices of human necessaries high (1). But since, in this century, the fixing of wages by custom and law has disappeared, the question has been amended to whether low or high wages have to be viewed as an economical advantage for a country; whether economical progress—and in this connection we think at the present time principally about the development of the centralised industrial system (2)—means the elevation or retrogression of the classes in its service.

---

1. R. Faber: " Die Entstehung des Agrarschutzes in England " (Strassburg, 1888), pp. 112—114.

2. That is, the factory system.—*Translator.*

B

I. The history of the question under discussion extends back, like that of so many national economical teachings, to that great observer, Sir William Petty, who first deserves, if anyone at all, to be called the Father of National Economy. In his "Political Arithmetic" (London, 1691) Petty defends taxes upon foods, etc., which he maintained increased the wealth of a country. Besides taking the view that with prices of food high men invested their money in less perishable articles, he gives, in proof of this statement, the experience of weaving overlookers who employed workmen on day wages. If wheat was cheap, labour tended to be dearer in the same proportion, because in such times the workers were so extravagant and dissolute that they thought simply about eating and drinking. For this reason an abundant harvest was a misfortune for the people if the Government did not keep the price of wheat high. But in a special manner, according to Petty, did this relation apply to Ireland. In that country the standard of living was such a low one, particularly after the introduction of that "root similar to bread"— the potato—that two hours' daily labour sufficed to satisfy all ordinary needs. In order to stir up the Irish people from their laziness, a heavy system of taxation was requisite (3). In another place Petty also demands in the interests of economical progress that the conditions of living should be made harder for the people. The working hours of those times were 12 daily, including two hours' stoppage, therefore in reality 10 hours, and three meals daily were customary. Petty demands that the time for dinner should be reduced by half-an-hour, and that Fridays should be fasting days. Herewith, he says, the English people will become richer, and the income of the State would increase (4).

The most celebrated writers of that time were of the same opinion as Petty. Sir William Temple recommended the taxation of food in order to enforce general industry in Ireland (Works, vol. I., pp. 60, 114) (5). In a fertile country industry does not as a rule flourish, because the cheapness of food makes it possible

3. William Petty: " Political Arithmetic " (London, 1691), pp. 35, 42, 45
4. William Petty: " Political Survey of Ireland"(London,1719). "Verbum Sapienti," p. 12.
5. " I conceive the true original grounds of trade to be a great multitude of people crowded into a small compass of land, whereby all things necessary to life become dear, and all men who have possessions are induced to parsimony ; but those who have none are forced into industry and labour, or else to want."

for the worker to abstain from labour, and consequently tends to raise its price (6). Petty, as well as Temple and many others, pointed to the example and teaching of the Dutch. Indeed De Witt had already demanded high taxes in order to encourage an inventive spirit, industry, and frugality, as well as a strict poor-law, with bureaucratic reduction of wages (7).

This point of view is most minutely justified by John Houghton, in "A Collection of Letters for the Improvement of Husbandry and Trade" (London, No. 6, June 16th, 1683, p. 174). In consequence of several bad harvests the price of wheat at that time had considerably risen. The result, Houghton thought, was in no wise to be viewed as a disadvantage, but rather as an economical advantage. If the price of wheat was lower the poor would work less, because with less exertion they could earn the necessaries of life. This, he says, follows from general psychological observation. The landed nobility spend their time mostly in recreation and sports, instead of working, because they possess means for years to come—for eating, for drinking, and for maintaining themselves. Should, however, one of their circle come to grief, he immediately looks out for some public post and occupation. The rich tradesman retires from business when he has succeeded in entering the ranks of the landed gentry. The poor craftsman, on the other hand, who can never hope to call a fortune of £10 his own, scarcely takes the trouble to get 10s. into his hand at once. If he can earn sufficient in three days to live up to his usual standard for a week, he does not work the remaining four days. The same thing is true of the labourer, who does not work any more than is necessary to earn his bare livelihood. Instances were provided by lace and stocking makers. As soon as their wages were high they were seldom seen at their work on Mondays and Tuesdays, scarcely even on Wednesdays and Thursdays. They spent those days preferably in alehouses, and in low debauchery. With high wages and cheap prices of food the majority of workmen employed in the various trades followed the same course. On the other hand, never did they work so hard as in dear times. By their lack of means the invention of useful labour-saving machinery received

6. Compare A. Young: "The Farmers' Letters to the People of England" (London, 1768), p. 35, where, in the preface, a number of further adherents to this opinion are given.

7 Compare "Essays on Trade and Commerce" (London, 1770), p. 49.

an immediate impetus; by their deep poverty "submissive servants" were formed from the working classes. In fact, competition
between the workers in such times caused cheap wages. When
left to itself, development moved in a circle.   Cheap prices
induced laziness; this, in turn, want and dearness; the latter
industry and abundance. If, on the other hand, by wise govern-
mental regulations high prices of food could be permanently
fixed, it would also enforce application to be constant, and thereby
a permanent surplus of production would be attained, which
creates the opportunity for the conquest of foreign markets.

Therefore, let it be the duty of the King to keep the price of
wheat high by the re-introduction of bounties or export-
premiums (8).

II. There had already arisen during the last century, in
opposition hereto, defenders of cheap food, especially opposers of
the artificial raising of prices. The first defender of this standpoint, as far as I know, is Josiah Child, as early as 1693.   He
attacks the custom of fixing remuneration, which was made in
the interest for low wages. This was possible as long as England
was not a country with handicrafts. At that juncture, however,
low wages must cause the emigration of the cleverest artisans to
better-paying countries, as already, indeed, numerous English
seamen had withdrawn to Holland (9).

More in detail Jacob Vanderlint advances the same view in
"Money Answers all Things" (London, 1734).   This writer asserts
that double proposition which has ever since been taken as an
axiom by the adherents of high wages and low prices of food.   At
some time or other—and herein he has a forcible argument on
his side—a population capable of consuming is necessary for the
development of trade. He turns against the writers of that day
who opposed the raising of the people's needs as being luxurious.
This was not the reason of the low ebb of trade—much
rather was it the lack of means of the great masses of consumers
(pp. 21, 160).   In addition to this, Vanderlint also casually draws
attention to the fact that higher wages for the working man are
an incentive for more work (p. 122).

---

8. The same opinion is given also in J. Houghton's "Husbandry and Trade
Improved."   Revised, corrected, and published by R. Bradle (London, 1727),
p. 266.

9. Josiah Child: " New Discourse of Trade "(London, 1693), pp. 10 and 11.

Postlethwait and Nathaniel Foster join with this writer in supporting the same view (10). Postlethwait starts on the same lines as Vanderlint, firstly in the matter of consumption. Wherever are many poor people, there, he maintains, the home market is insignificant. The luxury of the few cannot by any means replace the consumption of many ; therefore too great an inequality of wealth is against the trade interests of the country. From this point of view high wages and low prices of food are to be promoted. The latter caused, in addition, an increase of the population, and, therewith, of the quantity of work accomplished. In close connection appears also the second standpoint: the idleness of the working classes was not a consequence of an hereditary fault, but rather depended upon the fact that they lacked the incentive for labour. In order to make them work more there must be the motive of bettering their position placed before them (11). In like manner Postlethwait defends the granting of a cheap leisure time to the workers (12).

Foster (13), clearly influenced by Mirabeau, Rousseau, and kindred writers, takes a similar position. He is indebted to them for a criticism of the question more from the standpoint of the workmen. The opinion that high prices of food and low wages were desirable was "a teaching which avarice has grasped with eagerness and turned to account for its own object." Men believe nothing easier than an untruth which brings them personally an advantage. To prove this he points to the physiological experience that want certainly stimulated to energy, but only that want which could be overcome by energy. It was quite different if the exertion was not sure of success. A man who the more he laboured was so much the more highly taxed worked, according to experience, as little as possible. Foster,

---

10. Postlethwait, in his " Great Britain's Commercial Interest Explained and Improved " (2nd. ed., London, 1775), especially pp. 13, 16, 43. The Supplement to the " Universal Dictionary of Trade and Commerce," quoted by Marx, I have not succeeded in finding in the Library of the British Museum. N. Foster : " Enquiry into the Causes of the Present High Prices of Provisions " (London, 1767), pp. 56, 60. Similarly, Dangueille recommends (" Avantages et Désavantages de la France et Grande Bretagne." p. 293) high wages in the interest of consumption ; quoted by A. Young, " Farmer's Letters," p. 38.

11. " I take it for a maxim that no class of people will ever want industry if they do not want encouraging motives thereto " (p. 43).

12. " Dictionary of Trade and Commerce." I.—Preliminary Discourse, p. 751.

13. " Enquiry into the Causes of the Present High Prices of Provisions " (London, 1767), pp. 56—62

first linking himself to Mirabeau, points out, in confirmation, the peasant serfs of the Continent. The same, however, would apply to the English workman if by bureaucratic regulations, either in fixing wages or in making the necessaries of life dearer, the reward of working more was eventually withdrawn from him. Such a policy must lead, if not to rebellion, to general stupidity and lethargy. The author denies the proposition that with high wages and low prices less work would be done than under the opposite conditions. It is true that in an isolated case a sudden rise of wages might lead to less work being accomplished; but, generally, there would be more vigour and cheerfulness thrown into work the more the worker could better his position thereby. A similar view, though not clearly defined, and without sufficient proof, is taken by J. Anderson (14). The writers here mentioned as being friendly to the working classes are generally behind, when compared with the advocates of the opposite opinion, because they bring forward fewer results of observation than these latter, and limit themselves mainly to general assertions. Josiah Tucker, who judges the problem solely from the point of view of experience, and thereby arrives at a defence of high wages, draws attention to the fact that in a country with high wages and plenty of capital only those products were brought forth which required plenty of labour, whilst less cultivated countries with low wages had their strength in goods in the production of which Nature had a large and human labour a slight share. Tucker quotes an array of instances in confirmation of his statement. Scotland produced timber; England wheat, requiring more labour; certain portions of the South of England, garden products, needing still more labour; in spite of which agricultural wages in the latter districts were the highest, and in England higher than in Scotland. Horn, wool, and hides were produced in countries with low wages; their manipulation took place where the wages were high. Notwithstanding which, labour had in the first case a small, in the second a large share in the production. Holland, which did not produce a single log of timber, and where the wages were high, was pre-eminent in shipbuilding. Tucker ascribes these facts, in addition to the possession of larger capital, to the reason that more skilled and more trained labour was evolved in consequence of greater division of work. It may be cheaper to pay

---

14. James Anderson: " Observations on the Means of Exciting a Spirit of National Industry " (Edinburgh, 1777), p. 277.

a capable workman 2s. 6d. per day than to employ a bad one for 6d. The high wages of the richer country had, further, the result of attracting the most able workers from the countries paying less wages. Thus high wages were in no wise a disadvantage for a nation's economy, but were rather a sign of a higher stage of development (15).

III. But the writers mentioned represent by no means the predominating opinion until the time of Adam Smith. On the contrary, they evoked a violent opposition. Several anonymous articles appeared against Postlethwait; for instance, the "Essays on Trade and Commerce" (London, 1770), and "Considerations on Taxes" (London, 1765). The most ordinary knowledge of mankind taught that English workmen only worked for a bare livelihood. High prices alone impelled them to continuous labour. With low prices hours of labour were shorter, and still the workers were less industrious than with higher prices and longer hours, because in dear times the workmen were obliged to apply themselves to satisfy their masters. The French workman accomplished more, although he neither ate meat nor drank beer, to which the English workman believed he had a birthright. The latter was the laziest workman in the world. In order to improve him, the main point was to so raise the prices of food by legislative measures that he could not earn more by six days' continuous labour than a bare living. In addition, this writer demands authoritative fixing of wages and working hours—therefore, in other words, a normal wage and a normal working day, but in exactly the opposite interest to that in which these demands are put forward to-day ; a maximum rate of remuneration which might not be exceeded, and a minimum time of labour (14 hours, including meal-times) (16) below which might not be worked.

A. Young takes up the same position, also opposing the other view (17). He learned during his travels that business men and manufacturers in Manchester preferred high to low prices of

---

15. Compare Josiah Tucker: " Four Tracts on Political and Commercial Objects "(Gloucester, 3rd edition, 1774), especially pp. 30 and 40.

16. " The poor work only for the bare necessaries of life and for the means of a low debauch. When this is obtained they cease to labour till roused again by necessity."—The second of the works quoted in note 10.

17. " A Farmer's Letters to the People of England " (London, 1768), pp. 34-40, 201-210; further, " Political Arithmetic," pp. 110-111 ; further, " Six Months' Tour in the North of England " (1770), vol. III., pp. 242-50.

wheat—the cloth industry languished on account of the too great cheapness of corn.   He demands that food shall be made dearer and wages be lowered by bureaucratic control, in order to stimulate England's commerce and trade.

Young, and the anonymous writers just mentioned, differ from Houghton, who had noticed in a raising of the ordinary wants of the workers an incentive to increased labour.   They on the contrary believed that a raising of the standard of living was not possible for a workman.   Any balance of earnings above the necessary cost of living meant only more ale, more "spreeing," more headaches, and less work.   Therefore these writers wished to chain down the workman by legislation to the minimum standard of life.

Benjamin Franklin came also to the same conclusion in his "Observations concerning the Increase of Mankind," though he later on changed it for exactly the opposite opinion (18).

IV.   The writers mentioned were opposed by Adam Smith in his principal work ("Wealth of Nations," vol. I., chap. 8).   He teaches that high wages and low wheat prices mean an increase in labour capacity.   Well-nourished men worked better than those poorly fed ; those who were cheerful and contented better than the downtrodden ; healthy better than such as frequently succumbed to illnesses.   The opposite view depended upon the fact that in dear years the workmen were certainly more submissive and dependent, but by no means more capable of labour, than in cheap years.

Adam Smith based these statements upon the proofs given by Messance, Receiver of Taxes at St. Etienne, in "Notes on the Population of Auvergne, Lyons, and Rouen" (Paris, 1766).   The passages relating hereto are on pages 287-92 and 305-8.   Messance differed from the opinion that the workman only laboured for a bare existence, and that when this was attained he fell a prey to idleness.   On the contrary, after satisfying his hunger he worked on more diligently to satisfy the higher wants of his life.   He bought industrial productions, and spent his money on a better house and better furniture.   Especially in years of cheap wheat was more clothing bought, and therefore more cloth woven, than in bad years.   To the cheapening of wheat prices as well as the increase of wages during the last century was the prosperity

18 Compare Roscher : "Handbuch," vol. I., par. 173, note 3.

of French trade to be in the first place ascribed. Just
so the development in stock-farming and garden and vine
culture, the products of which now for the first time found consumers. Even the farmers themselves had not suffered to any extent
by the falling of wheat prices. Messance proceeds, like Postlethwait, in the first instance on the ground of increased consumption, although he mentions also the increase of industriousness and
labour power in consequence of lower wheat prices and higher
wages. In the cloth factories at Elbeuf and the silk and linen
mills at Rouen we have the proofs. Messance communicates a
number of tables, which, as Receiver of Taxes, stood at his service.
From these, indeed, it was clear during 1740 and 1763 that the
years of dear wheat had been mostly years of less production, and vice versa; that in every case the dearest showed the
least, the cheapest the largest production.

V. The teaching of Adam Smith was, however, far from taking
immediate root. The almost universally accepted wage-theory
of Ricardo stood as more important in opposition. Ricardo
certainly acknowledges clearly that the minimum standard of
living, to which according to him the worker was chained, depended upon the customary standard of living. But in his further
statements, as in those of his supporters, this customary limit,
though capable of being raised, disappeared behind the bare minimum of existence, solely decided by physiological_laws. The
economical prosperity of a country—i.e., according to the personal
economical standpoint of Ricardo, the profit of the employers—
depended, for him, on low wages. Therefore, countries in which
wages were low had an advantage over countries with high wages.
In the latter countries capital was to be led into the channels in
which the least labour in its own country was necessary—a step
backward from the theory of Tucker (19). According, therefore,
to Ricardo, centralised industrial development (20), which he had
already in his mind, does not necessarily at the same time mean
social development : for however much national economy advanced
and riches increased the worker remained chained to the minimum
standard of life. ' That which A. Young had uttered as a practical
demand was with Ricardo a law of nature.'

---

19. Compare, on Ricardo's position, Herkner: " Die sociale Reform als Gebot
des wirtschaftlichen Fortschritts" (Leipzig, 1891), p. 12.

20. Factory system development.—*Translator*.

Whilst Ricardo himself stands upon the platform of the capitalist, his wage-theory has become the basis of all those movements which, on principle, oppose the present economical development depending upon privilege and property—the starting-point of radical as well as reactionary Socialists. For both of these the maxim cannot be dispensed with that by reason of the existing economical arrangement the worker cannot raise his status in any case, but is irredeemably fettered down to the subsistence minimum. Only a complete upheaval of the groundwork of this arrangement, the abolishing of privilege and property, can bring deliverance to the working classes. But the turning of the tables will be made possible by the fact that in the present economical system the cleft between those possessing means and those without always becomes wider. The expropriated at last expropriate the expropriators.

The wage-theory of Ricardo is most clearly the foundation of the Communistic manifesto in which Marx and Engels first formulated the programme of Continental Social Democracy. The teaching appeared here in the definitely expressed form that it was modern centralised industry, especially the machine, which pressed down the worker unceasingly. "By the spread of machinery and the division of labour the work of the proletarian has lost its independent character, and therewith all attraction for the worker. The expenses of the worker limit themselves, therefore, almost solely to the necessaries of life, which he needs for existence and the propagation of his race. The price of an article, consequently also of labour, is equal to its cost of production. In the same proportion that adversity of labour increases do, therefore, wages fall." "The modern worker, instead of raising his status along with the progress of industry, always falls deeper below the condition of his own class." This teaching, which Karl Marx (21) as unconditionally supports in "Capital," has found an eloquent defender in Lassalle. "For you, gentlemen," he cried to the workers, "always the bare necessaries of life; for the employer's share, all the balance remaining from the result of labour." Lassalle does not recognise a social advance on the basis of an economical one; hence his scoffing at the English trade unions as "the ineffectual experiment of the commodity Labour to demean itself as Humanity."

---

21 K. Marx, 4th edition, vol. I., pp. 226-61.

The teaching of reactionary Socialism is nothing different with regard to the consequences of the modern economical system for the worker. Represented in England by the early novels of Disraeli and contemporary High Churchism (22), it has found its most spirited adherents in Germany. In the numerous volumes of the "Berlin Revue," and in Glaser's "Annuals," this tendency in the years of the "fifties" and "sixties" has culminated in a social-political programme which H. Wagener, in 1855, collected in the "Outline for a Programme of the Right." This party, as it on the one hand glances backward to the Mercantile-State of Frederick the Great and Frederick William I., has on the other hand become the basis of later State-Socialism.

Through all the volumes of the works mentioned the main thought shows itself, that the modern economical system founded on freedom and property, and especially centralised industry raised on this foundation, tramples down the worker irredeemably. Far from the fact that continuous economical development means at the same time social progress, the view is taken that deliverance depends upon banishing "the principles of 1789" and in going back to the old Guild trade-rights, coupled with the fixing of wages by the State.

The most important of these writers, Lavergne-Peguilhen, attributes an implacable struggle between Capital and Labour to the present economical system. It burdened the worker more heavily than the feudalism of the Middle Ages, and even than slavery (23). Similarly, Hermann Wagener speaks of the economical system of to-day as a "despairing and annihilating struggle which everywhere can only lead to the complete social and political subjection of the less powerful—to modern slavery without masters" (24). The bourgeoisie invited the worker, "like a lame man, to a race," and under the scornfully invented pretext of freedom of trade, by the overwhelming influence of their means shut him out from trade. Freedom of trade means for the worker nothing more than the freedom to seek out for himself that trade wherein he wishes to

---

22. Compare my book "On Social Peace," German edition, vol. I., pp. 377-99.

23. Lavergne-Peguilhen: "The Conservative Social Teaching," second number; "The Organic State Teaching," Berlin, 1870 (Collected Essays from the "Fifties" and "Sixties," p. 128). Compare also pp. 59, 60, 124.

24. H. Wagener: "The Small but Important Party" (Berlin, 1885), wherein the programme of the Right of 1855 is communicated, pp. 8 and 9.

suffer from hunger (25).   In fact centralised industry needed
pauperism, so that the price of labour power did not increase
beyond the cost of its production.   The modern industrial system
and its representatives had therefore the highest interest in preventing the advancement of the worker (26).   Similarly, says
Prof. Glaser, intimately connected with the writer mentioned, "No
real judge of the teachings of national economy will assert that
under the present condition of production in European States the
working class as a class can raise itself by its own power from its
position" (27).   England is, according to this writer, because
economically the furthest developed, in the worst social
position—the country of massed distress, close on the brink of
revolution.

To these fathers of the present State-Socialism Catholic authors
like Joerg, Bishop Ketteler, and others link themselves.   According to all of them the impossibility of an elevation of the workers
on the basis of the existing economical system is an axiom, and by it
they support their more or less far-reaching Socialistic demands (28).

VI. This teaching, like that of Radical Socialism, depends on the
common principle of view that the modern economical development
binds the worker to the minimum standard of life, and that on
this basis a continuous improvement of his position, especially by
increases of wages, is impossible.   This view, which is nothing
else than a condensation of Ricardo's wage-theory, has been abandoned in later literature.   The so-called Manchester school, as well
as the historical school, acknowledges the possibility, even the
necessity, of a rise in the standard of living of the workers, also
continuous increases of wages, on the ground and as a consequence
of economical progress.

25. Compare Wagener's speech on the occasion of the proposal of Schulze-
Delitsch regarding the coalition right of employer and employed, sitting of
the Prussian Parliament, 11th Feb . 1865.   Further: "Past, Present, and
Future of National Political Economy." by Oswald Stein (a known pseudonym
for Wagener). Berne and Leipzig, 1880, p. 126.

26. Wagener's "Staatslexikon," vol. XV., Art., "Pauperism."   Further,
the book just quoted, pp. 131, 132, 122

27. Compare Glaser: "Elevation of the Working Classes to Economical
Independence "(Berlin, 1865).

28. Jörg: "History of the Social-Political Parties in Germany"(Freiburg i.
Br., 1867), p. 36.

In this way Macculloch (29) explains the higher wages of America, of England, and of Holland as by no means an economical disadvantage compared with the lower wages of the Irish, Poles, and Hindoos. The difference was more than balanced by greater industry and increase in the amount of work done. Senior says the same thing—in spite of lower wages the price of labour was dearer in France than in England (30). Rau and Roscher are of the same opinion (31). The last-mentioned author supports it with an abundance of interesting experiences, gained in all countries.

We find a similar change of theory respecting the hours of labour. Whilst formerly the use of machinery as long as possible was considered desirable, and every reduction of the hours of labour was looked upon as a loss, later on the economical advantages of a gradual curtailment of the hours of labour were generally recognised. Especially well known is the change which the views of Senior underwent in this direction. Whilst he had declared, in his "Letters concerning the Factory Acts of 1837," the reduction of the hours of labour from twelve to ten would ruin the cotton industry, because just in the last two hours was the employers' profit realised, he withdrew this teaching in 1863, at the Congress of Social Science, in Edinburgh, as erroneous, and recommended the extension of the ten-hours law to a number of other industries.

The views of Macaulay changed in a similar manner. Formerly an opponent of the Factory Acts, he made, later, a brilliant speech in defence of the ten-hours law. He closed this speech with these memorable words, since so often quoted: "If we are ever compelled to retire from the paramount position amongst trading nations we shall not give way to a race of degenerated dwarfs, but to some other strong nation excelling us in physique and genius"— referring to the then extreme hours of labour of some German factories and the quoted bad results of recruiting in German industrial districts.

German national economists agree with the English. According to Emminghaus (32), for instance, the shortening of the hours of labour means in no wise always an economical disadvantage; fre-

29. "Principles of Political Economy," 2nd edition (London, 1830), p. 397.
30. "Political Economy," 5th edition (London, 1863), p. 143.
31. Rau: "Volkswirtschaftslehre," par. 201a; Roscher: "Volkswirtschaftslehre," I., par. 40, par. 173.
32. A. Emminghaus: "Allgemeine Gewerkslehre" (Berlin, 1868), pp. 78-90.

quently the same production was realised with shortened hours of labour. But if with shortened hours of labour the same amount in wages on piecework could be paid, this had at once to be recognised as an advantage for the employer.

The severest attack against the theory of Ricardo was made by Brentano, in the first instance in his "Arbeitergilden der Gegenwart." As a result the wage-theory of Ricardo became untenable also for those hitherto its supporters, whose interests were bound up with it. After Fr. Lange had already acknowledged this in the introduction to a later edition of his " Arbeiter-frage " (33), it was only a question of time until the representatives of German Social Democracy also acknowledged the scientific advance. This occurred at the Congress at Halle in 1890, where even the former wage-law was abandoned (34).

Brentano enforces in detail the teaching above described, that the gradual raising of wages and shortening of the hours of labour, being used for elevating the standard of living, is economically justified, in that they bring forth a higher capacity for work. Brentano has, in his writings as well as his lectures, given frequent expression to the conviction that the elevation of the working classes by continuous development of the existing economical system harmonises, indeed, even on the basis of economical progress, and follows as a matter of course—a teaching which must be the foundation of all social strivings after peace (35). It is necessary for me here to thankfully acknowledge that for the incentive to which the present work is owing I am indebted to the gentleman mentioned.

Herkner follows Brentano's steps, in his meritorious work— " Social Reform a Demand of Economical Progress" (Leipsic, 1891). Herkner expressly teaches the utility of all efforts with a tendency to the elevation of the working classes, especially of legislative enactments tending to the economical development of strength.

---

33. F. A. Lange: "Die Arbeiterfrage," third edition, 1875, p. 190.

34. Compare Brentano: Meine Polemik mit Karl Marx (Berlin, 1890), p. 7.

35. Compare Brentano: "The Teaching on the Increase of Wages— Annual for National Economy and Statistics," published by Hildebrand, vol. XVI. (1871), pp. 251-91; also "On the Relation between Wages and Hours of Labour to the Capacity for Labour "(Leipzig, 1876).

VII. Let us now interrogate practical men. Among them predominates by no means the same unanimity as at present exists in theoretical circles. On one side stand the English and Americans; on the other, many of the Germans.

Chief amongst them, the best known is Brassey, who, in his "Work and Wages," has gathered together the experiences of his father—the greatest railway contractor in the world. Brassey's conclusion I have spoken of in another place (36). It was a mistake, he says, that the higher wages of England meant an economical disadvantage; rather was the price of a defined piece of work in England by no means higher, in many cases certainly lower, than in the remainder of Europe, which exhibited a far lower standard of living of the workers. In a similar manner Lowthian Bell, a distinguished ironmaster in England, declares, in his "Manufacture of Iron and Steel," that the weekly earnings of the workers engaged at the English furnaces were certainly considerably higher than on the Continent, in spite of which a lower amount of wages was paid per ton of pig-iron in Cleveland than in Germany. The same result holds good, according to Schoenhof, in comparing the American production of pig-iron with the European (37).

Generally, the two Americans—Edward Atkinson and J. Schoenhof—support as decidedly as possible the opinion of Brassey. Both are men of business. Atkinson is engaged practically in the cotton trade of Massachusetts (38). Both declare that economical progress, which is at the present day progress from Isolated to Centralised Industry, from hand to machine work, necessarily brought in its train a continuous elevation of the status of the workers. The high weekly wages which countries the most economically developed exhibited were in no wise a disadvantage for them in the competition of nations. They were nothing more than a sign of technically-developed trade conditions—especially of the triumph of centralised establishments over antiquated methods of production. In spite of the higher weekly wages of the workers, in consequence of better machinery and of greater capacity for

36. "Social Peace," vol. II., pp. 261-5.

37. J. Schoenhof: "Industrial Situation"(New York, 1885), p. 77.

38. Edward Atkinson: "Distribution of Products," 4th edition (New York, 1890). Also: "The Margin of Profits." Further: J. Schoenhof, "Industrial Situation " (New York, 1885).

work, the cost of labour in America for most of the goods produced, especially by means of Centralised Industry, was lower than
in the competing industries of Europe.

The opposite view is held by numerous practical Germans.
According to the opinion of many of these, the sudden and considerable increase of wages which took place at the beginning of
the "seventies" has by no means resulted in economical progress. On
many sides was the view defended, in the press as well as
in the Reichstag, that these increased wages represented a
weakening of German industry compared with foreign, and a curtailment of exports.   Far from the increase of wages being accompanied by a corresponding raising of labour capacity, they had
rather in most cases caused a diminution in the work accomplished.
This view was taken, for instance, by the Prussian Minister of
Commerce, in a Rescript of 28th March, 1876, to the head Mining
Departments (39).   The same view is expressed in the "Memoir of
the Association of German Iron and Steel Employers" which
appeared in 1875 (40), and in the Government inquiries concerning
the Iron Trade, as well as the Cotton and Linen Industries, in
1878 (41), herein with special confirmation by German ironmasters
and some spinners.   As a means for raising the labour capacity it
is recommended, in the Rescript above quoted, to lower the rate
of piecework, by which the most effectual incentive for work
would be given—advice similar to that of A. Young and those
writers of the last century mentioned along with him.   If we
hie to the agricultural East of Germany, the teaching of the contrary relation between height of wages and labour capacity would
meet with few doubters.

We have, therefore, to record a variation between the older
theory and the younger, and also between practical men of
different countries.   Is it possible that one of the two sides is alone
correct—the other simply wrong?   Such an assumption is forbidden by the abundance of undoubted facts with which each of
the two views is justified by its adherents.   Rather is the variance
only to be solved by accepting it as the result of development.
One must accept that the theoretical view, from Sir William Petty

39. Compare Brentano: "On the Relation of Wages and Hours of
Labour to the Work Accomplished" (Leipzig, 1876), pp. 6-7.

40. Berlin: Printing Office of the "Berliner Börsenzeitung," p. 21.

41. In the original the author, in his foot-note, gives the pages and questions here referred to.

to A. Young, corresponds to an older, that of the newer national economists to an advanced stage of development. Could we still be doubtful about such a solution of the divergence, it is made a certainty by the fact that one of the most decided adherents to the newer theory himself denies its applicability for India (42). In India, says Brassey, one has observed, contrary to experience in England, that a higher wage lessened the capacity.

If, otherwise, the change in the teaching depends on a change of circumstances, this latter must extend back to that economical reversal encircling everything which distinguishes the economical life of the present from that of the foregoing century. Wherein did it consist? From a system of independent economical units regulated by privilege and birth was evolved, with the improvement of competition, an international establishment riveted into an independent whole by division of labour and by barter. This change caused, on the one hand, a change in the method of production. In place of hand-labour appeared modern Centralised Industry (43), and further, a certain psychological reversal. There arose new ways of thinking and, therewith, new men—new types of employers, and of workers.

To the degree that this alteration develops itself the changed theory corresponds. In purely customary circumstances, the old teaching obtains everywhere; to the extent that the conditions glide away from the ordinary average character and are drawn into the world's economy, the theory begins to waver. In the same degree that the reversal has developed with the triumph of Centralised Industry over the older forms of production, the new teaching becomes acknowledged, first by the theorists, then by practical men, of nations in which the economical reversal completely exists. In countries on the point of changing, many practical men cling to the old teaching.

This development should be followed closely in the most important branches of trade. It should be shown how this economical development on the one hand means technical, then social progress, and how the elevation of the working class necessarily moves hand in hand with it. Nothing should be more fitting to combat that social pessimism which supposes that modern development of

---

42   " Work and Wages," 2nd edition (London, 1872), p 88.
43.   The factory system.—*Translator.*

C

affairs leads to a breaking-up of society, or to a dilemma which is only to be loosened with powder and shot. Among great industries there are two specially adapted for this proof—the Iron Trade and the Cotton Industry. Both extend over the whole world, and produce everywhere the same, or at least similar, articles. The productions of both are measurable and comparable either by length or weight. Both are, in addition, the leading trades of the most important industrial countries in the world.

But the Cotton Industry has one advantage over the Iron Trade. In it machinery has for a century obtained the upper hand, and has more and more confined human exertions to the minding of the machine. The Iron Trade is different. The Bessemer and Siemens processes have only recently put mechanical power into a leading position, whilst with the puddlers of to-day that older type of skilled and strong-sinewed hand-labour dies out. But the English Cotton Industry, which presents the longest history of all modern Centralised Industry, is particularly suitable for an examination of the economical and social tendencies of the modern economical system. We seek in the history of the English Cotton Trade those traits which can everywhere be deemed of value as general characteristics of centralised industrial forms of production.

Therefore, if I beg the reader to accompany me yet again to England, this happens in the sense in which once Sir William Petty and other contemporary Englishmen studied Holland, and thereby helped to establish the greatness of their own native country.

CHAPTER II.

THE DEVELOPMENT OF CENTRALISATION IN THE ENGLISH COTTON INDUSTRY.

I.—The Origin of the Factory System.

India, the ancient seat of trade, is also the home of the cotton industry. Alexander the Great found, even in his time, the natives clothed in cotton garments. Indian woven goods have been from ancient times imported into Europe as articles of luxury. The Arabians brought many trades and arts, including the cotton industry, to Europe. Wherever they pushed their way they grew the cotton plant; especially did its culture flourish on all the coasts of the Mediterranean. Spain and Sicily spun and wove cotton in the 11th and 12th centuries.

When, in later times, the economical point of importance in Europe advanced north of the Alps, it was followed by the cotton industry. Flemish and German towns became its seat. England, at that time depending solely upon agriculture and its products, was not the place for an industry of luxury, as the cotton trade was at that time. It required, as essentials, trade, and consumers who had become rich by trade. Venice was the cotton market of the world—the Liverpool of those days; Antwerp the seat of manufacturing—the Manchester of that period.

As was often similarly the case, foreign immigrants also laid the foundation of the English cotton industry—refugees who sought a home in England after the destruction of Antwerp by Alba, in 1585. Many of them settled in Manchester and Bolton, which towns were at that time the seat of woollen weaving. Foreign weavers were particularly attracted to Manchester by the permission to fell wood for building and burning, as they wished, in the College woods situated in the vicinity of the city—

a sign of very primitive economical conditions. From that time the import of cotton into England is mentioned. But how little important was the manipulation of cotton, even at the turn of the century, is shown by the fact that in the Elizabethan poor-laws the various occupations, notably the spinning of flax, hemp, and wool, are recommended as employments in workhouses, whilst cotton is not mentioned by a single word.

It was the transference of the world's highways of commerce, in connection with political events, which caused Germany and Flanders to give way, economically, to Holland, and later on to England. On this basis is the flourishing of the English cotton industry to be understood. Already Lewis Roberts, in his "Treasure of Traffic," published in 1641, mentions the cotton industry of Manchester as a flourishing trade. Daniel De Foe finds, on his "Tour through the whole Island of Great Britain," in 1727, the town of Manchester in an astonishing state of progress. In a few years its population had doubled. This has to be ascribed, he says, before everything else, to the cotton in-dustry, which has flourished so exceedingly during the last 40 years.

The art and manner of manufacturing was at that time, according to Guest, as follows (1). The warp for the woven goods consisted of linen yarn, mostly imported from Germany. Cotton for this purpose could not yet be spun strong enough. The weft was cotton yarn, which was spun by country people in the vicinity of Manchester. The weaver was an independent hand-worker. He bought yarns, and brought the woven goods to the Manchester market for sale. In the degree that the industry produced not only for local needs but also for more distant markets, and the striving to cheapen the production costs extended with competition, the independent weaving master gave way to the wage worker who received the yarns for weaving from the merchant. The merchant origin-ally sold the woven goods himself, by carrying them on the backs of packhorses through the country. Up to this point merchant and weaver stood socially equal. But in proportion as the merchant became the giver-out of the yarns he began to get the sales effected by commercial travellers and pattern books. This change is put by Guest at 1740.

---

1 Guest: "History of Cotton Manufacture " (1820, p. 7).

With the extension of the market this method of selling was not sufficient. The merchant separated himself from the giver-out of yarns, who moved from Manchester to the weaving villages situated around Manchester, and this latter sold to the merchant. Thus worker, manufacturer, and merchant divided themselves into three separate functions which are still to-day the main essentials of the industry.

But, in spite of trading activity, England's cotton industry had to deal with a superior competitor. As the European Continent and America are to-day with respect to England, so was England at this time with respect to the Indian cotton industry—dependent on coarse yarns and woven goods. As to its further development it is important to note that the English cotton industry was already exposed to international competition in a larger degree at a time when bad country roads on the Continent still scarcely made this competition felt.

India was in the last century, compared with Europe, still an industrial country which chiefly interchanged trade products, especially cotton and silk goods, for natural products, principally metals. As early as 1708 De Foe complained about the importation of Indian cotton goods into England. It had become the general fashion for ladies to wear calicoes and muslin, following the example set by the Queen. Not only clothing, but also bedding and curtains, were made from foreign stuffs. De Foe's complaint is more worthy of attention as it happened at a time when the law prohibiting printed Indian calicoes already existed (1700). Again and again similar complaints appeared, such as that the "depravity of the nature of woman" by the passion for foreign clothing ruined the home industry (2). That throughout the whole century Indian competition existed very keenly is proved by the following occurrence. In the year 1775 a "Patriotic Society" was founded in Edinburgh with the object of opposing the fashion for Indian cotton apparel. It was determined to boycott every man who associated with ladies wearing cotton. It is also said that at this juncture the use of Indian stuffs was general—of course only in well-to-do circles of society (3). If, even, the complaints mentioned about the use of

2. Compare Baines' "History of the Cotton Manufacture" (London, 1885), pp. 79, 82, 104.

3. Ure: "The Cotton Manufacture" (London, 1836), I. p. 190.

cotton goods were first raised in the interest of the English woollen and linen industries—these were at the time still the more important industries—it is clear, that the pressure of Indian competition affected in the highest degree the English cotton industry.

What a revolution took place in the following decades is shown by a petition of Indian merchants in 1831. The petitioners complain that in India home productions were supplanted by English, and they demand, without promising themselves even by its aid much relief, the withdrawal of import duties in England, so that both countries might be at least treated on an equality (4).

In the interval the change to machinery and the modern factory system took place. In 1760, says Baines, machinery in England was as primitive as in India; after that time inventions followed each other rapidly. In the last decade of the past century the first muslin yarns—up to this time a monopoly of India—were spun in England. In that period occurred the tremendous revolution which first transformed the cotton industry of England and placed it at the head of trading as well as social development—that revolution which extended first to Lancashire, then to the whole of England, then to the West of Europe, and re-arranged the economical conditions of the world. This change raised up new classes, firstly the middle, which became the chief in the State—in the place of the old agrarian influence—followed by the upward-aspiring working class. To the extent that a nation makes such a change its own, and completes its productions by the machine, in that degree does it stand to-day ahead in economical power amongst the nations of the world.

From what causes did this change arise? Marx, who depicts the development of machinery in a very clear manner, has no answer thereto. He believes that machinery was invented because natural science was far enough advanced to create such inventions. How mistaken such a belief is Brentano has pointed out (5). He has specially called attention to the fact that by no means scientific searchers, but men of the most various callings, mostly of industrial pursuits—Cartwright alone was a clergyman—created the inventions, by reason of the practical wants of the time. A

4. Compare Baines, p. 82.
5. Compare Brentano: "On the Causes of the Present Social Distress" (Leipzig, 1889), p. 7.

further proof in contradiction of Marx's theory is, that similar-machines had already been used here and there for centuries without in their time attaining any economical importance. The application of steam power for lifting loads is centuries old. Peter the Great had applied, after the manner of the Dutch, a steam engine for the watering of his gardens. The combination of a number of spindles with bobbins in a creel or frame, and the setting into operation of bobbins as well as spindles by mechanical means, was an arrangement of Italian silk-spinning introduced by Sir Thomas Lombe into Derby before there was any mention of machinery in the cotton industry (6). The so-called Saxon spinning wheel—an old German invention—the forerunner of the later throstle—had already made the greatest portion of the spinning process mechanical ; for instance, the twisting of the thread and the winding-on of the same without the aid of the human hand (7). The woman spinning had only to perform the drawing-out of the thread by manual labour. This spinning-wheel was used for a long time in Germany for spinning flax, but a combination of this arrangement in some way with that of the Italian, which appears to have been somewhat similar, was not thought of. Johann Beckmann relates, in the first volume of his "Contributions to the History of Inventions"—and, with the exception of the date, Marx in "Kapital" makes exactly the same statement—that as early as about 1579, powerloom weaving had been invented in Dantzic.

Therefore it was not technical grounds which led to the economical reversal towards the end of the last century. Much more probably was it the accumulation of a number of economical moments which led to the technical developments. Long-created, or at least half-accomplished inventions, but, up to that date economically without influence, were first at this time applied to form modern centralised industry. This is not the place to give in fuller detail this economical foundation of the trade revolution, because this task requires a special examination. It is sufficient to name the main ideas of the development.

I. As mentioned above, society in the Middle Ages consisted of a number of independent isolated groups which were only in a slight manner connected to each other by interchanging. What-

---

6. Baines, p. 127.
7. Karmarsch: " Technologie " (Hannover, 1867), vol. II., p. 844.

ever flowed to each group in the way of riches was controlled by usage and privilege, especially by the position in which the representative of the group was born. The revolutionary element in Middle-Age society was the merchant—a stranger in the land, originally treated as an enemy. He represented, as opposed to the landed proprietary of the Middle Ages, a new modern line of thought. Whilst, then, the lots in life were settled by usage and privilege, the striving after the greatest possible profit filled his very soul—according to present ideas, the first " self-made man."

Commerce brings riches. In order to favour it a new system of law subservient to it must be created. Whilst justice for the rest was inherited privilege, a law freed from personality was created the commercial relations—a " jus gentium," as opposed to " jus civile "—a common right as opposed to the special laws of the Saxons, Franks, etc. The two events in the history of the Roman as well as German law just mentioned depend upon the development of the commercial element. Wherever this attains the upper hand it leads to legal conditions which are just the opposite to former ones ; in place of restriction of property, to free property ; in place of limitation of the person, to personal freedom.

But for a long time the influence of the commercial element was slight, and was confined to certain centres of communication, markets and towns. The difficulty of traffic, the badness of roads, the uncertainty of law, duties, staple rights, etc., confined commerce to a few valuable articles. With respect to the great majority of economical commodities, competition was not felt for a long time. Production and prices depended upon privilege and custom. How the individual persons participating in the production divided the products among themselves was regulated, in like manner, by authority. Only when competition, and therewith commercial ideas, seized industry, the old guilds yielded to freedom of trade, and that change of production occurred which led to the machine and centralised industry.

The development, for certain reasons, first occurred in England during the last century, and, indeed, earliest in the cotton industry. A helper at the birth of the new period was here, as in other places in Europe, the mercantile monarchy, which required money in order to pay civil servants and soldiers, and therefore favoured commerce. (Elizabeth, Cromwell, William III.)

During the last century England became the chief commercial country of Europe. Even into the camp of landed proprietorship the spirit of commerce entered, as is evidenced by the change from customary rents to so-called rack-rents. To a still greater extent was industrial production seized by the desire for the greatest possible profit. But, on the other hand, with the thriving of commerce, industry came under the pressure of competition. The maritime position of England, the number of her harbours, and the favourable conditions of the tides for shipping aided her traffic, whilst the bad communication on the Continent combined to maintain the monopoly of trade for a long period (8). But, as seen above, English cotton industry came first under the influence of competition. Therefore with competition arose the striving after cheapening the costs of production, which led to production in large masses, and to the application of labour-saving machinery. "Communication was the outer vehicle, Commerce the inner soul, which gave the impetus to Centralised Industry" (9).

II. The first essentials of commerce—personal freedom and security of property—were, during the last century, in England, as a commercial country, more realised than in the still mostly agrarian States of the European Continent (9a). In the supposed interest for the livelihood of the people State police-power has in other countries (10) hindered the coming into use of machinery. The hatred of the masses against inventions has also caused the persecution of inventors everywhere. The first English manufacturers passed through this experience; their mills were destroyed, their lives threatened. Kay, the inventor of the fly-shuttle (1733) had to leave his native country, and later inventors were mostly compelled to seek their fortunes in other lands.

---

8. According to Sir William Petty ("Several Essays on Political Arithmetic," (London, 1699, p. 173) carriage on land was at that time 15 to 20 times as dear as ship freights.

9. Schmoller : Ueber die Entwicklung des Grossbetriebs und die sociale Klassenbildung, "Preussische Jahrbücher," vol.. LXIX., part 4.

9a. Adam Smith acknowledges, thus early, political freedom and security of property as consequences of commerce, and even declares them to be the most important issues ("Wealth of Nations," vol. III., chap. 4). Petty points out, following the examples of the Dutch, that commercial and religious freedom go hand in hand.

10. Roscher : System, III., par. 125. Lotz : "Archiv für sociale Gesetzgebung," vol. IV., p. 560. Thus the people of Dantzic caused the inventor of the "Band-Mill" to be secretly drowned. Grassmann: "Entwicklung der Augsburger Industrie" (Augsburg, 1894). At pages 13, 14 there is a passage concerning a magisterial order against using machinery in the year 1826.

Thus, especially in Nottingham, and later in Lancashire, the seat of the textile industry, were their mills destroyed and their lives threatened. Thus it was with Hargreaves and Arkwright; even the elder Peel was personally in danger of his life. It is thus seen that the security of the law was in England also, at that time, only just so far advanced that inventions could be applied under great difficulties and dangers.

(III.) The revolution in industry could only develop itself in a branch which was free from legislative enactments of industry in the sense of the older period. The cotton industry of the Continent possessed such an enactment. One only needs to read the description which Bein gives of the industry of the Voigtland in order to see that under such conditions inventions could not come into existence. There everything was regulated. Spinning took place under the control of the State, and yarns were collected together by officials. The right to weave was vested in membership of the Guild. The method of production was strictly defined. State offices for inspection exercised control. Faults in woven goods were visited by punishment. In the same manner the right to dispose of cotton goods was also vested in members of the Commercial Guild. To be a trade employer had almost the character of a public office. Besides other essentials, a formal examination was necessary for it. The sale of goods was also minutely regulated; for a long time fixing of prices existed, and even a legislative fixed selling maximum for the retailer. The retailer was obliged to buy the weaver's goods, for which, in return, a monopoly of sale was guaranteed to him. Under such conditions the application of machinery was not to be thought of. Not only was the production itself defined by the State, and every deviation punishable, but, what was still more important, the incentive to technical progress was wanting, in that to everyone who possessed a lawfully confirmed position in the trade, to the weaver as well as to the retailer, a sufficient existence was guaranteed by reason of fixed arrangements, and every encouragement to technical improvement was lacking. The introduction of the modern working system would also have opposed the spirit of this legislative arrangement, which had for its object an equal division of riches and sought to prevent that advancement of the few which was certainly inevitably connected with the modern factory system. It was competition with the productions of English machinery which first overthrew this arrangement on the Continent (11).

11. Compare Bein: "Die Industrie des Voigtlandes," II., pp. 40-45, 73-86

A similar institution controlled the English woollen industry. There existed offices for the inspection of woollen goods in Manchester, Rochdale,, Blackburn, and Bury (12).

Josiah Child gives (in his "New Discourse of Trade," London, 1693, p. 130) a view of the trade privileges which he had already. opposed, and which regulated the woollen industry. According to him, the sort and quality of the cloth was exactly specified by law, so that "loyal cloth" might be produced. Deviations were settled by the inspecting offices. It was also defined up to what length a certain piece of cloth might be stretched. Cloth fulfilling the lawful conditions was marked with the magisterial seal, and every infringement of the existing regulations was punished. In addition to this, the law fixed the number of the workpeople and of the looms which one weaver might employ— that is, as by the aforementioned German law, it fixed a limit of production in the interests of property-equalisation. The author mentioned demands, instead, that a faculty inspection should displace the obligatory; everybody should be able to make cloth to his own mind, but only the cloth produced and examined according to regulations should receive the official seal and so go abroad on the "public good faith of England." On the other hand, Child is in favour of retaining definite bureaucratically controlled length-measurements of all cloth which was destined for export. Therefore, even an unquestionable reformer asks to what extent the old arrangement should be limited, as in fact this gradually occurred during the last century, especially by means of the movement of the industry from the towns to the country.

Whilst the woollen industry, therefore, only gradually loosened the bonds of the older trade-privileges, the cotton industry was a new trade, just brought into the country, which the State, in protection of the older industry, handled with disfavour. Whilst the one was helped forward by all the means possible—the law is known according to which no dead should be laid in the grave without a woollen shroud—the cotton industry was hampered with import duties only repealed by Sir Robert Peel (after a partial repeal, 1787, 1798); with prohibition of printed calicoes; later, in place of these, loaded with heavy taxes on its' use (the latter only repealed in 1831). In spite of which it was not the woollen but the cotton industry whose wonderful unfolding was to create the greatness of England.

12 Compare Ure: "The Cotton Manufacture," I. p. 187.

It enjoyed an advantage over the woollen industry in being able to develop itself in the field of the new time without hindrance. On the basis of property and freedom, the spirit of commerce launched this, the first modern industry. It was not by chance that the delicate fibre, its standard-bearer, was a child of the distant tropics. Commerce had first brought the fibre here, and Commerce had to be thanked for the freedom from ancient enactments which still strangled her home-bred sisters, the woollen and linen fibres   (13a).

The revolution first attacked spinning so early, because up to now the demand for yarns had by far outstripped the supply (13). Powerloom weaving could not be thought of until spinning by power delivered yarns in suitable quantities. The first factory, in the modern sense, was the spinning mill of Arkwright, in Nottingham, 1768.

The following moments are to be noted in the first decades of the cotton industry—I. The prohibition of Indian woven goods. In 1772 the first printed calicoes wholly of cotton were made in England; in 1822 the first twist was exported to India. II. The change of fashion to cotton among the wealthy as well as the working classes. Fustian, a sort of cotton velvet, became for a very long time the clothing of the English workman. III. The flooding of the Continent with English yarns and woven goods. In 1792 English yarns appeared for the first time in large quantities at the Leipsic fair. IV. The Napoleonic war, which hindered the flourishing of a Continental industry, and, with the tremendous extension of smuggling, scarcely harmed the English cotton industry. V. The quick realisation of large fortunes in the hands of the earliest manufacturing families. Up to the "twenties" there were, unless we except 1812 to 1814, no depressed business years.

As early as 1801, with total exports of 18 millions, cotton goods counted for 7 millions. Truly could Macculloch say that the rapid growth of the cotton industry had given England the

---

13. Compare Baines, pp. 115, 116.

13a. Qn the other hand the German cotton industry, because older than the English, was under Guild control, the Augsburg industry (compare Nübling Ulm's Baumwollindustrie in Mittelalter, Leipzig, 1890) as well as that of the Voigtland (compare Bein: " Die Industrie des Voigtlandes," Leipzig, 1884). Even in this century the existence of Guild trade limitation was a fetter preventing the development of the Augsburg cotton industry. Compare Grassmann: " Augsburger Industrie in Jahrhundert," Augsburg, 1894, pp. 12, 13, 27, 29, 31, 107. Only in 1861 did the Weavers' Guild cease to exist.

power and the means to withstand victoriously the long years
of war with France.

But this splendid economical development had another advantage, not less gratifying. It is known that England in the
first decades of this century possessed a social-revolutionary Labour party which exceeded in strength and harmfulness all later
similar movements on the Continent (14). This tendency, which
sought a forcible seizure of governing power by the workers, had
its chief adherents among the workers of the flourishing great
industry. Even Ure, depicting everything as favourably as
possible, has to acknowledge that nowhere in the world did such
bad relations exist between employers and employed (15) as in
the English centralised industries. This is interesting, indeed,
if we compare therewith the present relations of Europe.

In Manchester, in 1819, the massacre took place on "Peterloo"
field, caused by a charge of the yeomanry on a crowd of working
people which did not disperse on the reading of the Riot Act.
An attempt on the life of the Premier followed, and the answer
thereto was a coercion law, the so-called "Castlereagh's Gag
Bill," with extensive limitations of the right of public meeting
and the freedom of the Press. It was in Hyde, a stronghold of
spinning, and the seat of one of the oldest manufacturing families
—the Ashtons—where, in 1838, at a nightly gathering, the
workers, when asked by their leaders whether they were ready,
answered by volleys from rifles. At this time there existed in
Glasgow a system of terrorism advanced even up to assassination.
Houldsworth and other employers refused repeatedly to give any
evidence respecting workers' combinations, and the like, before
the Committees of Inquiry, because they would have feared for
their safety (16).

Without going more closely into the movement, we must get
to know its economical foundation.

About the turn of the century, according to the declaration of
the manufacturer Houldsworth, potatoes, and with them oatmeal,
were the chief nourishment of the workers; as an occasional
luxury a herring served. Indulgence in meat was almost unknown. It grew in proportion as the machines, becoming larger,

14. Compare my book, "On Social Peace," I., p. 55, also Brentano, in the
" Prussian Annuals " (1874).
15. Ure: " Cotton Manufacture," Intro., pp. 24, 25.
16. Ure: " Philosophy of Manufactures," pp. 348-65.

necessitated the meat-eating spinner, who was introduced from England into Scotland. On the other hand, the large majority of the workpeople were confined to the minimum standard of life. A weaver did not get more than 5 to 12 shillings per week, and the average wages of all, spinners included, was not higher than 10 shillings. Against this, having regard to prices in 1839, and to the indispensable minimum of clothing and nourishment, a weekly sum of 34s. 0½d. was necessary for a family of man, wife, and three children. If we assume that man and wife were employed at average wages in the cotton industry, they would together have earned 20s. There would therefore be a deficiency of 14s. to be covered by under-nourishment, debt, or both. "No wonder that we at that time heard about Chartism," remarks the best authority on the English cotton industry hereto (17).

That, indeed, both these means of aid were requisitioned is proved by the numerous instances contained in Blue-Books. During the last 25 years, related in 1834 a witness from Stockport—a town which was inhabited solely by cotton workers—the number of pawnbrokers had increased fourfold; the turnover of each threefold. A quarter of the population of the town regularly pawned their household goods, and almost all clothing, on the Monday, to fetch both back, as far as possible, on the Saturday, after receiving their wages. The same witness affirmed that the working classes bought nearly everything on credit, and, on account of the uncertainty of their paying, had to pay 50 per cent. more than buyers for ready cash (18).

It is not necessary here to give further details. On the other hand, it is to be pointed out that at that time the extensive mass of cottage workers stood behind the factory operatives as well; that also in England the question of the distress of the cottage weavers appeared to mock all efforts at solution. These conditions were the cause of numerous and unwieldy inquiries. They are full of telling analogies to the conditions of German cottage industry as they are depicted in numerous individual researches, and critically put together lately by Sombart in Braun's Archiv (19). That high-water mark in the development

---

17. Samuel Andrew: "Fifty Years' Cotton Trade"—paper read at the meeting of the British Association" (1887), p. 4. David Chadwick: "The Expenditure of Wages, 1839 and 1887"—paper read at the same meeting, gives the reckoning mentioned in detail.

18. Committee on Manufactures (1833), 10,547-86.

19. Braun: "Archiv für sociale Gesetzgebung" (1891), part I.

of cottage industry from handicraft, where the worker is still the owner of the means of production was long ago passed. In the years of the "thirties" the weavers were still mostly only hirers of the looms, or heavily in debt for them, and therefore at the beck and call and mercy of suffering employers (20).

The reason of the cottage weavers' decline was not, in the first instance, the power-loom. As early as 1808 there was an examination into the distress of the hand-weavers, and still there were in 1813 only 2,400 power-looms in Lancashire, as compared with 200,000 hand-looms (21). Much rather was it the marching of the cotton industry into the world's market that disturbed relations depending upon monopoly or usage. Guest is certainly correct in his "History of the Cotton Manufacture" (at the conclusion), when he ascribes the decline of the English cotton weaver to the tremendous yarn exports to the Continent, in conjunction with the cheaper prices of food there. The Continental cottage weaver thus in this way forced the English worker even below the Continental standard of living.

On average goods weavers in Bolton earned weekly (22) : —

					Lb. Wheat-flour.		Lb. Oatmeal.
1797-1804..	..	..	26	8	= 100	or	142
1804-11 ..	..	..	20	0	= 79	,,	115
1811-18 ..	..	..	14	7	= 60	,,	79
1818-25 ..	..	..	8	9	= 48	,,	64
1825-32 ...	..	..	6	4	= 38	,,	48

The stuff in question was at that time not yet produced by the power-loom. It permitted, therefore, the chance of far more favourable remuneration than the production, for example, of printing calico. There were even wages as low as 2s. to 3s. weekly (23).

"According to Blue-Books, potatoes and oatmeal were almost the sole nourishment of the cottage weavers." A housekeeping

20. Committee on Handloom Weavers in 1835 (3,375). Often did the employers say to the weavers seeking work : " We have no work ; if we give any, it is for God's sake. We would rather let it be undone ; but if you take it, it must be at a shilling less." But the hungering weaver thinks : " One potato is better than none," etc.

21. Compare Committee on Petitions from Several Cotton Manufacturers (1808).

22. Compare Committee on Handloom Weavers of 1834 (432).

23. Committee on Manufactures (10.065, 11.750). Committee on Handloom Weavers of 1835 (1,130-59) refers to linen weavers.

budget (24) of a man in a proportionally better position, because he possessed his own hand-loom, given in a Blue-Book, shows, for a family of 4 persons, only half a pound of meat weekly (on Sundays); for the other days weaker nourishment.   One is reminded of the conditions, noted by Rechenberg and Schlieben, of the hand-weavers in the Lord High Constable's district of Zittau (25).   Indeed Rechenberg's result may have acted in like manner for the weaving population of the North of England—that in many instances nothing at all would be left for the parents if the children had received as much to eat as was necessary for the formation of a healthy race.   A wavering step, a hollow-cheeked countenance, are given by observers at that time as typical of the English workers in general (26).   The average hours of labour were 14 to 16.   The children began to weave when 9 years old, and that after they had already been winders (27).

That under such circumstances the workers at that time were not consumers of the industry, follows as a matter of course. What the Blue-Books contain in this respect reminds us vividly of the accounts detailed by Herkner concerning German workers' budgets (28).

Thus says that weaver whose relatively favourable budget we touched upon above: "As regards clothing, I do as I can.   Sometimes I have some, sometimes very little.   I borrowed coat and waistcoat in order to appear before the Commission.   I never bought furniture in my life.   My wife is even as badly situated for clothing as I.   Cooking-utensils I have never bought since I was born. . . . . Cotton sacking filled with straw served as beds, and old tea-chests as chairs." (29).

---

24. Committee on Handloom Weavers of 1834 (7,256).   "The weavers subsist on the coarsest food : oatmeal, water porridge, onion porridge, potatoes. The parents may drink weak tea, and very little sugar in it, and eat dry bread. But even of the coarsest food they have no sufficiency."   Compare further, *loc. cit.*, 1834 (7,643-57); further, the evidence of Richard Oastler, 1834 (3,736-54); similarly, Committee on Manufactures (11,747).

25. Compare "Zeitschrift des kgl. Sächs. Stat. Bureaus," Jahrg. 31, and Rechenberg: "Die Ernahrüng der Handweber in der Amtshauptmannschaft Zittau" (Leipzig, 1890).

26. Compare Hermann Schulze: "Nationalökonomische Bilder aus Englands Volksleben" (Jena, 1853), towards the end.

27. Committee on Manufactures (11,764); Committee on Handloom Weavers, 1834, the above-mentioned evidence of Oastler; compare similarly, Rechenberg, p. 37.

28. Herkner: "Die sociale Reform als Gebot des wirtschaftlichen Fortschritts" (Leipzig, 1890), p. 55.

29. Compare Committee on Manufactures (11,801, 11,863); Committee on Handloom Weavers of 1834 (4,972-80).

It is extraordinary how long the cottage weavers, in spite of their distress, enjoyed the favour of many patrons. Thus, Sir Robert Peel has depicted them as loyal subjects, as opposed to the factory operatives. In fact, as the economical foundations of their existence were only tardily withdrawn from hereditary rule, so also the ideas accompanying them. But, under the pressure of high wheat prices and lowering wages, the inevitable revolution or change occurred here also, after the war. Instead of feelings of dependency towards the authorities above them, appeared doubt and hatred—hatred against the State as well as the Church. Blue-Books accuse the cottage weavers of disloyalty and atheism. Already, at the riots on the field of "Peterloo," in 1819, was this class numerously represented. They fell at that time into the hands of the Chartist leaders, and "would have greeted every upheaval, because it could only bring them an improvement." (30).

Similar conditions had just produced in the factory workers mental tendencies similar to those of the cottage toilers. But, whereas economical development led the former onward, it left nothing but a decline for the cottage toiler. The means were fruitless with which it was thought possible to help them, as, for instance, bureaucratic fixing of wages, etc. Especially was there demanded a return to the old trade system whereby, it was pointed out, new life was created for the silk industry by the Spitalfields regulations (31).

Indeed, even up to the demand for taxing of machinery, methods were resorted to (32) similar to those of the Frankfort handicrafts, which, in 1848, by forbidding the factory system, thought it possible to keep the world in the old grooves. But no regulation could cause the retreat of the economical development which had strangled the cottage weavers of Lancashire in the world's economy. (Wages and profits now put international competition in the place of officials) The English silk industry could withdraw itself from it, though unprofitably; but not so cotton weaving, which, more than any other industry, was interested in

---

30. Committee on Handloom Weavers of 1834 (5,351-6, 7,230-42, 3,821).

31. *Loc. cit.*, 1834 (7,577-97, 8,015-72, 5,389-5,403, 5,633-4). How wrong the idea is to lay the blame for the depression of handicrafts and cottage industry on freedom of trade is shown by the case of Prussia, where freedom of trade was introduced as early as 1810, whereas, on the other hand, the attacks mentioned upon it were only made in the middle of the century.

32. Baines, p. 501.

D

export. Therefore England stood, in the first decades of the century, in a social crisis of the most intricate nature, the blame for which was generally laid to the factory system. This is the reason for the attacks from all sides on its standard-bearers, the "bleeding mill lords." The workers were at one in the opinion that it was "King Steam" who had seduced them from the "old merry England." They had sworn revenge upon him. They considered him the great power of the upheaval which had destroyed all that had been; but under his iron rule the people were driven more and more to despair; they would at last destroy him, as well as all Governments in the world (33). Not much different was the opinion in the aristocratic seats of the South, which were still "undefiled by the breath of industry." The factory system was as opposed to Christianity as darkness to light; all social as well as economical evils were laid down to its account (34), especially that "even the Corn Laws were inveighed against."

What was the reply of Manchester manufacturers to such attacks from right and left? That the industrial system was not to blame for the distress in the country, but merely the circumstance that it was only half introduced. On the foundation of free property and contract, on competition and barter, it had developed itself; developed, further, on these foundations, the economical and technical peculiarities of centralised industry, and freed it from the pressure of an agrarian, interested order of things. Without examining here the correctness of this point of view, we next ask: How did both occur?

_____

II. *The Cotton Industry under the Influence of International Competition.*

The unprecedented advances of the industry came to a standstill in the "thirties"—at least according to the idea of the employers, whose profits during that period went down considerably. The long-lasting business crises of the "thirties" and of the beginning of the "forties" show, alongside of a series of bad harvests, peculiar economical conditions. By very detailed

33. Committee on Handloom Weavers of 1834 (5,588-9).
34. Committee on Handloom Weavers of 1834 (6,891).

Blue-Books, as well as by the works of Baines and Ure (1), we are in a position to obtain a clear picture of the position of the industry at that time—a much more detailed one than of the first ten years of its development. This is easy enough to explain; as long as everything moves smoothly mankind does not ask why and wherefore. But, since, according to the proverb of Socrates, death is the "museaget" of philosophy, so crises in the economical field cause the multitude to stand still and inquire into the conditions of their existence. Hence arose, in the decade under notice, a series of minute inquiries—"relief inquiries." Since they were undertaken according to the methods usual at that period in England—publicly, by means of witnesses from all interested parties, and with cross-examination—they form to this day, independently of their short-lived object, the most valuable, and still far from exhausted, mine of economical knowledge yet discovered (2).

Let us glance first at spinning, in which the modern method of production has the longest history behind it. Unsuspected figures show a remarkable falling-off of its profit (3).

	1784. s. d.	1797. s. d.	1812. s. d.	1822. s. d.	1832. s. d.
Price of 1 lb. of yarn, No. 40's twist ..	10 11	7 6	2 6	1 4¾	0 11¼
Price of the necessary cotton for this (18 oz.)	2 0	3 4	1 6	0 9	0 7¼
Balance for expenses and profits	8 11	4 2	1 0	0 7¾	0 4

How is this result to be explained? The English cotton industry was released earlier than other trades from the rule of privilege and monopoly. As a result the striving after cheapening of the costs of production had called machinery into existence. But the lucky possessors of machines, which in England robbed the cottage spinners of their curtailed and more or less protected markets, were themselves, as against the rest of the world, in a position of monopoly. One sign of this was the accumulation of

1. Baines: "History of the Cotton Manufacture" (London, 1835); Ure: "Philosophy of Manufactures" (London, 1835); Ure: "The Cotton Manufacture," 2 vols. (London, 1836) Further: The historical portion of Ellison, "Cotton Trade of Great Britain" (London, 1886), and J. C. Fielden, "Sketch of the British Cotton Industry" ("Co-operative Wholesale Annual," 1887).

2. On these "Enquêts" Friedrich Engels bases his "Position of the Working Classes in England" (Leipzig, 1848). Also Karl Marx: "Kapital."

3. Compare Ellison: "Cotton Trade" (London, 1886), p. 61, in connection with Committee on Manufactures (9,089).

fortunes by Arkwright, Peel, and others in an astonishingly
short time ; a proof of this is the quick and unopposable conquest
of, say, the Leipsic or Frankfort fairs (4). England's position
of monopoly lengthened the war in Europe, which occasionally
involved the United States. The countries mentioned were
at that time the markets for English cotton goods. Contemporary authorities were clear about these conditions. Thus Ure
speaks of a "silent monopoly" which England has possessed
during the war (5).

All this changed with the conclusion of the war. ' Local
spinning mills sprang into existence everywhere, partly under
the protection of duties, as in France, but also without such, as
in Switzerland. Switzerland became pre-eminently a strong competitor of Manchester, full of energy, not only in its own, but
also in other Continental and Mediterranean markets (6), for
which water-power and a relatively damp climate made it suitable. Switzerland also appears to be the first to have arrived
at the possession of fairly skilled factory labour. Thus Ure
remarks that in Switzerland the population preferred, in many
cases, factory labour to cottage industry, no easy, but so much
the more an important alteration in the people's usages.

Alsace also enjoyed advantages similar to those of Switzerland. Here there were already in the "thirties," even if isolated,
spinning mills which in number of spindles were equal to
the English ; for example, Nägeli's, in Mulhouse, with 80,000
spindles, and that of Schlumberger and Bourcart, at Guebweiler,
with 54,000 spindles. Notably was Alsace superior to England
in chemical knowledge, and in design for printed muslins. It
may certainly serve as a sign of industrial strength that the
Société Industrielle petitioned for the introduction of a Factory
Act, and that the president of the Chamber of Commerce, Jean
Dollfus, supported a reduction of the tariffs. In his evidence
before the Commercial Inquiry of 1834, and in his answer to
certain attacks on this evidence, in 1835, he declares, strengthened

---

4. Compare Bein : "Die Industrie des Voigtlandes," pp. 121-33. One is
compelled at once, by the appearance of English yarns in Leipzig, to give up
home spinnings and weave English yarns. But as early as 1797 an English
merchant put cotton goods also on the market at a reduction of 25 per cent.

5. Ure : "Cotton Manufacture," II., 398.

6. Ure : "Cotton Manufacture," I., Intro., pp. 31-33 ; Committee on
Manufactures (670).

by accurate reckonings of the costs of production, that coarse numbers could be spun in Alsace not only not dearer, but rather cheaper than in England. "It is clear that France, when everything is considered, possesses an advantage over England, which must increase in proportion as the duties on raw materials and machinery are reduced" (7).

America possessed another advantage—the cheapness of the raw material. This made it possible for that country to compete successfully with England in cotton goods, even in certain foreign markets, for instance, China, Chili, and Brazil. Thus, in 1834, the imports of American calicoes into China amounted to 134,000 pieces, the English to only 75,000 (8)—a state of affairs which since then has altered very largely in favour of England.

"The continents of Europe and America," says Ure in 1836, "possessed up to some time ago, after the peace of 1814, only factories in such a small degree that they could by no means be viewed as competitors in the world's markets. To-day, however, they manipulate 750,000 bales of cotton, which is about three-fourths of our consumption, and they have become dangerous competitors in many markets which up to now belonged entirely to us."

The economical worth of the facts quoted is nothing less than that the district of the earliest centralised industry had been attacked by international competition. This applies also with regard to countries of high protective duties, even to France, which maintained the importation prohibition against English cotton goods even after the Continental blockade. The economical importance of smuggling, which flourished at that time, must not be overlooked. It is certainly known that tremendous quantities of English yarns went to the Continent during and after the Continental blockade. Whole industries have to attribute their present situation to smuggling. Thus Ure declares—and he should know—that the spinning mills of Reichenberg, on the frontier of Saxony, were nothing else than establishments for reeling English yarns, and that the spinning mills of Lombardy

---

7. Compare the description of the Alsatian industry by the expert, Ure (" Cotton Manufacture," Intro., pp. 57-93). Compare also Engel : " Baumwoll-industrie im Königreich Sachsen ".(1851), p. 26. Further, Herkner: " Die ober-elsässische Baumwollindustrie " (Strassburg, 1887), pp. 71-115.

8. Ure, pp. 52-54. Committee on Manufactures (3,845). Compare, on the other hand, " Commercial Relations of the United States," No. 12 (Oct., 1881), p. 204.

also had no other object than to mask the import of English yarns. The value of yarns smuggled yearly into France alone is given as 15 to 20 million francs (9). Of the importance of smuggling we find in Bein's " Industry of the Voigtland " a quantity of proofs (compare pp. 88 to 91). The commerce of the Voigtland suffered for instance, by long-continued rainy weather, because thereby the routes for smuggling into Russia were made impassable.

International competition compelled England to cheapen the costs of production. This effort, as it had produced Centralised Industry, now drove this forward to further improvement. It was compelled to bear the consequences of its own existence. Even at that time also the egg-shells of decentralised industrial conditions clung to the oldest Centralised Industry—spinning. The brushing away of these egg-shells is the history of English cotton-spinning, which develops the peculiarities of Centralised Industry in proportion as it has to contend for the premier position in the world's markets. Looked at from this standpoint, the tremendous mass of entangled Blue-Book reports are quite clear. The complaints of textile employers and the troubles of the workers are understood—the conditions of changing from half to fully centralised industry. But clear also become therewith the social-revolutionary movements in the "thirties" and "forties." If, indeed, economical conditions are really the foundation of the social, the same conclusion harmonises for the latter : These social movements are the infantile sicknesses of Centralised Industry.

We now ask what was the result of international competition—how did the striving after the cheapening of the costs of production first influence spinning? It caused at once a concentration of the industry in the neighbourhood of Manchester. That this development occurred under the pressure of the world's market is proved by the fact that formerly spinning was much less concentrated than to-day. Spinning by means of rollers, the most important step to modern machinery, i.e., the arrangement for the mechanical drawing of rovings, which before this was achieved by hand, was transferred by the metal preparation. Thus the first yarn was spun " without hands " in the middle of the last century in Birmingham. The first large factories were situated near Nottingham, and the merchants of Manchester sought to

9. Ure : " Cotton Manufactures," Intro., pp. 34, 36, 63. Report of the Silk Committee of 1832, p. 586.

boycott them. Scotland, for a long time the home of Robert Owen, was originally one of the chief seats of spinning. The cotton industry was also pretty fairly extensive in Ireland at that time, although it has to-day disappeared (10).

The demand for cheap production forced forward concentration. The advantages of this are, apparently, the avoidance of expensive repairing shops and reserve stocks of machinery pieces, which isolated mills cannot dispense with (11). Everywhere the complementary machine works settled in the central points of the cotton industry, in proximity to the spinning-mills. Lancashire became, therefore, at the same time a chief centre of machine-making. Local concentration first made possible, as well, a class of workers highly and intelligently trained for the work.

But certain natural advantages made the southern portion of Lancashire the earliest centre for Centralised Industry. Marching from here, this industry conquered England—even the world. In the North and East the district in question, smaller than Saxon Voigtland, is bounded by hills, which, towards Todmorden and Rochdale, attain considerable elevations, and are there divided by deep valleys.

Keeping back the dry East winds, they subject the West to downpours of rain. The land is little suited for agriculture; therefore the population turned fairly early to cottage industry, especially woollen weaving. On all sides brooks and rivers hurry from these hills to the near sea. These streams provided the first driving power for the machinery springing up. But under the meadows, and easily accessible to men, lies that mineral whose presence allows the replacement of water-power by steam-power—coal. One of these water-courses—the Mersey—forms at its mouth, through the influence of the Atlantic tide, one of the best harbours in the world. As soon as the county possessed something for barter, a central point of the world's commerce could not help but spring up here, viz., Liverpool. But the county has to thank the proximity of the sea for something still more important—the damp sea-breezes which envelop the hills and produce rains. The degree of moisture of the air is, in fact, on those heights, only ten per cent. below complete satura-

---

10. Ure: "Cotton Manufacture," I., 287. Further, Baines, p. 219.

11. In these days also to dispense with special gas plant, etc. Compare Jannasch: "Die europäische Baumwollindustrie" (Berlin, 1882), p. 25.

tion (12).   This dampness was, later, to make it possible to spin cotton to such a fineness here as is impossible elsewhere, or only to be attained by large extra expense.   How much this advantage of climate comes into consideration is shown by the fact that spinning-mills more and more seek the declivities of those hills where the rains are the heaviest; thus, especially, Oldham instead of Manchester.

This local concentration of the trade is one of the striking features of Centralised Industry.   It strives after a condition in which every county, every country, produces that for which its natural essentials are most favourable, for an international division of labour.   But since the industry, then, more or less dispersed, settles all over the whole country, this wandering by the few unsuitably situated must be viewed in many cases as trade decline.   Thus, for instance, is to be attributed the particularly strong complaints, found in the Blue-Books, of the Scotch spinners.

In conjunction with the concentration just described, a similar one occurs within single mills.   Leaving out of consideration a few tremendous exceptions, spinning mills had formerly a small number of spindles—often not above 1,000.   They settled just where the necessary water-power existed.   The owners spun mostly on commission for the merchant, who delivered the cotton (13), and took the yarn, exactly as to-day small commission spinning-mills situated on the water-courses are still to be seen in the highlands of Saxony (14).   The pressure of the world's market made such people at that time impossible in England.   As opposed to them, larger mills sprang up (15)   With the modern method of arranging a mill a double amount of capital makes it possible to produce more than double the quantity.   The costs of establishment, for instance, of a double number of spindles are not double; and the cost of buildings, land, machinery, etc., is

12. Compare Edward Atkinson: "Science Monthly" (New York, Jan., 1890). Americans reckon the advantage which Lancashire possesses on account of its climate at 7 per cent. of the cost of production on all fine counts.   Compare "Commercial Relations of the United States" (23rd Sept., 1882), pp. 27-37, where are exact meteorological figures.
13. "Committee on Manufactures" (9,126).
14. Compare, concerning such small spinning-mills, "Government Enquêts on Cotton and Linen Industry" ("Shorthand Protocols," pp. 142-3). They have probably disappeared since then.
15. The reasons why the smaller spinning-mills everywhere succumbed to the larger have been already followed by E. Engel in his work, "Die Baumwollindustrie des Königreichs Sachsen" (1851).

less (16). The same thing applies to a portion of the costs of running; for instance, steam power, lighting, tending, etc. Entirely dependent upon steam power (16A), these great spinning-mills sought unrestrained the most favourable situation, especially the neighbourhood of similar mills. Thus arose those factory towns with workers solely trained for cotton manipulation.

Side by side with the concentration of the industry, the striving after cheapening the costs of production led to technical advancements in a more contracted sphere. These lay in various directions. Experience taught the spinner to use raw materials to a greater extent than before; to spin equally good yarns from poorer cotton by improved preparation machinery; to lessen the loss during spinning, and to utilise the waste itself for lower qualities of yarn. In spite of this, the percentage of loss, compared with to-day, was still high in every instance.

But the most important developments lay in the replacement of labour by capital and in the increase of labour capacity. Both developments require one another so much that with regard to greater production it cannot be said how much is due to the one or the other factor. Machines were originally small, and found occupation for a great many badly-paid and under-nourished workpeople, but who, on account of their great number, were expensive. But since the employers had to begin to defend the possession of the markets of the world, this pressure forced a continual lengthening of machines. The number of spindles in single frames was increased, the speed of the spindles raised, the traverse of the mule lengthened. Here children were not sufficient; grown-up workers were needed, who by means of an increased standard of living had to be made capable of attending to the increased demands of machinery.

In spite thereof, both developments allow themselves to be clearly separated into the development of technical matters and the consequential alteration of labour. The necessity for cheapening the costs of production demanded an increase in the quantity produced. This was to be attained, in the case of spinning ma-

16. Compare Committee on Manufactures (9,166). Also Jannasch: " Die europ. Baumwollindustrie " (Berlin, 1882), p. 21, according to which an engine of 100 h.p. costs only one quarter as much per horse-power as an engine of 10 h.p.

16A. Especially did the going over to the self-actor demand steam power Exclusive of preparation, according to Martin, a hand-mule spindle requires 0·004 and a self-actor spindle 0·0065 h.p. On the other hand, self-actors require more preparation machinery.

chinery, in two ways. One was a larger production of the single spindle attained by a greater speed. At the same time the loss of time by ends breaking, etc., was lessened by improvements in the spinning-machine itself, and by improved carding and preparation, in spite of the greater speed.

According to Ure and Kennedy, the capability of the spindle was tremendously raised in the very years with which we are at present concerned—with 40's yarn from 2 hanks daily in 1820 to $2\frac{3}{4}$ up to 3 hanks in 1830 (17). As early as 1834 the daily production of the spindle was $3\frac{3}{4}$ to $4\frac{1}{2}$ hanks, of course with the most improved, but at that time still little-known machinery (18). This latter increase was in consequence of the introduction of the Self-actor, invented by Roberts in 1830. Since the return traverse of the mule-carriage was achieved mechanically, the winding-on of the yarn spun took place concurrently, with less danger of breakages and in a shorter time. Besides this, mechanical power, by its regularity and freedom from fatigue, being superior to human power, built the cops firmer and better suited for the weaver. Only when the weaver received weft yarn spun on self-actors could an increase be considered in the hitherto low speed of the loom. By the introduction of the self-actor the last demand on muscular strength disappeared, but certainly not, as was then thought, the adult spinner, because the minding of the more and more complicated machines was not to be achieved with youthful helpers alone.

If by the introduction of the self-actor the production per single spindle was increased by 15 to 20 per cent., so also was the number of spindles per spinning frame increased. In 1779 the operatives smashed jennies containing more than 20 spindles. The water frames with which Arkwright founded the factory system do not show more than 8 spindles, in the illustrations given by Ure. The happy combination of both machines by Crompton—the mule—had also not more than 20 to 30 spindles (19). At the period when Baines and Ure wrote, 400 to 600 spindles were the common length, whilst both, so early, described machines of 1,000 to 1,100 spindles (20). Side by side with the raising of the number of spindles occurred, not an increase, but rather a decrease of labour power.

---

17. Ellison: " Cotton Trade," p. 65.
18. Ure: Cotton Manufacture," II., pp. 194-203.
19. Compare Baines. p. 201. Ure: " Cotton Manufacture," I., pp. 259-60.
20. Ure, II., p. 154. Baines, p. 202. Further, Ure: " Philosophy of Manufactures," p. 323

The consequence of the development delineated was an extra-ordinary increase of production. Since the costs of working did not increase in the same ratio, they were spread over a greater produced quantity. Especially could a permanent reduction in piece-wages be introduced. The cost of labour for a defined quantity was continuously declining, owing to the advancing technical skill.

Yarn counts.	Hanks spun per spindle per day.		Cost of labour per lb. of yarn.		Cost of similar labour in India.
	1812.	1830.	1812.	1830.	Unchanged.
			s. d.	s. d.	s. d.
40	2	2·75	1 0	0 7½	3 4
80	1·5	2·2	2 2	1 7½	6 10½
100	1·4	1·8	2 10	2 2½	11 11
150	1	1·33	6 6	4 11	25 0
200	0·75	0·90	16 8	11 6	44 7 [21]

What effect had this technical development on the worker? It is, in the first place, to be noted that in spite of continuous cheapening of work the weekly earnings of the worker went higher. This phase was hidden at first by the prices of food moving downwards. But it is certainly correct to measure the income of the worker, not only according to its face value, but also by its buying power in relation to the most important nourishing foods. Looked at in this light, there occurred also at that time, along with cheapening of labour, an increase in the earnings of the worker—a development which belongs to the most marked peculiarities of centralised industrial progress. The elder Houldsworth gave the following interesting statistics, in this respect, before the Committee on Manufactures.

	Weekly product'n of the Spinner.		Time worked. Hours.	Total wages.	Deduct for helpers.	Net earnings of Spinner.	Buying power of these net earnings.	
	Counts.	Lb. of yarn.					In lb. Flour.	In lb. Meat.
				s. d.	s. d.	s. d.		
1804....	180	12	74 to 80	60 0	27 6	32 6	117	62½
„	200	9	„	67 6	31 0	36 6	124	73
1814....	180	18	74	72 0	27 6	44 6	175	67
„	200	13½	„	90 0	30 0	60 0	239	90
1833....	180	22½	69	54 8	21 0	33 8	210	67
„	200	19	„	65 3	22 6	42 9	267	85
						(22)		(23)

21. Baines, p. 353. Ure: "Cotton Manufacture." II., 425.
22. These wages are applicable for fine counts. The average wage of the mule-spinner in Manchester at this time amounted to 27s. Ure: "Cotton Manufacture," II., p. 444.
23. Prices reckoned according to the invoices of the Chetham Hospital, Manchester

The high counts of yarn mentioned here were, at that time, as yet scarcely spun on the Continent of Europe, because it did not possess the needful skilled workers for them. They were spun, outside of England, only by Indian hand-spinners, whose dexterity up to then had been the wonder of Europe. These finest Indian muslins were termed "woven wind"; they were extraordinarily expensive, because counts of yarn up to 240's were not seldom in them.   But although the Indian female spinner of those fine yarns, up to then unattained on the newer Continent, received 9d. per week, the English spinner, therefore, earning 40 to 50 times as much, the latter nevertheless destroyed the ancient industrial art still existing at this time, which (paradoxical enough) succumbed to dear labour, to labour which, as the table on page 43 shows, was about four times as dear as in England (24).

But a similar process developed also within England, in that the place where the industry progressed most strongly was where piecework wages were certainly lower, but, on the other hand, the weekly earnings and standard of living of the spinner was the highest.   Thus at that time Manchester raised itself above Glasgow, which, notwithstanding considerably lower weekly wages, paid higher piecework wages (25).

It is everywhere a fact capable of proof that with Centralised Industrial development a continuous decline of piecework wages is accompanied with a continuous increase in the income of the worker.   Upon what does this result depend ?   In order to understand it, we must grasp it as a continuation of that old-time development which once raised labour from slavery to freedom. The fettered or slave worker, who acomplishes labour by external pressure, is chained to the minimum of life; the master does not, as a matter of course, spend more than is absolutely necessary for maintaining and perpetuating labour.   It has to be viewed as a permanent factor, that it was economical progress which emancipated the worker.   Only the most primitive tools can be put into the hands of slaves (26).   Economical progress de-

---

24. Compare Ure: " Cotton Manufacture," I., p. 45.   Compare also the work quoted by Roscher, I., par. 40: " La main d'œuvre est chère en Russie."
25. Committee on Manufactures (5,339), and Baines, p. 440.
26. Thus slaves in America could not be trusted with horses, but only with mules. Compare Roscher: " System," I., par. 71. Agricultural exhaustion of land can only be permanently connected with slavery. Compare Baines " Slave Power " (London, 1863); and Mackenzie Wallace: " Russia," where a similar state is reported in America and Russia.

mands an increasing interest of the worker in his labour, with
the object of improving and raising his capacity for work, and
these are only possible on the foundation of freedom. Thus the
free craftsman is evolved from the serfish industrial workers,
originally in the interest of the master; and the town from the
feudal establishment of the Middle Ages (27). But more especially clear, because only belonging to the last and present century,
is this development in the sphere of agriculture. The necessity
of more thorough cultivation compels the introduction of the free
labourer, whose work, though apparently dearer, is still cheaper,
on account of its extraordinarily greater capacity (28).

In the hand-toil of the Middle Ages, trade labour had reached
freedom early, and afforded not only an agreeable existence, but
also honour and position in society. But the foundation of this
position was insecure; it depended upon monopoly and law enactments. It vanished with the flourishing of the world's market
and international competition.

Cheapening of the costs of production was now the innermost
principle of trading. Hand-work was therewith succeeded by
Centralised Industry, the oldest form of which was (cottage industry, whose full attainment first created the modern factory
system.) But the worker sank exceedingly quickly from his
former height, under the pressure of the new world-market. His
law of life was again the minimum standard of living, beyond
which he had already appeared to have raised himself for good
with the abandonment of slavery. The time for labour, limited
by custom or law, in summer (including the stoppage for
dinner) 12 hours, in winter until the commencement of darkness,
was again lengthened to the bounds of possibility.

---

27. The same thing is to be seen, again, in Russia, where the serf was allowed
to engage himself in another's trade service, and only a payment was reserved;
in fact, he was freed with the exception of the payment.—Oprockbauern.

28. Compare, for instance, what Roscher (par. 71) says is the experience on
the Bernstorff estates. The experiences of Von Münchausen have a similar
tendency. This personage, along with Bernstorff, was one of the first to
demand the emancipation of the serfs from the point of view of economical
progress. Compare Münchausen: "Detailed Particulars of the Cessation of
Serfdom on the Estate Steinburg" (Leipzig, 1801). Further instances, for
Russia, are given by Roscher (par. 71, note 6). A free mower mows as much
as two or three serfs; an estate horse accomplishes as much as three to four
peasants' horses; with free workers instead of serfs rye produces 8¼ instead of
3, barley 9½ instead of 4, oats 8 instead of 2¾ standards. All are analogies of
the development to be depicted here.

This development, in the case of England, has to be followed up most minutely. Up to our century the standard of living for the worker stood authoritatively defined—the degree of labour as well as of remuneration. If he earned sufficient with three days' work to live six days in the ordinary manner, he did not work the other three. Therefore the merchants of Manchester told A. Young that they preferred high to low food prices; for nothing but the first compelled the worker to labour.

This customary foundation of existence fell with the appearance of the modern trade system. Broken-down farmers and cottage workers, workhouse children, discharged soldiers—in short, the poorest of the poor—were placed at the newly-invented machines. It is known that the workers applied themselves to factory labour only through the uttermost necessity. The iron discipline and regularity of this labour itself appeared worse than the untrammelled misery of cottage workers. Only by the lowest wages were those elements to be forced to regular work. This deterioration occurred so much the more without opposition because those first workers of Centralised Industry were thus first drawn from customary conditions, whereas, on the other hand, their employers had already completely realised the modern man. Certainly the power of that first generation of English large employers consisted entirely in carrying out the principle of economy, regardless of anything. The proposition : Satisfy thy wants with the smallest possible expense, produce at the lowest cost, was of so much value to them that the choir of national economists accompanying the drama declared it to be the everlasting law of human life.

The "white slaves" which the modern factory system has produced have been spoken of. This is more than a saying. Because, in spite of outward differences, the position of those factory proletarians certainly resembles inwardly that of slaves, in that they seem in a hopeless manner to be forced to the minimum standard of living, and that every interest of the worker in his work is lacking. Contemporary observers have therefrom derived the immobile wage-law. They had, as we see to-day, only that stage of trade before their eyes which belongs to the change from scattered to centralised industry, and has only extended itself where that change was retarded. On the other hand, Centralised Industry, which is no longer a monopoly compared with a declining industry, requires, as we shall see more in detail further on, for the purpose of cheapening production, a gradual raising of labour similar to that which formerly led from serfdom to freedom. That factory proletarian, whose position brings to mind serfdom, is put on one side by the Centralised Industry growing up.

This follows, as a matter of fact, because the first low-standing factory labour certainly did not work cheaply. As later, everywhere where the factory system was introduced, one had at that time to struggle in England with the irregularity of labour. A reliable authority informs us that at the turn of the century it was impossible to keep the spinners at regular work. " Frequently they spent two or three days per week in idleness and drinking, and made the children who worked under them wait for them in the alehouses until they decided to go to their work. When they went to it, they would often work quite desperately, day and night, in order to pay off their public-house score and to earn more money for ' sprees ' " (29). This description reminds us of that which Blue-Books to-day inform us about Indian spinning-mills—large centralised establishments with the latest machinery. In spite of all discipline it cannot here be avoided that the workers work irregularly, and stop to eat and rest themselves in between. One is therefore compelled to keep such a large number of workers that those who work can take the places of those who do not. It is allowed, under this arrangement, that the men go out and smoke during working hours, the women suckle their children, workers often remain away for weeks in order to do agricultural work at their homes, and so on, As compensation, there are no long stoppages during which the engine stands, no free Sundays, or only one per month in order to clean the engine, and the working day is from 12 to 14 hours (30).

Also in Lancashire—to-day the country of the highest working capacity—a similar condition existed at that time.

How little machinery had up to then entered into the people's consciousness is shown by the keeping aloof, by the often inimical position, of most writers, compared with whom Ure emphatically took the more progressive standpoint. Thus a well-known physician of Manchester complains at that time about the lot of the operative

29. Ure: " Cotton Manufacture," II., p. 448.
30. " East India Factories " (10th Feb., 1891), pp. 23, 27, 45, etc. Compare, further: Proceedings of the Manchester Chamber of Commerce—" Bombay and Lancashire " (1888), p. 57.

—" Whilst the engine runs the people must work. Men, women, and children are yoked together with iron and steam. The animal machine—breakable in the best case, subject to a thousand sources of suffering, changeable every moment—is chained fast to the iron machine, which knows no suffering and no weariness." (31) It is noteworthy how here the machine, as such, is accused of inhumanity; the almost mathematical precision which it requires from the worker is pictured as unendurable tyranny. In all the labour movements of the first ten years of the century the hatred of the masses turned against machinery.

But gradually a change came—a change by reason of economical progress. It was in the "thirties" that, on the field of the oldest Centralised Industry, international competition marched for the first time. If England would conquer it must lower the costs of production. How was this possible? No longer by pressing down the worker, because these were already reduced to the minimum of life's wants. The only means for economical victory lay, therefore, in technical improvement, as also in the lessening of the number of workers employed in comparison with the work accomplished. Both led to continuous lowering of piece-work prices, which was decisive in the battle of competition, and, on the other hand, raised the weekly earnings of the individual worker. Similarly, as one could not put better tools in the hands of slaves, neither were the increasingly complicated and more valuable machines to be trusted to miserable factory proletarians. In order to increase the speed of the spindle, to raise the number of spindles to be tended, and to lessen the number of operatives per spinning mill, a worker with a higher standard of living was necessary. Thus the unmeasured services of the serfs became measured, and from the latter came freedom, from the trade working slave the free craftsman, from the servant of the master the journeyman of the Guild; the servant rose, but the master had more than before. In the same manner, also, the economical need raised the worker of Centralised Industry.

This development on the part of the worker appears to have been followed by a psychological change similar to that which had produced the modern employer. Whilst the man of the Middle Ages was born to his standard of living, his wants authoritatively defined—

31. Dr. Kay: "On the Moral and Physical Conditions of the Working Classes" (Manchester, p. 24). Similarly: Göhre: "Drei Monate Fabrikarbeiter" (Leipzig, 1891).

a state of affairs which has survived for a longer period in the lower stages of society—the modern man now also grows up in the worker of centralised industry. Just as the enterprising spirit of the employer pervades the whole world, "insatiable" from the standpoint of a former condition of society, in the case of the worker the limits to economical attainment also disappear. His wants, up to now limited by custom, encompass the whole achievements of culture. That which he earns over and above what his bare existence costs he adds to his standard of living. In order to satisfy his increased demands, he increases his labour capacity. In this way he succumbs at last to the "law of the greatest possible profit," which first pervaded the merchant, then the trade employer, and had produced the modern regime. The best worker of the world at present is the one with the highest needs, just as the cotton worker in Lowell and Fall River excels, perhaps, all his fellows in labour capacity, but also in his wants (32).

It is true that this development in the "thirties" in England was only in its infancy. That, however, the later type of worker was also just beginning to be evolved is proved by occasional particulars in the Blue-Books. He comes upon the scene as the mule-spinner of Lancashire. Thus, for instance, attention is drawn to the evidence of a certain Edwin Rose, who in the "twenties" or "thirties" was occupied for some time in a spinning mill at Mulhouse (33). In this town at least double the quantity of hands were necessary compared with Lancashire. Labour was therefore dearer, in spite of lower wages. In Mulhouse there were, for low counts, mostly 3 persons per 200 ends; in England per 600 to 800. It is true, according to Ure, that

32: Compare Pidgeon: "Journal of the Society of Arts" (Jan. 1885). Miss H. Martineau had already described, in her "Mind among the Spindles," the high and well-regulated standard of living of the old race of labour in Massachusetts. Compare, on the other hand, the following story lately related to me. The proprietor of one of the largest and finest weaving-sheds in Germany wished lately to persuade the best of his weavers to mind three looms instead of two, as formerly. But as this arrangement met with opposition from the workers, he sent for one of them in order to inquire into the cause of the opposition. On being made aware that the new arrangement meant an increased weekly wage, the weaver answered: He and his wife earned 28s. per week; he did not wish to exert himself for more; more money meant a "spree more." That man stood, in the field of the customary standard of living, as opposed to that girl in Lancashire who to-day minds four, and that in Massachusetts who to-day minds six looms. —

33. Factory Committee: Report (1833), Part I., D. I., 121; also Mr. Cowell: Supplementary Report (1834), 119. Compare also Roscher: "Nationalökonomie," I., par. 40, and the therein quoted particulars of Mohl. Further, Senior: "Outlines" (London, 1863), 142.

E

especially in Alsace, at that time the number of spindles in the single frame appear to have risen quickly ; notwithstanding which the production remained less than in Lancashire. The daily production per 800 spindles of No. 40's yarn in England was 66lb., in France 48lb. From the evidence of numerous employers, given before the Examining Committee quoted, as well as before that on Artisans and Machinery, it appears that the master-spinners examined already looked upon the possession of better labour as their chief strength against Continental competition. " A spinner in England does twice as much as a Frenchman. The latter gets up at four o'clock and works until 10 o'clock at night. But our spinner does in 6 hours what he does in ten."

With the same tendency we have also the utterances of workers, as, for instance, that in spite of shortened working hours the labour had become far more taxing than formerly ; it was complained that some operatives were seized by a dangerous ambition to accomplish more than is fit for human nature (34). The same witness from Stockport reports that these workers, however, also developed wants unknown up to then. For instance, instead of going to the public-house they took to books and attended schools—all at that time still quite exceptional circumstances. Possibly this applied only to a town where, as in Stockport, the second generation was already spinning, and wherein numerous workhouse children had been introduced to factory labour. For nothing urges forward the development of the modern man as much as forced or willing transplantation to other fields (35).

A new type of man entered at that time into existence in Lancashire—the industrial worker, born and educated for the machine. He is the latest result of the modern method of working. and determines its condition for some generations ahead. But even then he is only developed under favourable conditions, as in the most advanced great industries, before all others of England and America, and still the economical power-position of a nation is dependent in an increasing degree on his possession. As the man of the future, he does not find his equal in the past. It is not bodily power which distinguishes him, for the movements

34. Committee on Manufactures (10,552).

35. We are reminded here of colonists, who generally develop themselves more quickly than their former countrymen ; also of how new-arising industries everywhere require foreign workers. How long the later increase of factory labour was fed from the poorhouses is proved by the Committee on Manufactures (11,412).

requiring strength are accomplished by the machine. He resembles not the labour virtuoso of the so-called manufacture
(division of labour without mechanical power) which,
by reason of extensive division of labour, requires few
hand-touches for perfection. Tools now accomplish these touches
more perfectly—tools which attack more and more the field of so-
called " mechanical " work. Freeing the man therewith from the
tie of the constantly developing division of labour, the perfect
machine simply requires watching. With increasing size and
speed, with their augmenting productive power and complication,
there is, on the other hand, a continuously increasing brain-
attention demanded from the operative—an understanding of the
therein embodied thoughts of technicality. The man attending it
should be a son of the century of natural science. The modern
method of production also tends towards the contraction of similar
or increased labour capacity to a shorter time; it is cheaper to
exhaust the working power in nine than in eleven hours. The
modern operative, as produced by the American and English
Centralised Industry, is the extreme opposite of that handworker
who, by reason of a real or legal position of monopoly,
" makes his customers wait."

This development has been, without doubt, hurried forward in
England by social moments, especially by the contraction of
children's work and the shortening of the hours of labour which
the Factory Acts caused. The workpeople's combinations, and
their struggles with the employers, are also to be taken into
account. For instance, it is undoubtedly correct that the Self-
actor, invented by Roberts in 1830, was designed as a weapon
against the spinner, and first came into general use in consequence
of strikes (36). Looked at from this point of view, the social
movements of that time, those of the philanthropic Tories, as
well as the workmen striving to raise themselves, first attain the
foundation of economical necessity. Both have done their quota
to urge forward technical development. This consciousness is
expressed unusually early in the "Edinburgh Review" of July,
1835. "If from the discovery of the Spinning Frame up to the

36. Ure: "Philosophy of Manufactures," 367. Ure: "Cotton Manufacture." II., 194. Committee on Manufactures (5,621, 5,421). On the other
hand, the so-called "cheap labour" (i.e. labour feeble, incapable of exertion)
held full sway on Saxon spinning up to the "sixties" with the ancient system
of hand-mule. Compare Martin, "Der wirtschaftliche Aufschwung der Baumwollspinnerei im Königreich Sachsen," Smoller's "Jahrbuch für Gesetzgebung,"
Band xvii., Heft 3, pp. 12, 13

present," it is there written, " wages had remained at a level, and workers' coalitions and strikes had remained unknown, we can without exaggeration assert that the industry would not have made half the progress." But economical development has still been the chief factor, in that it has first called Centralised Industry and machinery in general into existence. So it was also, side by side with social moments at that time, the pressure of the world's markets which in England led to technical advancement, and, therewith, to the uplifting of labour (37).

What has been said shows English cotton spinning in a peculiar condition of change. The lawful and real possibility of competition had evolved the existence of machinery, but this alone could only develop the tendencies existing in it to the extent that, with the entrance into being of international competition, the English spinner ceased to demand monopoly prices. It is in general the trading history of the 19th century which is here represented within a microscosm. All characteristic delineations of modern Centralised Industry present themselves in the tenets: Concentration of Capital, geographically as well as technically; Replacement of Raw Material and Labour by Capital; Increase of Labour-capacity; Upliftment of the Position of the Operative.

Far less developed were the conditions of cotton weaving, which had just taken the first steps towards centralisation. Up to now the manufacturers had bought yarns spun by the machine, and given them out to the cottage weavers. In the first years after the invention of spinning machinery, which allowed the English spinners to have monopoly prices simply at the expense of their Continental customers, the business of English weavers of necessity flourished. At that time a tremendous influx of men occurred in the hand-weaving industry, the wages in which up to the turn of the century were splendid. The so-called manufacture developed itself at that time side by side with the real cottage weaving. Capitalists built special weaving shops in order to find work therein for about 20 to 30 hand-weavers, whilst the preparation work was accomplished by children and old people in the same house. Everywhere in Lancashire, but especially in Bolton, one sees even to-day these now desolate weaving shops.

37. Compare, on the other hand, concerning the Continental industry, Committee on Manufactures (11,378, 11,382, 11,387, etc.).

All this changed with the end of the war and the beginning of international competition. The change was not merely a direct transition to the power-loom, but employers of hand weavers with plenty of capital built spinning mills, and spinners became at the same time employers of hand weavers. Especially was the latter often the case, because the increasingly unstable payments of the small manufacturers led the spinners to give out the yarns themselves. These were the persons who at that time drew large profits from the so-called elasticity of the cottage industry, and who, according to the state of trade, sold the yarns or got them woven. The richest in capital amongst them began gradually to build, in addition to their spinning mills, sheds for power-looms (38).

The first owners of power-looms made, like the first spinners, tremendous profits; as power weaving mills became general, prices as well as profits rapidly declined. On a piece of calico, for instance, 28 in. wide, $5\frac{1}{2}$lb. weight, ordinary quality, there was in 1829 still a sum of 5s. for the cost of production and profit, in 1833 only 3s. (39).

Only after 1820 did the power-loom make more important progress. But in spite of this there were still in 1830 only about 50,000 to 80,000 (40) power-looms, against 250,000 hand-looms. With the power-loom, also, the replacement of labour by the machine developed much more slowly than in spinning.

As long as the sizing of the warp had to be accomplished by hand during the weaving the application of the power-loom was scarcely an advantage. An alteration was for the first time effected by the invention of sizing and dressing machines. From that time weaving could go on without a break, and one weaver could mind two looms. It does not appear that more looms were anywhere at that time tended by one weaver. The increase of production by the power-loom was also not very important.

---

38. Ure: "Cotton Manufacture," II., p. 430. Committee on Manufactures (9,161, 9,280).

39. Committee on Manufactures (9,171-95)

40. According to Porter, 50,500; according to Ellison, 80,000 in the year 1829, and about 100,000 as early as 1833. Compare Baines, p. 236, where he gives the above number for hand-looms. Compare Committee on Manufactures (9,449); Committee on Handloom Weavers, 1834 and 1835 (371-4). The total number of all hand-weavers is given as one million.

In the year 1823 two power-looms produced weekly seven, in the year 1826 twelve pieces of shirtings, of which a hand weaver in the same time could produce but two (41)

Moreover the power-loom was at that time only used for the smaller portion of all woven materials—for common and plain goods. In 1822 a patent was first granted to Roberts for a power-loom with six shafts, in order to produce twill-like articles; and in the whole following decade experiments were being constantly made on arrangements for raising and lowering several shafts, with the object of producing the most simple patterns with the power-loom (42). That an advance in this branch was slower certainly was not on account of the greater difficulty of the technical problems to be overcome, but that in this branch the pressure of the world's market, and the necessity for invention, were not felt so soon.

In Blue-Books we find, accordingly, nearly all manufacturers of the opinion that the hand-loom could never be supplanted by the power-loom; but rather that with the increase of English commerce the number of the cottage weavers must permanently increase, as was in reality up to then the case (43). And yet the Frenchman, Jacquard, had as early as 1812 invented the arrangement called after his name, which, in connection with the power-loom, was to make it possible to produce even the most intricate art designs by mechanical means. At that time the production of such goods required a great quantity of labour—the so-called reader, who, according to the pattern, read aloud the figured points; and another worker, who, according to these instructions, connected the couplings to which the shafts hung with the hooks requiring to be drawn; and then, besides the weaver, the draw-boy, who during the weaving looked after the raising of the thus coupled shafts (44); also here, therefore, by the newer inventions an extraordinary replacement of Labour by Capital took place.

A peculiar similarity with the conditions just pictured is shown by the commercial organisation of the cotton industry at that time. Just as modern Centralised Industry developed itself side

---

41. Baines, 239-40.

42. Ure: " Cotton Manufacture," II., 306.

43. For instance : Committee on Manufactures (11,992, 1,212): "Hand-loom weavers increase and must increase"; further, 1,198, 9,434.

44. Ure: " Cotton Manufacture," II., 281-7.   Karmarsch: " Technologie," 973-5.

by side with spinning, the raw-material market was already the
most advanced product-market of the world, with which the
technicalities of the modern world's commerce were perfected. It
enjoyed already in the "thirties" a division of labour developed
in the highest degree. As, however, on the other hand, weaving,
being in closer proximity to the consumers, was technically still
behind, so was it also with the mediating commercial element
between manufacturers and consumers.

The reasons for these results are also similar. As Centralised
Industry in weaving required first that of spinning, so the whole
cotton industry required the cotton market. The investment of
large sums in centralised industries was not possible until the
investors were certain of the regular delivery of the raw material,
and an organised market already lessened the dangers of extreme
variations of price. But the possibility of such a market was
produced because purely commercial, calculating people came here
into contact with one another. It was otherwise with the relation
to the consumer. As long as the English factory owner, as the
representative of the oldest centralised industry, found himself
in a sort of position of monopoly as compared with his customers,
the formation of a highly developed organisation for sale was not
necessary. This appeared in proportion as these advantages disappeared, and it was solely economical superiority which assured
to the English industry its market for sale.

To the following of every industry, from the buying of the raw
material to the sale of the finished article, there are connected a
great many dangers of the most variable kind—dangers which,
however, allow themselves to be extraordinarily diminished by
an intimate practical knowledge of the controlling conditions.
Hence division of labour, wherever it is possible, in such a manner
that, for every risk which demands control of one of the groups
of certainties contained within it a special organ is created.

Now this was already in a high degree the case in the "thirties"
in the cotton market. Here, on the one hand, stood the importing
merchant with his office in Liverpool. His task was to make
himself conversant with the American market—a risk of such
greatness, with the difficult traffic and communication conditions
of the time, that he at first even imported the cotton, not at his
own risk, but on commission for account of the Americans against
cash on account. But already in the first half of the century
came, in place of the importing commission house, the real

importer, who imported the cotton at his own risk. To deal with him existed the inland merchant, mostly with his office in Manchester, who generally sold the cotton to the spinners, giving long credit. His task was to watch over the influencing industrial conditions—for instance, the demand to be expected, the paying capabilities of the spinners, etc., etc.

The more complicated the influencing conditions became the less were importer and merchant in a position to deal direct with one another—such would have needed also a knowledge of each other's business. Hence the formation of two mediums, the buying and the selling broker, each of which attended only to the interests of his own customers. The relation of these different classes of commercial life rested upon a code of unwritten laws. No importer could, as Ellison (45) assures us, attempt to deal direct with the buying agent; this latter would have referred him to the selling agent. Just as little could the buying agent contract direct with the importer. The importers, like the merchants, generally had one or more brokers, through whom they permanently transacted their business.

Whilst thus, as regards the raw material, an already extreme division of labour had arisen, it was absolutely wanting as regards the selling of the finished article. There was still wanting that, at the present day, important person, the export merchant, who relieves the manufacturers from a knowledge of foreign markets, of the paying capacity of foreign and home buyers, etc. The manufacturer still dealt direct with the home retailer or the foreign importer, the commercial traveller and the agent being the mediums.

The manufacturer searched for the home customer by commercial travellers. Richard Cobden was one of these in his youth. Similarly was the Continent of Europe attended to (46). At the most important places of the mainland the English manufacturer sold as well by agents on the spot.

The trade with India, China, and East India was conducted otherwise. This trade, on account of the great distances and slow connections of that time, was extremely risky. Originally the captain freighted his ship on his own account, so far as the trade was not by reason of privileges in the hands of officials.

45. "Cotton Trade," p. 273
46. Committee on Manufactures (2,148).

East India was only thrown open in 1815 (47). In the "twenties" and "thirties" this adventurous navigator disappeared. The manufacturer shipped the balance of his production at his own risk. The merchant who acted for him was in fact only a commission merchant, who attended to the shipping and generally advanced half the value of the shipment (48). When the goods arrived they were sold by native or English commission houses, or put up by auction. In the best case the English manufacturer could expect payment in 18 or 19 months after the departure of the goods. This came either in the form of return freight— indigo, coffee, tea, etc.—or in bills of exchange, often of a questionable nature. In this way nineteen-twentieths of the colonial trade was transacted, alongside of which shipments to order played but a slight part.

We find, therefore, as regards the selling, the manufacturer saddled almost alone with all risks. Instead of strictly confining himself to the inner development of his manufactory, he was obliged to take into consideration the political and economical variations of the whole world, especially the rate of exchange on India, at that time already very fluctuating.

The home market, in the last century the most prominent, was still always of larger importance.

Home Market.		Export in Cotton Goods.	
1766	£379,241	...... £220,759	according to Postlethwayt.
1819-21......	£13,044,000	...... £15,740,000	according to Ellison.
1829-31......	£13,331,000	...... £18,074,000	

We notice how the export interest at the beginning of the "thirties" predominated. On this basis was founded the position taken up by the manufacturers of Lancashire against the Corn Laws. This movement must here not be lost sight of; firstly, because it was the result of the centralised industrial development, as soon as the export interest was uppermost; then, because its success sealed the character of the English cotton industry as an export industry. The enormous increase in the export of cotton goods in the following decades was one basis of the further development of the centralised industrial form of production and the commercial organisation corresponding to it, the details of which we deal with below.

47. Compare Committee on Manufactures (2,066, 2,120) on the conditions which led to the withdrawal of the privileges of the East India Company.

48. Committee on Manufactures (2,117, 2,155).

The Anti-Corn-Law League was a capitalist movement, emanating from the cotton manufacturers and the Manchester Chamber of Commerce, after a forward movement by the London tradesmen in 1820 had remained without success. At its head stood the spinner and weaver, John Bright, and the calico-printer, Richard Cobden. The large sums which were used for the agitation—nearly £500,000, including the princely reward of Cobden for his services—are alone a proof of the capitalistic character of the movement. The immediate factor of the movement was the depression in trade from 1839 to 1843. In 1842 ten per cent. of all cotton mills stood idle part of the time (49). The manufacturers, so says Cobden distinctly, had invested a portion of their capital in the movement in order to save the remainder (50).

The working classes, up to then the most earnest opponents of the Corn-Laws, turned their backs to the movement as soon as it had got into the hands of the employers. Again and again they dispersed meetings of the League, so that Martineau thinks they went hand-in-hand with the supporters of the Corn-Laws. This is assuredly incorrect; shortsighted as they were, they turned themselves against their nearest opponents.)

We need not here go further into the movement, which under the name of Cobden is known all over the world. On the other hand it is necessary to make clear the inner moving reasons which drove the English cotton industry on to the political platform. These are to be separated from the arguments brought forward, which mostly predominate in the speeches.

The cotton manufacturers of Lancashire fought, in the expensive and wearisome agitation against the Corn-Laws, in the first instance in the interest of export. Export was only possible by import, because cash payments between economical nations play an exceedingly small part. If a nation was paid in cash for its exports, the store of precious metals must soon rise above the usual level, and this at once result in a raising of prices, facilitation of imports, and making exports more difficult. Further consequences must be the lowering of the rate of interest and the flowing away of cash reserves. In the stores of the precious metals of the world, such a levelling-up would follow of itself.

49. Compare " Ashworth, Cobden, and the League "(London, 1876), p. 34.
50. Compare " Ashworth, Cobden, and the League," pp 3.9,72-75,112.

As a matter of fact experience teaches that such a relation can really happen, but still not beyond reasonable bounds. A few millions in cash taken from or added to the stores of precious metals of a country accomplish of themselves alone a raising or lowering of the rate of interest which is sufficient to lead to the opposite result, and therewith cause an equality. Generally the money market is of itself very sensitive to the increase and decrease of amounts which do not come into consideration in comparison with the gigantic sums of international exchange of goods. The whole of the precious metal of a nation, including that used for ornamental and industrial purposes, would not be sufficient to pay, even for only one year, for the imports. Thus, for instance, in 1880 the whole stores of precious metals in England were computed at 140 million pounds, whilst the imports amounted to over 400 millions.

Looking from this point of view the cotton manufacturers of Lancashire asserted that it was immaterial whether the exports of their yarns and goods were placed under an export duty or the imports of the goods received in exchange were subjected to an import duty. As England satisfied its own industrial wants, the great mass of imports could only consist of nature's products; the dearer, and those natural products forming a luxury, are, however, only bought when the longing for food is stilled; therefore wheat was the most important exchange article of foreign and non-industrial nations for the English cotton and other industrial productions. Wisdom also demands that one should let in the chief exchange mediums of agricultural nations free of duty if one would not lead too early to the introduction of an industrial system (51).

That trade interests predominated is shown already in Cobden's first sentence in which he touches the question. The repeal of the Corn-Laws was the means to return to the battle in the world's market, under more favourable conditions to defeat the competition everywhere newly arisen. "To stem the import of corn into an industrial country is nothing less than to kill the living nerves of its foreign trade" (52). Industry has to bear the

---

51. Committee on Manufactures

52. Compare Richard Cobden: "Political Writings"(London, 1867), vol. I., 143, 288. Gladstone, in a debate on the 23rd March, 1842, expressed pregnantly the point of view under notice: "The import of 50,000 cattle leads to an import trade to the value of half a million. It therefore leads to an export trade of a similar amount, which makes increased industry and labour necessary." Similarly also, Ure "Philosophy of Manufactures," p. 448.

tremendous calls of the State debt caused by the war, and the taxes for the defence of the country as well as the colonies. That husbandry in the future will be more capable to bear these ever-increasing public burdens was beyond every possibility; therefore industry was to be strengthened in the common interest of the country.

The further point of view, that free imports, and therewith cheapening of foodstuffs, must lessen the production costs of the industry, is less seldom mentioned, perhaps because many manufacturers were short-sighted enough to introduce this advantage in the unpopular form of reduction of wages. But that it was thought about is shown by the writings of Ure and Cobden (53).

Ure lingers repeatedly on the advantage which the Continent possesses in the greater cheapness of foodstuffs. In January, 1836, the average price of wheat per quarter in Hamburg, Amsterdam, Antwerp, and Stettin had been £1 8s. 1d., against which in London it was £2 4s. 6d. A similar relation existed between England and North America. But even Ure does not arrive at a correct understanding regarding the influence of the prices of foodstuffs in the production costs of the industry. His gaze rests in the first instance on the possibility of reduction in wages. If in England the amount of wages just reached sufficient to guarantee the worker a scanty existence, this wage could not be permanently reduced. But where for the wages paid far more could be bought than was really necessary, there was created the possibility of a reduction in wages. Thus were the lower wages on the Continent explained by the cheapness in the prices of food.

The manufacturers of Lancashire were certainly correct when they considered that cheap food meant also cheap labour; they were, however, mistaken in confounding cheap labour with lower wages. Cheap labour, like low wages, is only in that beginning stage of centralised industrial development in which the worker accomplishes no more than is necessary for satisfying the scantiest needs of life. If the latter become cheap, there is therewith, indeed, the possibility given of reducing wages, and this is the only way to cheapen labour. It is otherwise where the modern worker develops himself from that extensive factory-proletarianism. The English manufacturers certainly knew already

---

53. Compare R. Cobden: "Political Writings," I., p. 286. Ure: "Cotton Manufacture," I., Intro., pp. 18, 36, 47, 56.

quite well, that their mule-spinner worked cheaper, although he was perhaps the only worker in England who at that time, measured in foodstuffs, received a higher wage than the worker on the Continent. For this modern worker cheapening of food causes at the same time a rise of wages, the latter, however, being added to the standard of living. The more nourishing food, especially the going over to wheat and meat nourishment which was the lot of the English worker after the repeal of the Corn-Laws, has certainly caused more than anything else the production of that high capacity for labour, the real " skilled labour," which to-day forms the strength of England in international competition. Up to the repeal of the Corn Laws English wages, at all events in money value, but not, which is the real factor, in purchase value of foodstuffs, had been higher than those on the Continent (54).

In conclusion, Ure draws attention to the fact that the antagonistical feeling between employer and employed, which injured the competitive capacity of England so much, was due in a great degree to the Corn Laws. Blue-Books, indeed, prove, by the printed evidence of the workers, how much the Corn Laws seemed to them as "a law for the rich," which had for its purpose the keeping down of the workers in their needy position—an irremovable source of hatred against the Government and society (55).

The manufacturers were also not wrong in thinking that the abolition of the duties would secure more peaceful relations between capital and labour. This did not happen, however, in the manner which they pictured to themselves, for the Chartists banished this hope at once by opposing the League. But by the repeal of the Corn Laws a stage of industrial development was prepared which made those political-revolutionary classes representatives of the past. Cottage-industrial and decaying hand-workers, along with that earliest, hopeless factory proletariat evolved by Centralised Industry. had been their foundation. While the path of centralised industrial development was opened by

---

54. They amounted, according to Ure, on the average to about one-third more than the Continental, just as the prices of food were just so much higher.

55. Compare Committee on Manufactures (10,614) : " They think it (repeal of duties) would cause a complete revolution in wages and profits; it would cause an unbounded extension of manufactures." Further, 10,618, 10,622, 10,627, 11,081

the victory of Cobden, it also aided not only economical but also social progress. The worker of Centralised Industry, as he was now formed, grew out of the political-revolutionary movement, which had been nothing more than a sign of extreme weakness. In consequence of technical development, and by reason of increased labour capacity, this worker rose in existing society to a middle-class position.

The victory of the League was the expression that bourgeoisie society, economically the highest in the State, had achieved this position politically also. The previous transition stage is noted thereby that the leader of landed-proprietorship, Sir Robert Peel, was himself the offspring of one of the oldest manufacturing families of Lancashire. On the other hand, it is not to be lost sight of that the manner in which the victory took expression, that of the autonomous duty repeals in place of the use of the Corn Laws to be given up, to get compensations from other nations, depended solely upon the commercial-political constellation of that time. It was hoped that the other nations of Europe would of themselves follow with lowering of tariffs. Then appeared at that time those enormous markets of the East for the cotton industry, India and China, which were ruled politically or commercial-politically, and with which that point of view of compensation did not come into question.

CHAPTER III.

THE PRESENT POSITION OF THE ENGLISH COTTON INDUSTRY COMPARED WITH ITS POSITION IN THE "THIRTIES" AND WITH THE PRESENT POSITION OF THE GERMAN COTTON INDUSTRY. (1)

In the half-century that has elapsed since the "thirties" England has become "the workshop of the world." "Where there is no English commerce there is no commerce at all"—is the report of the American Secretary of State (2). A number of centralised English industries have succeeded in obtaining possession of the neutral markets of the world; English exports have quadrupled and quintupled themselves since the "forties." The cotton industry progressed beyond all others, its exports exceeding those of the iron trade by about three times (3). We indicate at the outset the progress and the present position by statistics: —

	Spindles.	Power-looms.	Hand-looms.
1831	10,000,000	80,000	220,000
1856	28,000,000	298,847	some thousands
1885	45,000,000	560,955	some hundreds (4.)

About a third of the total exports of England falls to the lot of the cotton industry, and a not much smaller proportion of the English people live on the foodstuffs which are exchanged for

---

1. Where no sources are given in the following particulars they may be taken as originating from studies on the spot, and are, from their very nature, sufficiently authoritative.

2. "Commercial Relations of the United States," No. 12 (Oct., 1881), p. 71 .

3. 1887 : Exports of cotton yarns and goods, £70,959,766 ; of iron and steel, raw and finished, £24,992,314 ; total exports of home productions, £221,414,186.

4. These figures approximately agree with those given by Samuel Andrew, in "Fifty Years' Cotton Trade." They are taken for 1856 and 1885 from official statistics ; for 1831 from Ellison : "Cotton Trade." The number of spindles were averaged, because Ellison, by reason of commercial directories, declares the official figures far too small. He estimates the number of spindles in 1885 to be already 48 millions. Compare Ellison, p. 327-8. These statistics are confirmed by Elijah Helm, "Economic Journal" II. 737; according to him there were in 1891 in Great Britain 44,750,000 spinning spindles ; in addition, according to the Statistical Abstract, nearly 4,000,000 doubling spindles, besides the spindles not in operation, which, according to Ellison, are a few millions.

cotton goods. The English cotton industry, besides being the oldest, is also in many ways to-day the centralised industry which shows up most typically the peculiarities of the modern method of production in an economical as well as social aspect.

But still it has only to be accepted as a link of a people's economy depending upon centralised industry and world barter. As the flourishing cotton industry, before everything else, founded the trading dominion and capital power of England, so at present does it receive the harvest of the highly-developed economical life encircling it. We are thinking, firstly, in this connection, of the trade organisations of Manchester and Liverpool, of the development of English machine-making, etc.

The pressure of the world's market was the motive element. It compelled a continuous cheapening of cotton goods. With it a permanent lowering of the production costs became the leading motive of the whole development. This is shown by the following figures:—

	1779.	1830.	1860.	1882.	Jan., 1892.
Price per lb. of 40's yarn....	16/-	1/2½	11½	10½	7¾
Price of cotton, 18 oz.	2/-	7¾	6⅞	7⅛	4⅞
Difference in price	14/-	6¾	4⅝	3⅜	2⅞

And so with finer counts: a pound of No. 100's, which in 1830 still cost 3s. 4½d., was in January, 1892, sold up to 16⅛d. In the years 1880-85, which were by no means bad ones for spinners, the difference between cotton and yarn per pound amounted on an average to only 3$\frac{1}{16}$d., whilst in the "thirties" double the amount (for instance, 1830, for 40's, 6¾d.) was looked upon as unprofitable (5). Similarly with weaving, even though the comparison between the price of yarn and that of cloth is more difficult on account of the heavy and variable weighting of many goods with foreign matter, and on numerous other grounds. In any case one cannot be far wrong if the lowering of the costs of production is taken as at least one-half.

The possibility of this cheapening lies herein, that under the pressure of the world's market (competition) those tenets of a centralised industry before mentioned have been meanwhile fully developed.

5. Compare Ellison: "Cotton Trade," pp. 61, 310.

1.—*Arrangement and Division of Labour in the Industry.*

Marshall, in one portion of his last work, points to the connection between national economy and natural science. The latter has borrowed from national economical writers the representation of the struggle for existence; but to-day it pays back the debt by enriching national economy with its teaching of organic development. Marshall thinks, apparently, in this respect, about the development-teaching of Herbert Spencer, which allows happy analogies to be applied to the social and economical side.

Every development consists, according to this view, in the first instance in the formation of single centres for development by the collection of matter; it is in the first degree a history of increasing dimensions and accumulating positiveness, as compared with the surrounding state: Integration. Besides this, it is a history of growing inner variation. The homogeneous structure gives way to the improvement of parts, which develop themselves independently in an increasing degree and ever undertake more varied functions. But in proportion as the parts become different from one another their mutual dependence increases. The one cannot exist without the other; a change of the part alters the whole; a disturbance of the part disturbs the whole: Differentiation. This is applicable to physiological as well as social occurrences.

Thus the development progresses from the minute living form of the lowest class to the powerful phase of the higher animal world; from the protoplast, which is very little different from its surroundings, to definite wholes, complete of themselves, and sharply defined from their surroundings. Whilst in the lower stages of development the inner structure is homogeneous, an increasing variation of the parts is ever formed: in place of similar-shaped cellular formations appear complicated organisms. Originally every part performs all functions; thus the original particle performs the functions of nourishment and perpetuation at the same time. Later on there is developed for every function a special organ. Therewith the mutual dependency of the parts upon one another increases; for instance, of the heart upon the nerve system, and of the whole upon the parts. Those lower stages of life can be separated at will; they still live on. The mutilation of one of the organs of the higher organism is detrimental to all the other organs, indeed can kill the whole organism (6).

6. Compare, for this, Herbert Spencer: " First Principles " and " Principles of Biology," part I.

F

Economical development is also principally a history of enlarging dimensions and increasing separation from the surroundings. Firstly, small works are spread over the whole country; as against these stand the modern gigantic mills, which localise themselves geographically.

There is also here the same increasing division of labour. Whilst originally all trades are joined together in one works—the self-providing farm, the ancient municipality of the past—the farming interest separates itself from the textile industry, this from the preparation of metals, etc. But therewith increases the mutual dependency of the single works. The original isolated establishment can be separated without disadvantage from its like; the establishment founded on division of labour and exchange, if torn from its connection with the whole, perishes or falls back to the former basis of existence.

The same thing applies if we take only one trade into consideration—say the textile industry. Originally its inner structure is uniform; every one of the small establishments produces the raw materials, manipulates them, and uses them. Also where barter later appears, the small trader is producer and merchant concurrently. As against this stands modern industry, in which all these functions are separated—the production and the consumption, the technical and the commercial element. A special market is formed for the raw materials, a special one for the articles produced, and both markets are separated from the manufactory. All three links are joined by connecting ones. Also in the manufacturing process there is progressive division of labour; it is cheaper to produce 1,000 of A than 500 of A and 500 of B. But here, also, with progressive division of labour there is an increasing dependency of the single establishments upon one another. A disturbance of the raw-material market exercises its damaging influence on the manufacturing and selling; while sale stagnations are inimical to the two preceding links. The industry becomes more and more a complete organisation, made up by a number of isolated organisations dispersed over the whole country, but remaining similar to one another—a complete organism, which is formed out of different kinds of units, geographically concentrated, depending upon one another.

No industry is more fitting to confirm these principles of Herbert Spencer than the English cotton industry.

In this respect the concentration of the industry and therewith the developing division of labour is most striking. Lancashire, or rather the southerly portion of the county, not 25 English square miles in extent, becomes the sole seat of this world-industry, which was originally by no means so arranged (7). The once not unimportant Irish industry has ceased; Scotland, which at one time entered into competition with Lancashire, has been confined to some specialties. The population of England has increased threefold since the beginning of the century, that of Lancashire sixfold; some of the single industrial towns—Oldham, for instance—twenty-fold (8).

As Lancashire to-day is the seat of the industry, Liverpool is the world's market for cotton, Manchester that for yarns and woven goods.

But, closely allied with the local bringing together of the industry, we have the concentration of the single mills. According to official sources these were on the average in England (8a):—

In 1850, per mill	10,858	spindles.
,, 1885, ,,	15,227	,,
,, 1856, ,,	155	power-looms.
,, 1885, ,,	213	,,

But these figures do not nearly represent the real conditions. Remote mills scarcely coming into consideration for the industry are included, as well as such as still combine weaving and spinning. If we only bring those mills into consideration which solely spin or weave, there were already in 1878, per mill, 24,738 spindles and 305 power-looms (9). But much more do these figures increase if we consider the real seats of the industry. According to a personal communication from Mr. Sam. Andrew, the Master-Spinners' Secretary at Oldham, the average number of spindles in his district amounts to from 60,000 to 65,000; for the "limited" concerns, so early as the middle of the "eighties," to 65,342. There are in this district spinning mills up to 185,000 spindles. I am also indebted to a personal communica-

---

7. Compare Baines, pp. 19 and 238.

8. Compare " Co-operative Wholesale Annual " (1884), p. 106; do. (1887), p. 332.

8a. These statistics are based upon figures which do not distinguish between spinning and weaving mills, because the official census of 1850 was so arranged. The number of spindles per spinning mill is, of course, greater.

9. Ellison : " Cotton Trade," p. 72.

tion from Mr. Rawlinson, Secretary of the Weaving Association of North Lancashire, for the following information. According to him the average number of power-looms per weaving-shed is 600; the highest number in one building, 2,200; those belonging to one firm, 4,500. The lowest number is 110 to 130, because with such mills the employer requires only one overlooker, whom he would have to pay if even less looms were at work. There is an exception in Burnley—a weaving-shed with 60 looms; in this instance, however, the employer was formerly an operative, and is his own overlooker.

One circumstance is to be noted here which has helped forward the concentration of the mills: the extension of the "limited" principle. It appears especially advantageous for spinning concerns whose working is uniform and whose market is continuous. At the present time limited concerns have the upper hand in spinning. In Oldham more than 80 per cent. of the whole spindles belong to limited companies. It is generally acknowledged that this development, which has occurred since the "seventies," has led to an extraordinary accumulation of capital. Thus the best authority on the English cotton industry, Mr. S. Andrew, said before the Royal Commission on Depression of Trade:—"The limited principle has brought many benefits to the country. It came into existence with us at a time when the lowering of production costs in the cotton industry was a question of life or death. Private firms at the time did not quite keep pace with the requirements of the time: limited concerns arose and undertook the lead, which they have never yet lost since that time." In another portion he mentions how the very great accumulation of capital secured the acquisition of the most improved technical arrangements by these companies (10). The limited principle seems to be less suitable for weaving-mills, because these demand adaptations to fashion and market variations, especially those weaving-mills making fancy goods for the European markets. In the latter branch an employer following

---

10. Compare also Ellison: " Cotton Trade," p. 136; further, " Co-operative Wholesale Annual " (1884), which, on page 174, contains a list of the limited spinning-mills at work in Oldham at that time, along with the number of spindles. A similar list is published periodically by the Oldham Sharebrokers' Association, which, in addition to the number of spindles, gives also the market value of the shares. the amount paid per share, nominal value and number of shares, as well as the last dividend, etc.

the market, and with a taste for art, is to be desired (11). On
the other hand the regularity of Oriental conditions grants to the
greater portion of the cotton-weaving mills of Lancashire the
advantage of a similar regular staple industry. If European
taste changes according to months and seasons, that of the
Hindoo changes only after hundreds, even thousands of years.
It is therefore correctly stated in Lancashire that the demand
from India year by year for certain cotton stuffs is as sure as that
the English nation requires every year a certain quantity of
wheat.

In the weaving branch the limited principle is, by reason of
the causes mentioned, less extended, and is certainly confined to
the staple industry for the Eastern markets. Still, according to
Mr. Rawlinson's communication, about 10 per cent. of the weaving-mills of his district are also limited concerns.

The value of this concentration of the industry is best understood if one takes into account the division of labour made
possible by it. The latter, first developed in the "thirties" for
the raw-cotton market, has since then taken hold of the whole
cotton trade—the manipulation as well as the market for yarns
and woven goods.

We will follow the cotton on its way from the importer to the
export merchant. The cotton market in Liverpool, highly developed as early as the "thirties," has entered since then under
the influence of modern traffic facilities—i.e., the application of
steam power to transport. In the continual development that
has necessarily followed it has been an example in general for
the technicalities of the world's commerce (12).

The first of these occurrences was the opening of the railway
from Manchester to Liverpool. Up to this time the spinner
chiefly bought from the dealer in Manchester, either from his
warehouse or according to samples provided. From this time
Liverpool and Manchester became practically one city. The
spinner could go just as easily to the broker in Liverpool as to
the dealer in Manchester, and choose there and then on the spot

11. Herein consists, for instance, the strength of certain German industries.
Not only the director, but also his wife. are here often personally engaged in
designing patterns, often of remarkable beauty, as, for instance, in many
export goods of the Saxon Voigtland.

12. Compare, for instance, Fuchs: " The Organisation of Liverpool Cotton
Commerce" (" Schmoller's Annual," 14th year, part 1.), and the second portion
of Ellison's " Cotton Trade," which is devoted to the cotton market.

what he wanted. At the same time the paying capabilities of the spinners had increased sufficiently to dispense with the giving of credit on the part of the dealer. Since that time, therefore, the spinners began to buy direct from the brokers in Liverpool; the old dealer gradually disappeared altogether.

An event of far greater importance was the laying of the transatlantic cable (1866) and the consequent improvement of a network of telegraph wires encircling the whole world. Liverpool had now approached nearer to the American Continent than it had been before this time to the neighbouring city of Manchester. Therewith disappeared the necessity of a special class of business people, whose particular forte had been the knowledge of the raw-material market. In a similar direction tended the opening of the Suez Canal and the extension of Indian railways. The brokers themselves partly became importers, the importers partly sold without consideration of the brokers, and there followed a blending of both classes. This development reached its climax, after heated contentions between the Cotton Brokers' Association and the Liverpool Cotton Exchange (formed by the importers in opposition), by the formation of the Liverpool Cotton Association, consisting of both classes (1881). Therewith the old difference was in reality banished, even though the older merchant firms, backed up strongly by capital, frequently sold through brokers, in opposition to those younger firms which were at the same time brokers and merchants. As modern technical skill only puts aside the hand-worker understanding a particular work, so it puts aside also the merchant controlling only one closed market; it unites the markets.

There are, therefore, only the importer and the spinner, and, between both, the buying broker left remaining as different types. The buying broker so far justifies his existence that he is superior to the spinner—a non-commercial man, even to-day—in his knowledge of the market. The existence of the broker makes it possible for the millowner to concentrate his attention on the progress within his factory, and to trouble himself as little as possible about commercial conditions.

But the relation between spinner and broker had so far changed to the disadvantage of the spinner that the class which up to now had kept the buying brokers within bounds had disappeared. As long as the selling broker existed in the opposite interest, the separation was strictly kept intact, whereby the selling brokers solely represented the interests of the importer, and the buying brokers those of the spinner, by the separate class restraint which the business world regulates more than any other. The latter had thus the services of a class of people whose interests were identical with his own, and who represented only the buyer's side. With the merging of the selling brokers and importers into one class nothing hindered the buying brokers any longer from selling the cotton on their own account, or at the same time transacting business as selling brokers for importers. Instead of buying as cheap as possible, their interest was now very often in selling as dear as possible.

Some means were therefore necessary to force back the broker to the interests of the spinners. This was only possible by a section of the spinners banding together, and by means of paid expert servants regulating the transactions of the broker.

This was achieved by the formation of the Cotton Buying Co., a limited company originally consisting of 20 to 30 limited cotton-spinning concerns (13). Its object is to buy cotton in the Liverpool market, for which the members have to pay the ordinary broker's charges; the balance above the expenditure is divided at the end of the year in the shape of a dividend. This company encountered at the beginning the most violent opposition of the brokers. It only succeeded in holding up its head by a clever application of the antagonism—not yet vanished—between the brokers and importers, by the new company combining with the latter against the broker. The company has since then made its way on the Liverpool market under the direction of Samuel Andrew—whom we have several times mentioned—secretary of the large Master Spinners' Association of Oldham. If it only includes a minority of the total number of spindles of Lancashire, it has certainly compelled the brokers to attend to the interests of the spinners more than before—in the same way that the Co-operative Societies forced down the extreme profits of the retail shopkeepers. The possibility also of an extension of the operations of the Buying Company to America already influences similarly the importers. Corresponding to the development delineated, the burdens laid on the price of cotton by the Liverpool market have become less and less since

---

13. For this development, which Ellison and Fuchs did not describe, compare the business reports of the said company (12, Clegg-street, Oldham), and "Co-operative Wholesale Annual" (1883), p. 183.

the " thirties."   At that time cotton, even when the old merchant
had disappeared, was still made dearer by $3\frac{1}{2}$ per cent.; $2\frac{1}{2}$ per
cent. went to the importer and $\frac{1}{2}$ per cent. to each of the two
brokers.   To-day Liverpool demands only 1 to $1\frac{1}{2}$ per cent. for
the importer and $\frac{1}{2}$ per cent. for the buying broker (14)—not
too high a payment for the advantages which the Liverpool
market secures to English spinners.

If the market, when compared with the "thirties," shows a
simplification of the commercial routine, this is due to the
lessening of the risks by the influence of modern improvements
in communication, which brought the countries of the world
nearer together.   But as well as the traffic there was a second
moment which lessened the dangers of business; the progressing
improvement of commercial life itself, especially the introduction
of business in "futures."   This weakened, as Ellison distinctly
points out, the risk of imports so much, that a section of import
merchants existing solely for this purpose, and standing in connection with the market only through the broker, became
unnecessary.

In the next place it is certain that the flourishing of business
in futures neutralised the too violent fluctuations since the
"sixties."   Human intelligence is successful in an increasing
degree in foreseeing want and abundance, and by means of
speculative transactions compensating for their influences (15).
Therewith a formerly unknown equality of prices was attained
for the most important raw materials of human use, especially,
next to wheat, for cotton.   But independently of this, business
in futures helps the importer directly, as an assurance against
risk.   If he buys cotton at a favourable price in the producing
land he can immediately sell in Liverpool the same quantity for
the date at which the cotton, as far as can be seen, will really
arrive; by a further fall in cotton prices and loss on the real
business he can then recoup himself by the speculative profit on
futures; by the rising of prices he can balance the speculative
loss by the profit on the real goods.   He is placed in the same
position as if prices since the transaction of business had not
changed.

Thus, side by side with the development of communication,
the progressive development of commerce led to a simplifying

---

14. Compare Ellison, p. 280.

15. Compare Sonndorfer : " Technik des Welthandels," p. 14.

of that division of labour shown by the "thirties." On the other hand, this development called new organisations of commerce into being. First, in this respect, comes the founding of the "Cotton Clearing-house," in 1876, whereby the clearing system was applied for the first time to trade in products; then the formation of the "Settlement Association" in 1882, with the object of making certain, by periodical balancing of the parties, the final payments of the differences in "future" transactions; lastly the formation of the "Cotton Bank," for facilitating the method of payment. Without going further into these institutions, it is sufficient here to point to the fact that since the "thirties" the structural features of the already (at that time) many-linked cotton market have become to-day still more complicated. The result of this development was a regulation of extreme price variations and cheapening of the raw material for the cotton industry.

This far-extending linking of the market has been followed by a similar linking within the industry, whereof in the "thirties," even, scarcely a trace was to be seen. In the first place, weaving and spinning have separated themselves. Only firms which date from the older period couple both together; new mills are devoted either to the one or the other trade, and are arranged under the most favourable conditions for it. Herewith there comes at once the advantage of not needing any longer managers who are expert in both branches. Therewith weaving has also separated itself locally from spinning; whilst the latter clings to circles nearer Manchester, weaving describes a semicircle further north. The one seeks the declivities of the hills, with the level ground beyond, the other the valleys cutting through the hilly country. But division of labour has advanced further. Oldham is the chief seat of the great staple industry which produces the medium counts of yarn. There alone revolve 11 millions of spindles. The district of Oldham extends to Ashton, Middleton, and the factory places situated to the south of Manchester. Bolton, Chorley, and Preston, which border on the central point of commerce in the North, spin, on the other hand, fine counts, which, owing to climatic advantages, form a monopoly for England. The chief mass of weaving-mills seek the towns situated to the north of these, especially Blackburn and Burnley, in front of them, and extending to Todmorden and Rochdale. Burnley makes ordinary printings; Blackburn clothes India and China

(so-called dhooties and T-cloths); Preston produces finer plain
calicoes for the home and Continental markets. The factory
places lying nearer to Manchester, and the first customers for
spinning, have mostly their specialty in more complicated woven
goods. Thus Oldham has cotton velvets, Bolton figured goods,
Ashton and Glossop printing cloths cf the first quality, the district
of Colne, situated between these and the northern weaving district, makes ordinary coloured goods.

On the other hand, in Manchester, the central point of the
industry, manufacturing is gradually disappearing. The mills
there are mostly of an elder date, but are still of historical
interest as former cradles of the great industry. Manchester is
constantly becoming more and more simply the seat of the export
trade. Thirty years ago goods were packed in the northerly
weaving districts for export. At the present time this takes
place in Manchester—in many cases in the cellars underneath
the high warehouses, which often go down several stories into
the earth, and in which, by means of steam engines and hydraulic
presses, the bales of yarn and woven goods are pressed into half
their bulk, and even less. The continually increasing value of
the land (16) drives the industry away from the city of commerce. But the environs of Manchester are also abandoned by
the industry. It is generally admitted as the reason that only
in places which are quite exclusively devoted to the industry are
working populations, highly trained and thoroughly to be depended upon, to be found (17).

How important is the existence of these exclusively industrial
localities, which, situated in the neighbourhood of the centre of
commerce, combine the advantages of centralisation with those of
decentralisation, is confirmed by Marsden (18). "It can easily
be demonstrated that it would be more profitable to plant a mill
in a locality possessing skilled labour and in proximity to the
markets, paying full prices for buildings and machinery, than it

16. Compare "Auswanderung der Industrie nach dem flachen Lande"
(Jannasch: "Europäische Baumwollindustrie." 11 and 12). There is, however, by no means a decentralisation in Lancashire, but rather an organisation
of the industry round its central point.

17. Compare J. O. Fielden: "Sketch of the British Cotton Industries"
("Co-operative Wholesale Annual," 1887). p. 330.

18. Marsden: "Cotton Spinning" (London, 1888), p. 60.

would be to accept one of the same capacity as a free and untrammelled gift, but located in a place not possessing these advantages."

The division of labour which exists between the industrial places extends to the single mills. One employer produces at the present time few specialties. The large spinning-mills of Oldham and Bolton spin, for instance, not more than one count, or at most but a few counts, and these from year to year. In the same way many weaving-mills of North Lancashire produce only one sort of current staple goods (19).

This far-reaching division of labour is only made possible by the certainty of sale which is guaranteed by the organisation of commerce in Manchester. This also has made the principles of centralisation and division of labour useful in a high degree. The most important in this respect is, that the millowner does not himself go to customers, but the wholesale merchant or exporter acts between both.

We have above followed cotton up to its buying by the spinner through the broker. A highly-developed railway and canal net-work assists the traffic from the market of the raw material to the centres of production. Whilst the older spinning-mills are almost always situated on canals, and the cotton is raised from the boat to the immediate neighbourhood of the mixing-room, the newer spinning-mills are more and more dependent upon railway com-munication, often being connected by railway sidings with the main line.

The opening of the Ship Canal now being constructed will mean a further facilitation of traffic. Already at this time one sees those tremendous docks excavated in the neighbourhood of Manchester which only now require connection with the sea in order to receive here, in the middle of the seat of industry, its raw materials direct from the producing land. (19a.) A ten-years agitation in speeches and writings—carried on by employers as well as employed—preceded this colossal undertaking. It was authorised on the 30th July, 1885, with aquisition rights, along with which, as a condition, the authority of Parliament had fixed

---

19. Compare "Protokolle der Reichsenquête für die Baumwoll und Leinen-industrie," p. 389. Eighty thousand English spindles have spun, since the commencement of the "sixties," the same two counts—32's twist, 40's weft—an example of many.

19a. Now in full operation.

a maximum-rate tariff. According to this, the carriage from Liverpool to Oldham, up to now just as dear as from Bombay to Liverpool, will be cheapened at least by one-third (20).

Since the spinner mostly buys the raw cotton for cash or on short credit (21) it is to his interest to sell the yarn in the shortest time. Therefore the time during which the cotton is in the mill is always limited to a short span—even to only a few days. In the same way, as little cotton as possible is to be kept on stock. The English spinner generally goes every eight days to Liverpool (22) in order to buy there his weekly wants, just as he once or twice in the week sells his yarn on the Exchange in Manchester. Losses of interest therewith disappear, and the essential working capital is lessened. Only under extraordinarily favourable cotton prices does he buy on stock. This development of the conditions of payment has a further advantage for the English spinner: since the exchange prices for yarn generally follow cotton prices, he suffers so much less under the fluctuations of the raw-material prices the nearer the buying of the raw-material and the sale of the yarn approach each other as regards time.

A necessary condition for this system of production is the Exchange in Manchester, which determines the prices of yarn for the world (23). The spinner does not need to seek for his customers, but he can sell his production daily at 'Change prices. The spinners sell partly themselves and partly seek the aid of agents. Cash payments on short credit predominate. The weaver or the exporter are buyers. The agent receives, as the medium for business, a simple commission, in which case he gives the spinner the name of the buyer, and the spinner takes all the risk. The relation is similar if the agent has a fixed salary. It is, however, more frequent to-day that the agent undertakes "del credere," in which case he bears, for an increased commission, all

---

20. Compare J. C. Fielden's articles during the Days of the Agitation. in the *Manchester Examiner;* further. "Co-operative Wholesale Annual" (1889). p. 394.

21. "Protokolle" just mentioned, p. 90. The German buyer has, according to these. to pay cash in ten days at Liverpool; in Holland and Bremen in three months.

22. This is confirmed as an advantage for the Englishman by the German Examining Commission, p. 36.

23. "Protokolle der deutschen Enquête," pp. 353, 399. (The yarn prices in Germany follow those in England, *plus* expenses, freight, and duty.)

the risk, and, as the spinner frequently does not get to know the name of the third party, in reality acts as buyer for himself. In this case the agent pays the spinner, within 14 days, in cash. Therefore there is also here the formation of a special organisation for a special risk.

In the same way as yarns, plain goods, which form the great staple industry of Lancashire, and are produced by manufacturers principally on their own account, are sold through brokers at 'Change prices. "Del credere" commission and cash payment (3 to 7 days after delivery) predominate also with these goods. These brokers play a great role on the field of weaving, as they in many cases, even before the payments are due, give payments on account after receipt of the goods, and also look after permanent employment for the weaver and inform him of changes in the demand.

It is otherwise with fancy goods, which are not 'Change articles. They are produced to the order of wholesale merchants. Similarly, the printer mostly prints to order; he only prints his excess of production to designs on his own account.

All manufactured articles of the cotton industry, yarns and woven goods as well as printings, move at last into the hands of the wholesale merchant. He is at the present time one of the most important personages in the whole trade. He has developed himself from that agent who in the "thirties" attended to the consignments of the manufacturers. But he has become a buyer for himself, and the risks have been transferred to him. This is the case even when the foreign customer personally chooses his goods at the manufacturer's warehouse, because, as customary, the business is still settled with the export merchant, who is a guarantee to the manufacturer for prompt and certain payment. Therewith the choosing of customers, the taking into account of foreign fashions, of business conditions, and differences of exchange in the whole world, is taken from the manufacturer's shoulders.

Only a few firms, mostly such as have existed from olden times, have continued to export on their own account and risk (24) and this possibility keeps the business profits of the merchants within reasonable bounds. If the average value of English yarn exports

---

24. Compare Royal Commission on Trade, Second Report, part I. (5,673).

stands to-day at 4d. higher than the average 'Change prices in
Manchester, this is not too high a charge for the risks to be
incurred, bundling, packing, etc. (25). But the wholesale merchants in Manchester, also, do not sell by any means to the retail
merchant, but, apart from home wholesale houses, to foreign
export houses. The latter have very often English partners in
India, China, and Africa, who further the distribution of English
industrial productions with all their power (26).

The English cotton industry therefore at the present day also
couples extreme combination with extreme division of labour,
technical as well as commercial. Compared with it, the German
industry stands on a step of development which reminds us of
England in the "thirties." Certainly, Germany also shows a
certain geographical division of labour. German spinning and
weaving of plain calico have their seat in the South, especially
in Alsace, Baden, and Suabia. They need protective duties against
England, and supply only inland wants. Alongside exist the
North German finishing branches and fancy-weaving sheds,
especially on the Rhine and in Saxony. But in the North as well
as in the South the industry is dispersed over more extensive
districts, and is lacking in commercial centres.

Also in the size of the single mills Germany stands behind
England. According to the Commission for Cotton and Linen
Industry, in 1878, the average number of spindles had increased
from 15,000 in 1859 to 21,000 in 1877 (27). The average
number of looms given in 1877 for weaving-mills is 287 per mill.
These particulars refer, however, solely to those mills which gave
returns to the Commission, therefore mostly the larger ones—
economically coming into consideration—whilst those not drawn
into account would materially reduce this average.

Unfortunately there are in Germany no statistics taken of the
number of spindles and looms. We are therefore for the present
time dependent upon private sources ; as far as the information
given by W. Rieger (Stuttgart, 1893) goes, concerning the

---

25. Compare Andrew : "Fifty Years' Cotton Trade," p. 7.
26. " Commercial Relations of the United States," No. 12 (Oct., 1881),
p. 102.
27. Report "Stat. Ermittelungen," Heft II., pp. 4 and 5.

number of spindles and looms on cotton in Germany—of 877 firms only 748 have given particulars—the following figures are applicable :—

District.	Cotton Spindles.		Cotton Looms.	
	Total.	Average per Spinning Mill.	Total.	Average per Weaving Mill.
Alsace and Lorraine	1,187,738	28,280	27,110	467
Baden	402,088	19,148	11,966	307
Wurttemburg and Hohenzollern ...	499,492	19,980	11,865	237
Saxony	741,246	16,450	19,403	185
Silesia	74,600	6,782	5,630	268
Rhine Province and Westphalia ...	1,052,048	13,663	24,987	209
Remainder of North Germany ...	265,032	26,503	7,619	169
Rhine Palatinate	98,570	19,714	1,628	203
Bavaria	1,075,735	44,822	19,745	420
Totals ... ... (27a)	5,396,549	20,756	129,983	264

The total number is rather too little (27b) the average number rather too high, several firms, and probably the smaller ones, have furnished no particulars (27c).

German State statistics for 1882 show a further extension of small industrial concerns in the textile branch, although here a direct comparison with English figures is imposible. It is stated that per spinning establishment there are not more than 10 persons. This statement must only, however, be taken along with the consideration that amongst these spinning mills cottage industrial concerns which reel, as well as establishments engaged in manufacturing wadding and candle-wicks, are included. On the other hand, there are in England, according to Mr. Drage, secretary of the Labour Commission, at the present time no special mills for reeling. as formerly 20 years ago. These operations are performed either in the spinning mill before the yarn is sold, or in the weaving mill after it is bought (27d).

27a. The 600,000 German spindles spinning Vigogne yarns, also cotton, are not included.

27b. A great difficulty in giving a comparison with the English figures is the circumstance—which wrecks nearly all international comparisons statistically—that in England the single mills are counted, whereas in Germany, only the firms. It is certain that many firms have several mills, and therefore the average number of spindles and looms per firm must be greater than per mill.

27c. I myself, as well as the author, from personal observation, have little confidence in these figures. (Translator.)

27d. Concerning these statistical difficulties compare my contribution in Schmoller's "Jahrbuch für Gesetzgebung u.s.w.," 1893, pp. 1,224 to 1,226.

In a much greater degree than spinning does weaving bear a cottage industrial character. But since first cotton, then woollen, then half-woollen goods are produced on the same looms, special figures concerning cotton weaving are scarcely possible in this direction.

In the whole German textile industry there were in 1882 still 42 per cent. of the operatives occupied in small mills (mills with under 5 persons), and 38 per cent. in large mills (over 50 persons).

The relation between cottage industry and factory work in the three most important branches of the textile industry are given in the following table:—

	In Factories.		Employed, without further occupation. In Cottage Industry.
Preparation of spinning materials, spinning..	103,750	..	28,391
Weaving	171,095	..	178,060
Needlework, knitting, and lace	23,077	..	68,248
Totals	297,922	..	274,699

Losch (28) remarks, concerning these figures, that the total production of the persons mentioned, if applied to centralised industries, would require a far less number of operatives, and would make possible a far higher standard of living for the individual worker, and a far greater capability for competition on the part of German industry. Indeed, these figures include the hunger-suffering of the German cottage weavers, the banishment of which is only to be hoped for by the banishment of cottage industry itself.

The advantages which flow to English industry on account of its greater concentration are manifold and real. England has at once the advantage of the cotton market. That Germany has freed itself from Liverpool and buys direct from the producing land is certainly a step forward; for the foreign spinner had always to pay more in Liverpool than the Englishman—according

28. H. Losch (Leipzig, 1892), pp. 171-2. The value of this book is that it examines the backwardness of the technical conditions of our industry, and points out the tremendous waste of human power by the principle of small establishments. " No law for the protection of the worker ultimately influences the relation of the worker to technical skill," p. 20. The author most zealously advises that centralised industry should be under the control of the State. Does he not remember how Prussia, in fact, tried this during the last century, and, according to Herzberg, Humboldt, and others, nearly came to grief therewith? Did the productions of State industries ever show themselves capable of competing in the markets of the world?

to the Enquete (Protok., p. 389), 3½ per cent. more. But therewith the German is now met with all the disadvantages caused by the lack of division of labour. Instead of buying every eight days, he must buy months ahead. Besides the loss of interest, he is entangled in the variations of the cotton market, and is forced to speculation. Much too often is he the prey of bad shipments, not according to sample (29). How unfavourable is the position of the individual German spinner can be concluded by the fact that the Cotton Buying Company, representing several millions of spindles, at present does not yet venture to do what the individual German spinner is forced to do—to buy direct in the producing land—so great do the advantages of the Liverpool market (where Egyptian cotton is mostly cheaper than in Marseilles) appear to be to the Company (30).

Some of these disadvantages have been avoided by the formation of a cotton market at Bremen. The same came into existence by reason of an agreement between the associations of German spinning mill proprietors and Bremen importers in 1886.

Although it was recognised that the Bremen cotton market possessed splendid regulations for the business in futures, also that classification and arbitration could be depended upon and were impartial, four representatives of the German cotton spinners were placed upon the cotton market committee. German spinners have therewith understood how to curtail the dangers of conjuncture losses to the slightest degree. The development of this Bremen market is so much the more hopeful when we consider that to-day almost 12 million spindles belong to its natural territory, viz., the German, Swiss, Austrian, Polish, and (partly) Belgian mills.

The disadvantages of division are not slighter with respect to the mill itself. Whilst in England the spinner and weaver in many cases only produce one or two specialties, the German employer has hundreds of patterns. Therefore he is compelled to frequently alter his machines and to accustom his workmen to new work, which not only means less total production and more

---

29. Compare Report of the " Enquêtekommission," p. 22 ; " Protokolle," pp. 36, 286, and others.

30. Concerning the disadvantages of buying in the producing country, " Protokolle," p. 358. Concerning the position of the Liverpool market to the Continental markets, compare Jannasch, p. 60.

working costs, but also greater wear and tear (31). Add to this
that in Germany the combining of spinning with weaving in the
same business—clearly only because the difficulties of selling
occur in this case but once—pays the best, exactly as reported by
the English Commission in the "thirties"; to-day, however, the
organisation of the market in England makes possible that technical separation between weaving and spinning which is preferable
(32).

Lastly, without concentration highly capable labour is impossible, because such demands as an essential the sole employment of a population for generations in the same industry.
Further, only in the seat of a concentrated industry is labour also
with certainty to be met with, whilst German manufacturers often
on this ground also must work on at a loss, in order that the
laboriously taught labour may not vanish from their grasp, of
which instances are supplied from Alsace and other places (33).
Especially must South German spinning-mills, mostly situated in
isolated places, always attract afresh workers from other branches.
Scarcely in working trim, they often leave the mill again in order
to go back to agricultural work, to hand-labour, to house service.
This complaint is often repeated in the German Enquete; only
few workers think about devoting their lives to factory labour.
In the possession of a permanent operative population exists the
great advantage of England, where such a frequent change of
occupation is unknown. The German manufacturers are also
agreed that it is not want of capacity which makes the German
operative less capable than the English, but much rather the lack
of tradition, since he adheres to a decentralised industry. 'Such
circumstances decide," says one of the skilled witnesses examined,
after he had taken into account certain social-political advantages
for the dispersion, "that we can never have the trained workers
of England, where children and children's children devote them-

---

31. "Protokolle." p. 387, gives 15 per cent. as the disadvantage which
results to the manufacturers of Alsace as a consequence of having to spin a
larger range of counts than formerly.

32. Compare "Protokolle," pp. 29, 409, 452.

33. For instance, "Protokolle," pp. 360, 387. (A mill which just for the
moment wishes to spin fine counts cannot dispense with the thereby unnecessary
operatives, because if it goes back to coarse counts, which give employment to
more labour, it would not find the operatives at its call.) Also Grassmann's
"Augsburger Industrie," p. 176, informs us of a frequent change of operatives,
specially pointing out the custom of the younger workers to change their situations in spring. The compulsory military service has also a disturbing influence in this direction.

selves for their whole life to factory labour, and where the factory owners, by means of the great training which is there developed in such a form for the tending of machinery, can manage, for instance, 1,000 spindles with 3 to 4 operatives, whilst we need for this number from 6 to 10 " (34).

Centralised industry possesses a further extremely important advantage; it alone develops machine-making specially and solely for the cotton industry and its technical progress. This makes possible an important cheapening of establishment as well as working costs compared with mills which introduce their machinery from afar and must keep special repairing shops with highly-paid mechanics, often not fully occupied. In England the erection and repairing is done by neighbouring machinists, who at the same time guarantee the possession of the most highly-developed skill. As in Alsace the concentration of the industry is more extended than in Germany, it alone possesses also machine makers devoted solely to cotton, which certainly are, however, by no means capable of supplying all Germany. The latter remains dependent in the first degree upon English machinery (35).

The advantages of dispersion are, in comparison, slight. Extremely doubtful is the advantage of lower wages, which represents only too often bad, and therefore dear, labour. This advantage becomes so much weaker the more food becomes cheaper in the centres of traffic than in remote country towns. More important is the possession of water-power, on which the dispersion of the German industry is chiefly founded. But also in Germany the gradual going over to steam-power is developing itself (36).

But especially disadvantageous is the decentralisation in respect to the sale. Here also the German manufacturer stands under the same disadvantages with which the English had to struggle in the "thirties." The German manufacturer still seeks his customers through travellers and agents, and in many instances through retail sellers, whose financial standing is often questionable, whose necessity for credit is always certain. Hence the complaints about

34. Compare Report of the " Enquêtekommission," pp. 31 and 49 ; " Protokolle." pp. 19, 36, 74, 296.

35. Compare Jannasch : " Die europäische Baumwollindustrie " (Berlin, 1882), pp. 24 and 25.

36. Compare Report of the Commission, p. 27 ; further, regarding the necessity of going over to steam-power, Engel : " Cotton-Spinning in Saxony " (1851), p. 11.

the bad conditions of payment in Germany which crop up continually in the Enquete. The manufacturers had to wait three,
four, or six months, and even 12 months and longer for payment.
In reality there existed "termless terms"—a "complete anarchy
in the method of payment" (37). Sir Walter Raleigh once
similarly complained to the English that the economical greatness
of the Dutch was founded on the system of cash payments.

The disadvantages pictured are only to be avoided by progressive division of labour. The manufacturer cannot be at the same
time commission agent, banker, merchant, and retail dealer (38);
he needs sound customers capable of paying. He fares best if the
sale is concentrated in one market, and 'Change prices simplify
the struggle between buyer and seller. The search for customers,
foreign as well as home, and the bearing of all possible risks of
disposal are in any case difficult enough to necessitate the whole
strength of a man. The wholesale merchant alone is in a position
to pay the manufacturer in cash or on sure, short terms. But
especially where export is in question is the dispersal of sales an
extreme impediment. The manufacturer cannot follow the
fashions in Australia and South America; the foreign buyer
cannot travel from mill to mill.

There are undoubtedly at the present time in Germany arrangements made for the improvement of this important connecting
link between manufacturers and consumers (39). In Alsace there
has existed from the French period a commission agent (40) for
mediating the sales, a function performed in England, later on,
by the wholesale merchant. In North Germany exporters have
acted in many cases as sellers on their own account, as, on the
other hand, large home houses have begun to attend in many cases
to distribution on the inland market. Thus German industry
strives for that greatly advanced division of labour which in
England has developed itself only gradually, and not without diffi-

37. Report, pp. 100 and 101. " Protokolle," pp. 51, 52, 75, 197, 206, 211,
225, 292, 314, 413, 450, 499, etc., etc.

38. " Protokolle," p. 434. Even the largest spinning-mills sell lots of
100-200 lb., p. 469. Many weaving-mills supplied to measurements in ells
required.

39. " Protokolle," pp. 51, 206, 248, 360, 410, 477.

40. There existed in Alsace, before the war, a cloth market, on which the
chief articles had a 'Change-like value. Since then it has disappeared, and
the manufacturers of Alsace, in many cases, are just the ones who appear to
visit the retail sellers. Report, pp. 100 and 101. " Protokolle," pp. 314, 351.

culties in individual cases. Without successors, especially on the field of commercial organisation, competition in open markets is apt to be impossible.

But the comparison with German conditions just shows how the English development, which we have followed, is nothing exceptional, but is rather the consequential improvement of the existence of centralised industry itself under the pressure of the world's market. A concentrated industry with division in labour is, in the world's mart, plainly supreme over one decentralised and split up.

As the first developing tendency of centralised industry, one can set up the following: Striving after concentration and division of labour (Integration and Differentiality).

II.—Replacement of Raw Materials and Labour by Capital.

A.—SPINNING.

If we look at raw materials, labour, and capital as the most important producing elements, the progress of skill in every industry develops itself first in that wherein the material element is eclipsed by labour and capital, as already described by Josiah Tucker (1). This shows itself in several directions. On the one hand we learn to use inferior material, and then to produce the object desired with a less quantity of given material. For both of these assertions cotton spinning provides proofs. At the present time there are spun, on an average, qualities inferior to those spun in the "thirties," notably East Indian cotton, whilst formerly only the better American was used. Especially was this tendency influenced by the American Civil War, which also taught us how to treat shorter staple with success (2). We have also, in addition, made progress in the more minute using-up of the material. Thus in 1834 waste formed one-seventh of the raw material; to-day it only counts for one-tenth (3). Besides this, a great portion of the waste is now successfully utilised by mixing with better cotton, or

------

1. " Four Tracts on Political and Commercial Subjects."

2. S. Andrew: " Fifty Years' Cotton Trade," p. 6.

3. This is, of course, only a surmise based upon the particulars of Ure and Andrew ; as a matter of fact, the percentage varies considerably according to the class of cotton spun, the counts of yarn, etc. Germany appears to have rather more waste. Compare Protokolle of the " Reichsenquête," p. 9.

by spinning it into inferior yarns. It is also in many cases, for this latter purpose, sent out of Lancashire.

But in another respect also did raw material lose its position. More and more were articles taken up in which the cost of production out-balanced the element of raw material by the amounts for labour and capital. This development was aided by the climatic advantages to which we have drawn attention. Whilst the degree of moisture contained in the atmosphere comes less into account with coarse counts, it is an important advantage with fine numbers. England has thereby gained a monopoly in fine spinning (4), whilst home spinning in the lower grades was developed on every side, partly with protective duties, as in Europe and America, partly without, by reason of certain natural advantages, as in India and China. The quantities of raw cotton used per spindle at the beginning of the "eighties" were (5):—

			(1885)	(1891-2)
The Indian spindle used yearly	..	..	111 lb.	.. 118 lb.
,, American spindle used yearly	..	..	74·5 lb.	.. 79 ,,
,, European Continent spindle used yearly			61·2 ,,	.. —
Of the latter the	Austrian spindle used..	..	88 lb.	.. 97 ,,
	German ,, ,, ..	..	67 ,,	.. 86 ,,
	French ., ,, ..	..	52 ,,	.. 55·5 lb.
	Swiss ,, ,, ..	..	26 ,,	.. 35 .,

The English spindle used yearly 34·5 lb. (1885) and 34·2 (1891-2).

The difference in favour of England is of far greater extent than is to be assumed from the foregoing figures, because the English spindle produces a greater quantity of yarn in a given time than most of its competitors. Since, according to the above statistics, it can be concluded that England spins yarns twice as fine as Germany, so, for the reason given, the average English counts must in reality be more than double those of the German (6). The average English counts may at the present time be taken as rather above than below 40's, whilst the Indian spinner—the

---

4. Protokolle of the " Reichsenquête," p. 5.

5. According to Ellison and Andrew p. 8. The figures for 1891-2 are from Merttens' Paper read before the Manchester Statistical Society, April 18th, 1894. An interesting trait of international division of labour, is that against a generally increased consumption of cotton on the Continent per spindle, the spinning of fine counts in England increases.

6. According to the "Reichsenquête" for the Cotton and Linen Industry, Germany could not compete with England in counts above 36's, whilst lower English numbers did not come on the market in South Germany.

strongest competitor of the English—only successfully spins counts up to 20's (7).

Less apparently does the same development arise in weaving. For in this respect the buying power—as yet only slightly developed—of Oriental nations enters too much into account, and necessitates the coarse nature of the staple woven-goods of Lancashire. Excellence in art, design, and dyeing have, on the other hand, in fine goods for the European and American markets too great an influence to allow of England being able in this branch to form a monopoly. For just in these directions lies, up to the present, the advantage of Continental nations.

Technical progress further develops itself in the replacement of labour by capital, by the increase of production with closely-allied diminution of labour power. Both results are at once to be verified by mule-spinning, which in Lancashire has always up to now played the chief part alongside the throstle. Whilst both kinds of spinning have in common the drawing-out of the yarn by rollers, the peculiarity of the mule consists, as is well-known—as in its forerunner, the jenny—in the spindles first twisting the thread and then winding it on. The spindles are on a carriage, which goes backwards and forwards from and to the portion of the machine which is fixed and contains the rollers. During the first movement the thread receives the twist, as well as a slight stretching, during which the rollers that deliver the thread to the spindles are revolving. During the back traverse the rollers are, however, out of operation, so that no more yarn is produced, but that which is twisted is alone wound on. The inward traverse of the carriage (as also the necessary regulation of the fallers) was originally accomplished by human power (hand-mule) : with the self-actor both of these are attained mechanically.

Since the " thirties " the capacity of the single spindle has been extraordinarily raised, partly through improving, partly by speeding, the machine. Even so early as the middle of the century the self-actor had attained the upper hand in England, whilst in Germany this revolution first appeared in the " seventies " (8). In England at the present time the hand-mule is only used in

7. Compare " Bombay and Lancashire " (Manchester Chamber of Commerce. 1888).

8. Report of the " Enquêtekommission " for the Cotton and Linen Industry, p. 14. In 1877 about 76·90 per cent. of German spindles were self-actors.

isolated cases for the very finest counts, the production of which requires special skill on the part of the operative, and which scarcely come into competition. The hand-mules are even here gradually dying out; in 1883 their number in the whole of Lancashire was estimated to be 80 pairs.

The quantity produced by the self-actor is determined by the time in which the carriage travels backwards and forwards and the length of the traverse which it makes. In this direction progress since the time of Ure has been important. The following may be considered as ordinary conditions of speed : —

				1836.		1890 (9).
Length of traverse	..	No. 40's	..	58 inches	..	65 inches
		„ 120's	..	—	..	58 „
Time for travelling back-		40's	..	20 seconds	..	14 seconds
ward and forward	..	120's	..	60 „	..	21 „

Similarly, England possesses, in comparison with Germany, a not unimportant superiority, although, especially with regard to the conditions of speed of machinery, in Germany itself extraordinary differences exist. Regarding the finer counts, which are very little spun in Germany (in Alsace), it is easier to point out instances which show a picture of the conditions of production generally :—

				Length of Traverse.		In and out.
Bolton	..	60's twist	..	66 inches	..	17·7 seconds
Alsace	..	60's „	..	60 „	..	22 „

Ure draws attention to the following as a wonderful achievement, only possible by a remarkable capability of the management and quality of machinery, in a factory at Manchester. No. 170's were spun with a speed of 60 seconds (in and out traverse); at the present time I have found cases, and not exceptional, in which, with the still finer counts of 200's, the backward and forward traverse does not take up more than 38 seconds (10). Since the beginning of the "seventies" alone, the speed of spinning machinery has been augmented 15 per cent. (11).

The weekly production depends, though, not only on the speed and size of the machine, but also on the real loss in comparison

9. Ure: "Cotton Manufacture," II., p. 400. The figures for 1890 are based upon personal inquiries in Oldham and Bolton.

10. Karmarsch gives, on the other hand, the ordinary speed for 200's to 240's at 100 to 120 seconds—a speed at that time purely theoretical for Germany, because these counts were not spun. Compare Karmarsch, "Technologie," II. (Hannover, 1867), p. 1,091.

11. Commission on Depression of Trade, Second Report, part I. (5,079).

with the theoretical production. Before everything else, the number of breakages of the ends comes, in this respect, into account. Upon the skill of the operative depends the time which is taken up by the piecing of the broken threads, and the doffing of the full and putting on of the empty bobbins. But the quality of the raw material, the perfection of the preparation and of the spinning machine itself, especially the roller arrangement, come also into consideration. In the German "Enquete" a millowner says that whilst in England the spindles actually run during 95 per cent. of the whole working time, in Wurttemberg, on the other hand, they only run during 90 per cent., although the spindles were arranged to run 10 per cent. slower (12). Another, from Alsace, also confirms this, stating that in England 92 to 95 per cent. was produced, in Alsace only 80 per cent., of the theoretically possible production.

Since the "thirties" the actual weekly production in England, which at that time already exceeded the figures given by Karmarsch for Germany in 1867, was enormously increased:—

| | | | Weekly working hours. | | Weekly production per spindle, in hanks. | | |
					40's twist.	60's twist.	200's weft.
1812	..	England (13) ..	.. 74	..	12 ..	10·5 ..	4·5
1830	..	,, (13) ..	.. 69-70	..	16·5 ..	15 ..	5·4
1890	..	,, (14) ..	.. 56½	..	28·30 ..	23·5 ..	17·18
1867	.. {	Germany (according to Karmarsch) .. }	76	..	21 ..	18	{ Not spun in Germany,

Ure tells us of an average production, as early as 1834, of 20 to 22.5 hanks of 40's twist per week; but though the differences at that time between good and bad machinery were far greater than at the present time, his statement refers only to the few spinning-mills at that period which had already introduced Roberts' self-actors (15). In 1866, 32's Oldham twist had attained a production of 22½ hanks per spindle and week; in the middle of the "eighties," 28 hanks (16).

The most remarkable fact in the above table is, that not only is the capacity of the spindle increased, but that it has increased in spite of substantially diminished working hours.

12. "Protokolle," pp. 81, 290.
13. Compare Baines, p. 353.
14. From my own observation in Bolton and Oldham.
15. Ure: "Cotton Manufacture," II., pp. 201, 399.
16. Andrew: " Fifty Years' Cotton Trade," p. 4.

A similar development is shown by those spinning-mills in which the twisting and winding-on of the thread—differently from the mule—is continuously taking place, whether it be by a throstle or by ring spindles. The twisting of the thread is achieved in this case by the spindle and flyer traveller respectively running in the same direction, but with different speeds.

No. 32's twist.	Speed of spindles per minute.	Working hours per week.	Weekly production (17).
1834 .. Throstle ..	4,200 ..	65-70 ..	24 hanks
1891 .. Ring	9,000 ..	56½ ..	40-50 ,,

This higher capacity of the throstle and ring spindle, which is so very apparent, is balanced by the greater cost of buildings and increase of power—therefore, in this respect also, a replacement of labour by capital. Ring-spindles are advantageous up to 40's. Above these counts they can scarcely supersede the mule, at all events not in the softer weft yarns (18).

The machines used for preparation also show an increase in their capacity similar to that of the actual spinning-machine. But the progress in both is developed not only by the greater productive power of the single machine, but at the same time by a lessening of the number of operatives per machine. This was made possible partly by technical progress, partly by raising the labour capacity. An operative to-day attends to more than twice, in fact nearly three times, as much machinery as his father did. The number of machines in use has become five-fold since that time—the number of operatives has not quite doubled (19). Instead of 10,000,000 spindles and 80,000 looms in the year 1831, England possesses to-day, for cotton alone, about 50,000,000 spindles and 600,000 looms. The number of operatives has, on the other hand, only increased from 220,134 (first official census in 1835) to 504,069 (1885). From 1856 to 1885 the number of spindles have increased 58.6 per cent., power-looms 87.5 per cent., and the number of operatives only 32.8 per cent.

Of especial importance is the decrease in the number of operatives in the spinning of fine counts. This process was still in the time of Ure in a high degree an art which demanded great prac-

---

17. Ure: " Cotton Manufacture," 11., p. 131. The particulars for the present time were received from the spinning-machine makers, Howard and Bullough, and Brooks and Doxey.

18. Compare R. Marsden: " Cotton Spinning " (London, 1888), p. 312.

19. Andrew: " Fifty Years' Cotton Trade," pp. 2, 5.

tice and much hand labour. In 1850 there were in Houldsworth's fine spinning-mills 7·5 operatives per 1,000 spindles; as early as 1885, in the same mill, not more than 3 operatives.

By the following figures is clearly shown the great advantage which Lancashire enjoys by reason of this state of affairs, even in comparison with its own past days, as well as against its present competitors. Per 1,000 spindles and accessory preparing machinery there were at the commencement of the "eighties" (20):—

In Bombay	..	25 operatives	In Germany (1861)	20 operatives
,, Italy ..	..	13 ,,	,, ,, (1882)	8·9 ,,
,, Alsace ..	..	9·5 ,,	,, England (1837)	7 ,,
,, Mulhouse	..	7·5 ,,	,, ,, (1887)	3 ,,

According to the Enquete, there were in Germany itself the most extreme variations. Whilst in Baden and Suabia only 6 operatives were employed to 1,000 spindles, this number increased in Silesia to 14·75 operatives (21).

On the other hand, India shows us, since 1884, extraordinary developments, about which details follow. There can be no doubt that Germany also has reduced the number of operatives per 1,000 spindles since the Enquete. From a great quantity of materials lying before me for 1891 and 1892 I cull the following, which, however, refer solely to leading and technically distinguished spinning-mills. The average for Germany is certainly higher :—

Switzerland, per 1,000 spindles	6·2 operatives
Mulhouse ,, ...	5·8 ,,
Baden and Württemberg, per 1,000 spindles ..	6·2 ,,
Bavaria, per 1,000 spindles	6·8 ,,
Saxony (new and splendid spinning-mills). per 1,000 spindles	7·2 ,,
Vosges (old spinning-mills)	8·9 ,,
Russia	16·6 ,,

The average counts of yarn spun by all the spinning-mills mentioned are between 20's and 30's. The table shows the most favourable conditions for the south-west corner of Germany, where

20. Compare Manchester Chamber of Commerce ("Bombay and Lancashire." p. 2), according to which 30,000 spindles in Bombay require 750 operatives; and Jeans: Statis. Soc. (Dec. 1884), p. 665. Similarly Merttens; Manchester Statistical Society, April 18th, 1894, p. 169. The report of the German "Enquêtekommission" for Cotton and Linen Industry, p. 8, gives the figures for 1861. Further, compare Jannasch: "Die europäische Baumwollindustrie" (1882), p. 53; Andrew: "Fifty Years' Cotton Trade," p. 2.

21. "Protokolle," pp. 3, 33, 307 ; further, pp. 19, 54, 73, 98, 289. Statist. Ermittl, I., 16.

spinning is the oldest and the operative the most skilled, whilst newer spinning-mills towards the east (Bavaria, Saxony, and Silesia) require an increasing number of operatives per 1,000 spindles.

In order to prove the saving in labour in detail, I put together the labour power utilised in a new spinning-mill at Oldham with 70,000 spindles (Oldham medium counts), for which I examine all the necessary processes for spinning in their order. The spinning-mill chosen is a suitable average instance, which we can very well compare with the one given by Ure in his time, one just about as large—rather smaller if anything.

The first process to which cotton is subjected is "mixing." There are for this, in the case in view, two grown-up men necessary, who manipulate 12,000 lb. of cotton daily. The next process is "opening," i.e., loosening the fibres, which have been pressed together in the packing. For this purpose a machine is applied which tears the cotton apart by means of revolving teeth, whereby the heavy and coarse impurities fall out. In the spinning-mill described there were not more than two women engaged in opening. Then follows the "scutching" process, in order to separate the single fibres one from another and to remove the finer impurities by means of a fan. The cotton leaves this machine in the form of a wide, connected sheet (lap), in which form it is brought to the "card." The cotton is generally subjected twice to this latter process. Each time four—therefore, together, eight—machines were at work for this purpose. They were, together, tended by two grown-up men.

Next follows the important process of "carding," which, along with the further removing of impurities, serves the object of laying the fibres parallel. This is achieved by two cylindrical surfaces working against one another, and which surfaces are clothed with fine hook-shaped wire points. At the mill in question there were 50 carding-engines, each of which manipulated 800 lb. of cotton weekly. These engines were attended to by seven men—an average of one man for seven engines. This number is, however, even under the average; frequently, in Oldham, eight or nine engines are tended by one operative. The cotton leaves the cards like a small loose band (sliver), which is collected in revolving cans.

The "drawing" of the cotton next follows. The slivers produced by the cards are drawn out under stretching rollers. At the mill under examination there were 7 drawing frames, each with 3 heads and 7 deliveries. Each of these frames was attended to by a girl.

The cotton drawings produced are made by the next process into "rovings," by which they are further drawn out and then given a certain twist. The manipulation before finally spinning is subdivided into three operations (slubbing, intermediate, and roving frame). In this particular spinning-mill 7 slubbing frames, 13 intermediate frames, and 30 roving frames were brought into operation. The first 20 frames were tended by 10 young women and 10 children. The children—so-called back-tenters—stand behind the machine and have to fill it with bobbins, to clean it, etc. The 30 roving frames are served by 15 young women, each of whom minds 328 spindles. They have as helpers eight children. In Oldham the number of spindles in the slubbing frames frequently reaches up to 96, in the intermediate frames up to 150; accordingly a rover frequently looks after 360 spindles. I have, however, noticed even higher numbers; for instance, roving frames up to 200 spindles. The whole preparation work does not need more than two overlookers.

Finally follows the fine spinning ("finishing" process). In the spinning-mill described by me there are, for 30 pairs of mules with 70,000 spindles, 30 spinners and 60 piecers, as well as one overlooker. Therefore, one spinner and two piecers mind 2,330 spindles. Besides these there are a few young operatives engaged in carrying bobbins. The yarn spun is packed by six packers.

If the instance given can be taken as the average for the large and new "limited" concerns of Oldham, a comparison with the spinning-mill of about a similar size described by Ure shows the enormous advance in technical skill, as well as in labour capacity. There are :—

	According to Ure (22).			At the present time.		
	Men.	Women.	Children.	Men.	Women.	Children.
For preparation ..	26	—	27	13	2	—
„ roving	—	58	14	—	32	18
„ spinning (includ-) ing overlookers)	105	—	403	32	—	65
Totals (excepting) packers) ..	131	58	444	45	34	83
	653 operatives.			163 operatives.		

22. Ure gives also, in addition, 90 grown-up women as engaged in cleaning and choosing cotton. But since this hand labour, according to him, was only employed at that time for the production of a special quality, I have left them out of account in the above comparison.

The great number of children and young workers in 1830, compared with the present, is worthy of notice. At that time a great portion of them were under ten years of age, and for the most part were only there to sweep up cotton waste—those poor little "scavengers" which Lord Shaftesbury has handed down for the pity of following generations. Those Factory Acts, therefore, which made child-labour more difficult have in no way injured the advance of the great industry; it was in no wise, as was frequently argued by his opponents, dependent on an increase of child-labour.

After reading the works of Baines and Ure, let us visit such a new fireproof (23) spinning-mill in Oldham, in order to view the advances since their time. We find ourselves in one of the outer exits of those polypus arms which extend the factory town into the meadow-lands of Lancashire. As far as the eye reaches, on the meadows there are dispersed five or six storeyed spinning-mills— neat brick buildings, with overtowering chimneys. Certainly there are 40 to 50 of such chimneys to be counted in one view, until they disappear on the horizon, for the towns dovetail one into the other. Add a clouded sky and that damp atmosphere the possession of which an American expert reckons to be, with fine counts, an advantage of 7 per cent. We enter into the factory immediately from the street, without a special yard and gateway, as is customary in Germany.

The foreigner looks about, as soon as he is inside, and asks himself: Where are the operatives? Less human labour than even given in the above instances may be required. For mixing, as for opening, I have myself observed only one grown-up male operative, and this in a spinning-mill at full work, with 68,000 spindles. There is a similar saving of labour at the carding engines, which are connected by rails with the drawing room for the easier removal of the revolving cans (24). Whilst the air in the carding rooms was formerly filled with fibres of cotton flying about, the introduction of self-cleaning cards for the saving of

23. At the present time only fireproof mills are built, whereby the insurance charges are lessened.—Marsden's "Cotton Spinning" (London, 1888), p. 64.

24. "Double carding-machines" mean a great saving in labour power. The spinners are, however, by no means agreed that double cards are to be preferred to the old system, by which the cotton is carded twice successively— first by the so-called breaker, and then by the finisher. In the latter case the roller or Wellman card is chosen as the breaker, and the revolving flat as finisher.

material has alone already banished this nuisance. In the preparation, also, the advances of skill have, since the time of Ure, made more complete utilisation of material possible, as well as replacement of labour by the machine to a large extent. The regularity of the slivers, on which depends the quality as well as the quantity of the yarn to be produced, is, for instance, here accomplished by mechanical means. Not only does the drawing-frame stop when a sliver breaks or the can from which it is taken is empty, but the relative drawing is also increased or diminished without human aid in proportion as the disappearing sliver turns out too thick or too thin.

Large, light, and well-ventilated rooms open to our view when we at length enter into the spinning departments. They have such a width that a spinning-frame with 1,250 spindles can stand comfortably therein. Two such frames are tended by the mule-spinner with his helpers, the two piecers.

At the finish we are led into the engine-house. The boiler is of selected steel, standing a pressure of over 100 lb. to the square inch, and capable of converting 8,000 lb. per hour of water into steam. The piston travels 800 ft. per minute, compared with 240 ft. in the "thirties."

There is no sight within the whole modern industrial system which is more worthy of wonder, or so rich in teaching for the tendencies of our economical development. On the one hand the giant steam engine; on the other, splendid machinery which produces the most delicate results. By well-designed arrangement of shafting the gigantic power is transmitted, led, and suited to the machinery. Scarcely anywhere does the human worker give a lift, except in watching, correcting, and feeding with material. In comparison with the era of hand-mules, the work has become easier rather than harder. For this reason is the enormous increase of production, compared with former times, to be looked at as the work of the genius of the past, of the thousands of thoughts, ideas, and experiments which are embodied in the machines.

Let us compare the instance we have just spoken about with an average one, which has been communicated to me by the

"Industrial Society of Mulhouse" as representative of spinning there. Both instances refer to self-actors alone.

	Oldham. 70,000	Mulhouse. 32,000	Vosges. 56,000
No. of spindles in the mills ...			
Operatives for—			
Mixing	2 men	2·3 men	
Opening	{ 4 men and women }	7·6 men and women	} 120 operatives
Carding	7 men	15·5 men	
Drawing	7 women	12·6 women	50 ,,
Slubbing, intermediate, and roving	} 43 women and children {	44·3 women and young workers ... ...}	202 ,,
Spinning	{ 95 men and boys {	87·0 women and young workers ... ...}	— ,,
No. of overlookers	3	4	
,, jackers, etc.	6	12	117 ,, (25)
Totals	167	185·3	498
Operatives per 1,000 spindles	2·4	5·8	8·9

These results show that in Oldham fewer operatives are required for 70,000 spindles than in Mulhouse for 32,000. Yet by these very figures Mulhouse shows, in this respect, the most favourable conditions of all Germany. Much more unfavourable is the state of affairs in the valleys of the Vosges, as the instance given proves. It is true that the figures given for Oldham and Mulhouse do not refer to the same average counts of yarn; Oldham medium is from 36's to 40's; those which are given for Mulhouse refer to No. 20's French (metrical). But this circumstance does not come into account in the extraordinarily high difference of the fore-going instances. This is also shown by the following fairly repre-sentative mill in Switzerland, compared with Oldham—both spinning the same average counts:—

40's twist.	Oldham.	Switzerland.
No. of operatives per 1,000 spindles ..	2·3 ..	6·2
Thereof for preparation	0·31 ..	1·7
,, slubbing, roving, and inter-mediate .. ..)	0·62 ..	1·2
,, spinning proper	1·37 ..	3·3

The comparison on page 93 between the instance from Ure and the Oldham spinning of to-day shows, in preparation as well as in spinning, the most important reduction in labour power. In the first instance this results from the invention (in America) by Wellman of the self-acting carding-engine. Whilst formerly the cards had to be freed by hand from the cotton remaining behind—the operatives were called strippers—this is now done by the machine (26). The card which is to-day becoming more and more pro-

25. This number refers at the same time to the operatives who are engaged in the factory workshop, because such are indispensable in the Vosges. Labourers and firers-up are not included.

26. Compare Marsden: "Cotton Spinning," pp. 120-2.

minent in Lancashire is a further improvement of Wellman's invention—the so-called "revolving flat card."

In spinning proper the saving in labour compared with the instance given by Ure results from the replacement of the hand-mule by the self-actor, as well as from the lengthening of the spinning-frames and increase in the number of spindles. In the time of Ure the latter varied from 400 to 600, whilst only occasionally mules up to 1,000 spindles were met with. For each of these machines there was a spinner with two or three helpers; or, if the spinner looked after two mules, with four to six helpers (27). At the present time the spinner in Lancashire always minds two machines (a pair of mules), and he has not more than two helpers for the work. Here and there we find also, instead of one spinner with two helpers, two adult spinners (so-called joining system). Therewith the number of spindles per mule has so much increased that the lowest number of spindles to-day is about that which Ure admired as the highest accomplishment of skill. From my own observation in 1891 at Oldham and Bolton, the average number of spindles per mule is about 1,000; so that 2,000 spindles are tended by one spinner and two helpers. The largest machines which I have discovered have 2,700 to 2,800 spindles per pair of mules. When finer yarns are spun with these highest numbers of spindles the spinner has frequently three helpers; thus, in Bolton, on fine counts, with 2,208 spindles and upwards. In the spinning of fine counts at Bolton the number of spindles given above as the maximum is not attained; 2,520 spindles per pair of mules, as far as I know, is the highest number reached. With 1,200 spindles and under, which now only seldom occurs, one spinner and one helper are employed.

England shows also in this direction an extraordinary increase of labour capacity when compared with Germany. It is the more remarkable because technical differences scarcely come into account. The self-actors in both countries are certainly on exactly the same principles; indeed those in Germany have, in many cases, been made in England. Whilst in England about 2,000 spindles per pair of self-actors is to be looked upon as the usual number, about 1,300 to 1,600, with a great variation in some cases, are to be taken in Germany as the mean; 1,300 to 1,800 are given as the average in Mulhouse. In Germany this number

---

27. Compare Ure: "Philosophy of Manufactures," p. 312; also "Cotton Manufacture," II., 449.

of spindles is generally tended by more operatives than the greater
number of spindles in the English machines. In Mulhouse 1,300
spindles require one spinner and four helpers (two piecers, two
fillers); in England, 2,000 spindles require only one spinner and
two helpers; 2,000 spindles in one of the finest spinning concerns
of Saxony require one spinner and four helpers, whereas in the
smaller spinning-mills of Saxony there are even one spinner and
five helpers needed for a pair of self-actors with only 1,600
spindles.

But quite especially is it to be mentioned here that the English
spinner does not need overlooking the same as the German. In
England 60,000 to 80,000 spindles—i.e., the whole spindles of a
mill—are entrusted to one overlooker (50s. to 60s. per week). In
Germany, in favourable cases, there is an overlooker to 15,000
spindles; also in this respect is the South-West more favourably
placed than the East. In England there is one overlooker for
60,000 to 80,000 spindles; in Alsace and South Germany there is
one for 10,000 to 20,000 spindles; in Saxony there is one overlooker for 10,000 spindles: in a smaller spinning-mill of the
Saxon highlands there is one for 3,000 to 4,000 spindles.

In consequence of the development delineated the production of
yarn per operative in England has greatly increased since the
"thirties," and the cost of labour per given quantity of yarn has
considerably lessened. Let us compare, for example, the instance
given by Houldsworth, in 1834, before the "Committee on Manufactures," with figures which I have found in a spinning-mill in
Bolton in 1890. They are for 200's counts:—

	Weekly capacity per spinner.	Weekly hours of labour.	Cost of labour (spinners and helpers) per 1,000 hanks.	Weekly earnings of spinner.	Buying-power in flour.
1837..	3,800 hanks	72 hours	200 pence	42/-	267 lb.
1891..	34,500 ,,	54¼ ,,	23 ,,	44/-	406 ,,(28)

28. The price of flour is that of August, 1891. The comparison is rather
in favour of the spinner in 1837, because the price of flour at that time
is according to the invoices of a large hospital, therefore wholesale, whereas
the prices taken for 1891 are retail prices of a co-operative society. The
latter, in order to pay a dividend of 10 per cent., demands rather higher
prices than the shopkeeper.

A similar result is shown by ordinary 40's twist:—

Cost of spinning per 1,000 hanks in 1812 .. · .. 300 pence
  ,,   ,,   ,,   1830 .. .. 180 ,,
  ,,   ,,   ,,   1890 .. .. 12 ,, (29)
  ,,   in Alsace per 1,000 hanks, accord-⎱
    ing to the Enquête in 1878 (43·58 c. per⎰ 43 ,,
    kilogramme).. .. .. ..)

Whilst the foregoing particulars for the finest and the average yarns show the reduction of the cost of labour in detail, the following table—in which, based on the particulars of Ellison, all counts are included—may give a general idea of the development mentioned:—

	Yearly yarn production, in 1,000 lb.	No. of operatives in spinning-mills.	Yarn production per operative, in lb.	Cost of labour per lb. of yarn.	Average annual earn-ings per operative.
				d.	£ s. d.
1819-21	106,500	111,000	968	6·4	26 13 0
1829-31	216,500	140,000	1,546	4·2	27 6 0
1844-6	523,300	190,000	2,754	2·8	28 12 0
1859-61	910,000	248,000	3,671	2·1	32 10 0
1880-82	1,324,000	240,000	5,520	1·9	44 4 0

Especially within the last 20 years has a lowering of piecework prices by 15 per cent. left its impression (30) in that the operatives to-day look after 15 per cent. more machinery, which runs from 12 to 15 per cent. quicker. Weekly wages increased in the same period by 8 to 10 per cent.

Undoubtedly a similar development is taking place also in Germany, which means a replacement of labour by capital, and a raising of labour capacity. This is made clear already by the fact that the considerable increases of wages at the commencement of the "seventies" by no means brought a corresponding increase of

29. The figures for 1812 and 1832 are taken from the particulars of Ure ("Philosophy of Manufactures," p. 341); those for 1890 from my own experience in Oldham; those for Alsace from the Enquête. Regarding the cost of labour, compare "Die Stat. Ermittelungen," p. 24; Protokolle, pp. 54, 387, etc.

30. Committee on Depression of Trade: See Report, part I., 5,077, 5,114, 5,164, 5,167. Even since 1877 the Oldham list has gone down 8 per cent., whilst the weekly earnings of the spinners are 2/6 to 3/- higher than at that time.

the cost of labour in its train. For instance, according to the Enquete, the wages in Alsace rose about 50 per cent. from 1860 to 1878; the amount of wages, however, falling annually per spindle, was lowered from 4'75 to 4'65 marks, whilst the yearly production per spindle had remained at least equal.   It is certain that wages have gone up tremendously in the German textile industry. The associations of Alsatian and Bavarian textile employers give the following particulars as regards the average wages paid : —

	1887	1888	1889	1890
Alsace ..	589 m.	590 m.	602 m.	606 m.
Bavaria ..	505 ,,	593 ,.	601 ,.	618 ,,

The hours of labour have also been reduced; whilst in 1868 these were 78 hours per week in Augsburg, in Chemnitz even 84, they have now been reduced by legislation to 65.   A greater production per operative, as well as per spindle, has also resulted

Grassmann, in his work on the Augsburg Cotton Industry, p. 95, gives the following figures . —

Yearly Production and Quantity of Cotton used per Spindle.

	lb. Yarn.	Counts.	lb. Cotton	Operatives per 1,000 Spindles	Hours of Labour
1855 ..	37·86	30·5	42·9	15·6	82
1869 ..	42·89	29·84	59·75	11·7	78
1891 ..	54·14	26·47	53·5	8·4	66
1866 ..	25·3	34	31·85	9·12	78
1875 ..	32·6	34	39·3	9'7	72
1885 ..	33·6	34	41	8	77
1891 ..	35·9	34	42·4	7·8	66

A cheapening of labour, corresponding to that in England, has, however, not been generally observed for Germany.   This is due to the circumstance that since the "sixties," along with the increase of wages, there has been a corresponding increase in the price of food (30a)   In later periods, however, in which, as is well known, a beginning has taken place in the reduction of the duties in food, cases have been noticed which quite correspond to the English as regards German cotton spinning.   Thus Grassmann relates, p. 173, "An establishment has alongside of the shortening of hours made a considerable increase in the earnings, and.chiefly hereby gained better and more capable operatives, the threatened reduction in the production was warded off by the simplification of working, whereby it was possible to reduce the working staff

30a. Compare Grassmann, pp. 163, 172.

by 25 per cent." Similar instances are given by the German Enquête in 1878 (31). But in spite of this the cost of labour in English spinning mills is still cheaper than in German.

In a similar direction there are also the following facts of a later date. The weekly earnings of the operatives engaged in the textile industry, as far as these have a centralised industrial character, have increased slowly but surely, as proved by the reports of the accident assurance associations. Even in 1892, when the hours of labour were reduced by legislation to 65 hours per week, the weekly earnings of the operatives remained at the same level, in fact rather increased, without the reduction in piecework prices (31a).

This is proved, indeed, by the tables attached, which contain cases for the present time. They make clear at once the advantage of the conditions of production in England, but at the same time they prove also the fact, still to be more closely examined later on, that there, where the cost of labour is the lowest, the conditions of labour are the most favourable, the hours of labour are the shortest, and the weekly earnings of the operatives are the highest.

We examine briefly the instances given on page 103. Cases 1 and 2 contain comparisons of conditions of production between a valley of the Vosges and Mulhouse. We see how the lower weekly wages of the Vosges are counterbalanced by the greater number and the less skill of the operatives, which latter brings in its train a greater loss compared with the theoretical capacity. Therefore a higher sum is paid for labour in spinning a kilo. of yarn in the Vosges than in Mulhouse.

Case No. 3 treats of 20's twist, the counts which are probably mostly spun in Germany. A fair approximation is shown between the relation of wages in Bavaria, Wurttemberg, and Saxony. The relatively high cost of labour in the spinning-mills of Wurttemberg is explained by there being a larger number of operatives employed (5 per 1,200 spindles). The difference in wages between the spinning-mills of Saxony and Bavaria is, in comparison, very

---

31. Report of the " Enquêtekommission," p. 31 ; " Protokolle," 175, 397 (an instance of the lowering of piece prices accompanied by the earning of the same weekly wages as before). Economically an interesting controversy, whether the rise in wages during the " seventies " has resulted in a corresponding increase of labour capacity. Compare the introduction.

31a. Compare Grassmann : " Augsburger Industrie," pp. 163, 164.

trifling, and is counterbalanced by the considerably higher cost of overlooking in Saxony. If we compare herewith the instance in Oldham, we find, in spite of shorter hours of labour (55 instead of 64), a little less weekly production than in Saxony, and a larger than in Wurttemberg and Bavaria. In spite of the far higher weekly earnings of the English spinner (45s. instead of 22s.) the difference in the cost of labour is extremely slight (1·8 in Oldham, against 1·7 in Saxony). But this insignificant advantage in Saxony is reversed if we take into consideration the cost of over-looking against it. This is the more important, as in Oldham the corresponding overlooking costs are generally not to be taken into account, because the one overlooker there simply corresponds to a technically-trained employee in German spinning-mills.

Case No. 4 shows the same things for 30's twist, in a com-parison between South Germany and Bolton. In the latter town there are fewer operatives for a greater number of spindles, in spite of which we find a greater speed of the machinery, and by both means the far higher weekly wages of the operatives and the far shorter hours of labour more than compensated for. Already, apart from the overlooking, the cost of labour in Bolton per lb. is lower than in the South German case. Exactly the same thing results for 36's twist in case No. 5.

Especially interesting is case No. 6, which compares two in-stances of 40's twist in Oldham with one another. The one refers to old, the other to the latest machinery. From these we see in the clearest way that it is technical development which really demands higher capabilities from the operatives, but also in return betters their position. Although spinners as well as helpers stand better in the second instance than in the first, the cost of spinning is considerably less.

Finally, just the same result obtains for the finer yarns (cases 7 and 8), which in Germany are only spun in quite isolated in-stances. Especially noticeable is the difference in the conditions of speed between Bolton and the splendid spinning-mill in Alsace. This difference is also to be ascribed to lower capacity of labour; greater speed would not be economical in Alsace, on account of increase of loss in comparison with the theoretical capacity.

Let us condense the results shortly. In England the operative minds nearly double as much machinery as in Germany; the machines run quicker; the loss compared with the theoretical

PARTICULARS RESPECTING SPINNING BY SELF-ACTORS

Places	No. of sp'dles per pair of self-actors.	No. of operatives — Spinners	No. of operatives — Helpers	Length of traverse	Seconds for traverse back'w'ds and forw'rds.	Weekly working hours.	Weekly production per pair of self-actors	Spinning prices	Weekly earnings of spinners	Average weekly wages of the helpers.	No. of spindles per overlooker.	Weekly earnings of over-looker.
				Metres.			Kilos.	Pfennige per kilo.	Marks.	Marks.		Marks.
(1) 12's metric warp												
Vosges	1272	2	3	1·6	13	66	1980	3·9	21	10·80	10,000 to 20,000	35 to 40
Mulhouse	1200	1	3	1·55	12·5	66	2050	3·15	21	13·50		
(2) 25's metric warp												
Vosges	1272	2	3	1·6	15	66	900	8·89	21	10·80	...	...
Mulhouse	1200	1	3	1·55 (In., Eng.)	14	66	740 lb.	7·02 per lb.	21	13·50	...	...
(3) 20's twist, English												
Bavaria	1568	1	3	64	15	65	2420	1·9	18	10·70	13,000	27
Wurttemberg	1200	1	4	65	15	63	1980	2·6	21	10·50	10,000	:::
Saxony	2000	1	2	66	14	64	3600	1·7	22	11		35
Oldham	2288	1	3	63·8	16	66	3432·5	3·37	43	15·25	15,000	20 to 30
(4) 30's twist, English												
Bolton	1472	1	3	64	14·6	65	1340	3·25	21	7·70		
S'th Germany	2064	1	2	63·8	19	65	2200	4	46	12·75	15,000	20 to 30
(5) 36's twist, English												
S'th Germany	1200	1	2	65·2	17	65	1055·5	3·9	21	7·70	11,600	21·60
Switzerland	1704	1	3	66	15	61	1560	3·35	18	7·50	5,000	20 to 25
Saxony	2000	1	3	67	13	55	1880	3·2	22	8 to 13	10,000	35
Oldham	2576	1	2	67	13	55	3182	3·25	38	9 to 13		
	2688	1	3				2725·6	2·88 (Peace.)	40·15	17·75		
									s. d. 33·5 / 36·0	12·9		
(6) 40's twist, English												
Oldham	1560	1	2	65	13	55	1222	0·6	40 (Marks)	*s. d.* 14·2 / 16·2	12,000 to 15,000	23·50
Oldham	2400	1	2	64	13	55	1650	0·5	21	17·50 (Marks)		
(7) 60's twist, English												
Alsace	1248	1	2	60	22	69	530	9·75 (Pfennige)	40	11	8,000	28·50
Bolton	1632	1	2	66	17·7	55	653·3	9·75	21·60	10·33		
(8) 120's weft, English												
Alsace	1764	1	3	65	28	69	256	22·75	43	11		
Bolton	2250	1	3	58	21	55	333·3	22·28				

capacity is less. In the latter respect it is to be borne in mind that in England doffing and filling with bobbins take place in a shorter time, breakages of ends occur more seldom, and the piecing of broken threads requires less time. From these it results that the cost of labour per lb. of yarn—especially if the overlooking is included—is in England decidedly less than in Germany. The wages of the English spinner are, as well, nearly twice as high as in Germany, and the hours of labour a little over 9 hours (32), compared with 11 to 11½ in Germany.

WEAVING.

Similar to the progress of spinning was that of weaving. Cotton manufacturers, before the Committee on Manufactures (1), in 1834, advanced the theory that hand-weaving was increasing, and must increase as long as British commerce expanded. Especially had the manufacturers of Bolton—which at that time was the centre of weaving—thus expressed themselves.

In spite of all prophecies to the contrary, hand-weaving, at least in cotton, has, as a matter of fact, died out in England. Not without much difficulty—because in Manchester even the largest merchants in cotton goods knew nothing more of them—I have still found hand-weavers in Lancashire. Let me here dedicate a word to the last of the race. If the death-struggles of hand-weaving often extend themselves in a sad manner throughout decades, its death itself is a comparatively easy one.

A great portion of the operatives' outlying districts of Bolton comprise, even to-day, those houses which at the beginning of the century were built for hand-weavers—cellars for weaving, lighted from both sides by an unbroken row of windows, over which are dwelling-rooms accessible by steps fixed outside the house, now small houses for single weavers, then larger ones with space for about 20 to 30 looms, where cottage weaving had developed into division of labour establishments. Most of these houses have at the present time lost their original object, and have become dwelling-houses for the operatives under the rule of

32. Spinning machinery in England generally runs 55 hours per week ; the Factory Act grants 56½, of which 1½ hours are devoted to cleaning the machinery. The clause for regulation of German trades shortens the hours to 65, because, out of the 66 hours allowed, one is necessary for cleaning.

1. (1,212).

tho factory system (centralised industry). But in a detached environ here and there we still hear—of course isolated—the sound of the hand-loom.

If wo descend into one of these cellars, which, as mentioned, are very well lighted and contain about four looms, we are greeted by grey-haired men and women. They seem to belong to another world, especially if the visitor has just wandered through one of the gigantic fine-spinning mills of Bolton. Here, as everywhere else, the dying hand-weaving clings to a specialty for existence—counterpanes of peculiar patterns and with words woven in, mostly Bible verses. The patterns are formed by the weaver raising the weft, at the proper place, with a small hook to form a shed. Similar patterns could only be produced by the power-loom with complicated jacquard arrangements, and in large quantities. But here it is only a question of a limited supply for people who still cling to the old fashions, perhaps mostly for customers who, in point of age, do not stand much behind the producers. For their requirements it would not pay to introduce costly machinery.

The weavers work with extremely coarse weft—about 90 yds. to the lb.—which is spun from cotton waste. This enables a quick production, because there are no more than 12 picks per quarter-inch. The warp is 12's twist. Similar counterpanes are also woven with coloured cotton—in every instance old-fashioned goods with a very limited circle of buyers.

We see, therefore, how the cottage industry has at last withdrawn itself to a sphere specially suited for it, which also becomes more and more contracted, but not more quickly than the hand-weavers die off. Therefore the position of these, the last of their race, is a better one than that of their parents in the "twenties" and "thirties." They have taken their share in the general progress of the times; a 4lb. loaf, pointed out one of the weavers, 40 years ago cost 10d., now only 4d. The hours of labour are still 12 to 14, but with longer stoppages for meals. The rate of wages is also better than formerly. A weaver receives 1s. 7d. for one of the counterpanes described. He can weave 8 in a week, so that his earnings amount to 13s., of which, however, 2s. to 3s. goes as rent for the loom, etc. As soon as goods come into question which are not specialties, the earnings sink far below —to 7s. per week and less. But the most astonishing fact in regard to the condition of wages is that the hand-weavers in late years even succeeded in obtaining an advance. Since the old men possess a monopoly of their hand-labour, the threat of a strike was sufficient, as long as old maids still bought their goods.

An astonishing thing is this guild of the cottage weavers, which once comprised the whole neighbourhood of Bolton, and had thousands of members. Even 30 years ago it had 1,800 members; to-day it has only 50. The youngest member, 50 years of age, is secretary, with whom, apparently, at some time the guild will die out. Most of them are far older, and to our questions about the trade the answers often went back 50 years. If their condition is tolerable, it depends upon the almost fanatically spoken-out determination to be the last of their trade, and to teach their handicraft to no younger person. Even winding is not done here by children, but by the oldest of the old. The grandchildren work in the factory, where they earn three times as much—thus solving the hand-weaver problem.

If we compare the conditions of the hand-weavers in Germany with those just delineated, they stand also on about the same economical footing as those of England in the "thirties"—in the midst of the death-struggles of the cottage industry, whose fatal character is well known to the thinking observer. There are, indeed, also voices not wanting like those of the manufacturers of Bolton who thought the home hand-weaving could only cease altogether with English commerce (2). For instance, an advertisement lies before me, in which hand-weaving is declared to be as capable, indeed in many articles superior, to power-weaving. It ill fits in therewith, however, if at the same time the sympathy of the public is appealed to, and an advertisement made of the poverty of the weaver.

Opposed thereto E. Engel (3) deserves special recognition, for in 1855 he already called attention to the fact that there was only one remedy for the misery of the hand-workers—the replacement of the hand industry by the factory system. So early as that, Engel spoke with great foresight of a certain "conservative calling of centralised industry." Even at this day this expression will appear paradoxical to most people. Where, however, the

---

2. Compare Report of the " Enquêtekommission," p. 76.

3. E. Engel: " Süchsisches Obererzgebirge " (Dresden, 1855), especially pp. 10, 14, 15.

change to the factory system has been possible, hand-weaving in Germany has also been put aside without extreme sufferings. Where it still exists, conditions are the most favourable where it confines itself to at least a specialty. But it wrestles most severely with death where it does not bend before the factory system in the direction of a specialty, but lives on by tampering with the quality, as in many cases in Silesia and partly in Saxony (4).

Power-weaving, compared with hand-weaving, means a replacement to a large extent of labour by capital. A weaver on the power-loom accomplishes about as much as 40 good hand-weavers (5). But also in power-weaving itself, as in spinning, the quantity produced per loom as well as per operative is continuously increased.

First comes into account, since the "thirties," the considerably increased speed of the loom, which at the present time in Lancashire has in some cases reached 240 picks per minute (6). The average speed on plain goods is approximately as follows:—

In England, in 1830 (7)	80 to 90 picks	
„ „ to-day	195	„
„ Alsace „ (8)	140	„

The advantage of England in this respect is given in detail by the following table:—

APPROXIMATE SPEED OF LOOMS ON PLAIN COTTON GOODS.
Picks per minute.

Width.	England.	Switzerland.	Alsace.	(9)
80 to 85 cm. ..	240	190 to 200	150 to 160	
110 „ 115 „ ..	200	160 „ 170	130 „ 140	
135 „ 140 „ ..	180	150 „ 160	120 „ 125	
165 „ 170 „ ..	180	120 „ 130	110 „ 115	

Similarly, however, as in spinning, the number of the really completed movements of the machine within a working day is far less than the simple multiplication of the picks by the number of minutes. The loom is not in operation during the whole of the

4. Report of the "Enquêtekommission," p. 77; "Protokolle," pp. 223, 306, 405, 411.

5. Andrew: "Fifty Years' Cotton Trade," p. 7.

6. Compare Andrew, p. 2.

7. Ure: "Cotton Manufacture," II., 310.

8. Jannasch: "Europäische Baumwollindustrie" (Berlin, 1882), p. 54.

9. These figures are from private information. The particulars for England are, however, confirmed by Brooks: "Cotton Manufacturing" (Blackburn, 1889), p. 79.

working hours, but time is lost by breakages of ends and similar disturbances. Thus in England, with a theoretical speed of 240 picks, not more than 200 picks are on the average effective—i.e., the loss amounts to 16·6 per cent. With lower speeds the loss sinks down to 8 per cent. In comparison, 20 to 30 per cent. has been given me as the average loss for Alsace in plain goods; for Switzerland even a little more. Karl Grad mentioned before the " Enquete-kommission " a not exceptional case, in which on plain goods, and with a speed of 160 picks per minute, the loss amounted to 34 per cent. He founded this emphatically on the want of highly-skilled labour (10).

From the facts mentioned we find that English looms produce considerably more than those on the Continent in the same time. Unfortunately a comparison in figures, as in spinning, cannot be given, because I have not succeeded in getting details for exactly the same goods in England and Germany—by the way, an interesting instance of international division of labour. If, however, English looms run about 30 per cent. quicker than the German, and show at least 10 per cent. less loss, it follows that in spite of 15 per cent. shorter hours of labour, the weekly production is not less, but rather must be greater.

In spite of this increase of production per loom, the number of operatives, compared with the number of machines used, has, as in spinning, continually decreased. If we take the particulars given by Ure as a basis for reckoning, there were still in 1820 more operatives than looms; in 1878, on the other hand, there were more than two looms per operative, both including all the people employed on the preparation machinery : —

In 1820 there was one operative per			0·9	loom
., 1850 ,,	..	..	1·6	looms
., 1878 .,	.,	,,	2·1	,, (11)
.. 1893 ,,	,,	,,	4·6	,,
In comparison, in India. only			0·22	loom (12)
,, . in Alsace. only			1·5	looms (13)

10. " Protokolle der Enquete," p. 372.

11. Compare Birtwistle before the Labour Commission. 1891.

12. Compare " Bombay and Manchester " (Manchester Chamber of Commerce, 1888), p. 3. Report of the " Reichsenquête," p. 109. Whereby, however, it must not be forgotten that on the average Alsace produces finer goods than England.

13. Brooks : " Cotton Manufacturing," p. 47.

We find the same thing if wo leave the preparing machinery out of the question and take only into account the number of looms which the weaver minds. Whilst during the time of Ure the weaver did not mind more than one loom, or at the most two looms, the average number at the present time in Lancashire on plain goods is four looms. This number is confirmed to me by Mr. Edward Rawlinson, the secretary of the large Association of Employers in North Lancashire. In his district one person minds on the average 3·9 looms.

That we can accept four looms as the average number has been confirmed to me, in a similar manner, by Mr. Birtwistle, secretary of the Amalgamated Weavers. He writes: "The larger number of our best weavers (in Blackburn and Accrington) mind four looms per person, some with, some without, help." It is, however, to be borne in mind that these statements are not only with respect to plain, but also to simple fancy and bordered goods, especially the so-called dhooties—the clothing of the Hindoos. Six looms per weaver are in Burnley very frequent; in this case the weaver has mostly a young assistant.

Compared with the foregoing, the number of looms per weaver in America has increased still more. A weaver in Massachusetts frequently minds 6 to 8 looms, as a letter of Mr. J. Howard, secretary of the Cotton Operatives of Fall River, informs me (14), and Mr. Edward Atkinson, of Boston, confirms.

In a weaving-shed at Lowell, Massachusetts, there were employed in the "eighties," according to a communication from the manager—Mr. Dupre:—

| 11 women weavers with 5 looms | 43 women weavers with 7 looms |
| 232 ,, ,, ,, 6 ,, | 20 ,, ,, ,, 8 ,, |

In Germany a weaver scarcely anywhere minds more than two, in Mulhouse and Switzerland, on plain goods, often three looms. Also in Augsburg this latter has, according to Grassmann, been lately successful (15). The highest capacity there is that four looms are given to two operatives—one adult and one young

---

14. Reprinted in the *Cotton Factory Times* of March 22nd, 1889. The same is given in "Commercial Relations of the United States," No. 23 (Sept., 1892), p. 43.

15. Compare Grassmann: "Die Entwicklung der Augsburger Industrie, 1894." On the other hand, the story on p. 49 was related to me a few years ago.

person.   In Silesia (15a), on account of the lower standard of weekly earnings, it has been found more economical to confine a weaver to one loom.

In order to bring the degree of labour-saving which has been attained in England before the eyes of the reader, let us visit one of the weaving-sheds in North Lancashire.   It contains 602 looms for plain printing calicoes.   The looms are arranged on a flagged ground floor, with light from above.   This is at the present time the usual arrangement in England for weaving, because thereby the vibration, and therewith the wear and tear of the machinery, as well as the number of ends breaking, is the least (16).   The remaining rooms attached to this light and roomy weaving-shed are small, and are built with the utmost regard to economy.   There are the following operatives :—

16	Females at winding machines, at	.. ..	18/-	per week,	piece-work
2	Operatives for beaming, at	.. .. ..	33/-	,,	,,
1	,, for sizing (for the coarser and white yarns), at .. .. }		40'-	.,	day-work
5	,, for dressing (for coloured and finer yarns (17), at .. .. }		40'-	,,	.,
5	Females for drawing-in warps, from	.. 35/- to 16/-		,,	piece-work
180	Weavers and tenters, mostly females, including six-loom weavers, at .. .. }		33/6	,.	..
	These pay the tenters ..	.. .. ..	6/6	.,	day-work
	Four-loom weavers, at ..	.. .. ..	24/-	,,	piece-work
6	Overlookers, at ..	.. .. ..	38'-	..	,,
	[These latter receive 1/4 for every pound which the weavers under them earn.]				
	Then, in the warehouse :—				
1	Cloth-looker, at ..	.. ..	33/-	,,	day-work
3	Labourers, at	.. .. 22 -. 18'-.	14/-	..	.,
4	Youths, at	.. ..	10/-	..	..
	In addition :—				
1	Clerk	.. .. ..	38/-	..	.,
1	Labourer ..	.. .. ..	18/-	..	,,

225 operatives, all told. or per operative. including all preparation. 2·7 looms.

15a. "Protokolle der Enquête," p. 410.   Compare also p. 180.

16. Compare B. Shaw: "The Cotton Manufacture of Lancashire"; "Commercial Relations of the United States," No. 12 (Washington, 1881), p. 129.   In America this method of building is impossible, owing to heavy snowfalls in winter—also another climatic advantage of England.   Compare the same, No. 23 (Sept., 1882), p. 42.

17. The difference between dressing and sizing is that in the first case the warp is spread out thread by thread; in the second it is subjected to the strengthening ingredients in the form of a small coil.   Compare Karmarsch, II., 883.   In the case before us, partly one system and partly the other was used.

In similar first-class weaving-mills of Baden and Switzerland there are, in comparison, on plain goods only 2·1 to 2 looms per weaver, whilst on the average this number is much less.

A weaver in the weaving-shed we have examined earns 5s. 6d. per loom per week, whilst the average in Burnley probably amounts to 5s. The weekly wage varies between 22s. and 27s. The six-loom weaver earns 33s. 6d., but pays from this to his young helper, who, by the way, is generally a member of the family, 6s. 6d. The width of the printings produced varies, as generally in Burnley, between 32in. and 46in. The yarns used are so-called mediums—that is, warp 28's to 45's twist, weft 30's to 60's. The weekly production per loom is 250 yds. on the average, therefore the cost of weaving is 0·26d. per yard, whilst in Burnley it is reckoned at 0·22d. In comparison, a weaver of similar plain printings in Germany and Switzerland earns about 12s. weekly. His labour is, in spite of this, by no means cheaper.

Quite another aspect is shown by one of those art weaving-sheds in the neighbourhood of Manchester—for instance, Bolton. Here no loom is weaving the same thing as another. There are towels, table-cloths, counterpanes, so-called fancy goods, especially for the home market. But in spite of the fact that the majority of the looms have jacquard arrangements, even here one weaver minds on the average two looms, whilst in all Continental weaving-mills one weaver has only one such loom. Only a few of the weavers in Bolton have tenters—among 250 weavers perhaps about 50. On the 500 looms at work, which represent a considerable amount of capital (a loom costs £5 to £150), there are 300 weavers and tenters, in addition to 150 operatives on the preparation work, cutting of jacquard cards, and in the repairing shop, which is necessitated here by the complicated machinery. The average, therefore, per single operative, including all the accessory preparation mentioned, is 1·1 looms—a remarkably favourable result.

The woven goods which the dexterity in art of our German hand-weavers still produces are in many cases the same. The English weavers earn on the average 25s. per week, and on the real art-looms 8s. per day easily, and still the productions of these highly-paid operatives have killed the old cottage weaving of Bolton, in which their fathers and grandfathers once eked out a not less miserable existence than the German hand-weavers.

What we have said shows how the technical progress in weaving also caused a permanent increase of production per operative, and therewith a continuous lowering of piece-wages. Thereby, as in spinning, the weekly earnings of the operatives have risen. This can be proved by figures. The following instance is taken from a large weaving-mill in Hyde, which since the introduction of the power-loom has remained in the hands of the same family : —

	Weekly production per operative.	Cost of labour.	Hours of labour.	Weekly earnings per weaver	Buying-power in flour.
1814...	Yards. 130·7	Per Yard. 1·3d.	Per week. 80	14s.	Lb. 56
1832...	221·2	0·6d.	72	12s.	65
1890...	540	0·13d.	54½	{ 3-loom weaver, 17s.3d. 4-loom weaver, 22s.6d. }	} 151½ (18) } 208

The goods to which these figures refer are ordinary printing calicoes (31½ in. wide, 72's reed, 26's twist, 30's weft, 20 picks per quarter-inch) (19). Figures comprising the whole of cotton weaving, on the basis of Ellison's estimates, have like results : —

	English total production in cotton goods.	Number of operatives.	Capacity per operative.	Cost of labour per lb.	Yearly earnings per operative.
1819-21 ..	In 1,000 lb. 80,620	250,000	Lb. 322	Pence. 15·5	£ s. d. 20 18 0
1829-31 ...	143,200	275,000	521	9·0	19 8 0
1844-6 ..	348,110	210,000	1,658	3·5	24 10 0
1859-61 ..	650,870	203,000	3,206	2·9	30 15 0
1880-82 ...	993,540	246,000	4,039	2·3	39 0 0

The apparent irregularities of the table (20) are explained by the decline of hand-weaving being included in it. To this the lowering of the yearly earnings between 1820 and 1830 must be ascribed.

18. The prices of flour are the same as before (p. 98). In Hyde, south of Manchester, the weavers, unlike those in the districts of the staple industry in the North. only mind three to four looms.

19. The figures for 1816 and 1830 are reckoned from the particulars of Baines ; those for 1890 emanate from private communications.

20. Compare Ellison: " Cotton Trade," p. 69.

This development has been repeated in the States of Massachusetts and Rhode Island. The following particulars emanate from the well-known writer, Edward Atkinson, who at the same time is a practical man in the cotton industry (21). Here also the same decrease is shown in piece-wages, the same increase of production per operative, and the same raising of weekly earnings.

Even if the still remaining colonial character of America (higher cost per spindle and loom per mill, stronger demand for labour, dearer capital, etc.) should make the industry there appear not suitable for extracting general economical principles, the American instance is nevertheless, in respect to the replacement of labour by capital, extremely instructive. The particulars of Atkinson refer to two mills which since 1830 produced unchanged the same goods (standard sheetings, width 36 in., No. 14's yarn), and spun the necessary yarns themselves. In the cost of labour the cost of spinning as well as of weaving is included. The particulars are taken from the business books of the firms in question.

	Yearly production per operative.	Cost of labour per yard.	Annual earnings per operative.
	Yards.	Cents.	Dollars.
1830	4,321	1·9	164
1850.........	12,164	1·55	190
1870.........	19,293	1·24	240
1884.........	28,032	1·07	290

In the case of Germany, also, a similar development can undoubtedly be shown. Although the looms run more slowly, in spite of this the losses (22) are larger and the production per loom less than in England. This is a consequence of the want of highly-skilled and highly-capable labour. But this fact is easily explained by the still comparatively youthful age of power-weaving in Germany. In the eastern portions of Germany, especially in Silesia and Saxony, the power-loom has only been settled since

21. Edward Atkinson: "Address upon the Labour Question" (Boston, 1886), p. 11. The same: *Popular Science Monthly* (January, 1890), pp. 316-7. The same: "Distribution of Products," 4th ed. (New York, 1890), p. 118. Compare, further, Jeans: Statist. Society (December, 1884), p. 617.

22. That is, the difference between the theoretical and real production.—*Translator.*

I

the "sixties"—in 1861, for instance, the first powerloom mill was got to work in Plauen (23).

Grassmann gives the following table regarding plain calico weaving (23a) : —

Yearly Production per Power Loom in metres.		Weavers per Loom.	Annual Production per Weaver in metres.
1861	8,588 (93 cm. wide)	0·5	17,176
1875	8,966 (130 ,, ,,)	0·494	18,153
1891	9,202 (130 ,, ,,)	0·43	21,447

On account of the disparity in the goods produced, an exact comparison of the cost of labour in weaving between Germany and England is more difficult than in the case of spinning. I confine myself to the following instance, which is based on the authority of Schoenhof (24), and has been confirmed to me in Lancashire. It refers to ordinary printing calicoes, 15½ yds., 64 by 64 standard sheeting : —

	Weekly production per operative.	Cost per yard.	Daily hours of labour.	Weekly earnings per operative.
	Yards.	Pence.		s. d.
Switzerland and Germany ...	466	0·303	12	11 8
England	706	0·275	9	16 3
America	1,200	0·2	10	20 3

That on the field of weaving, however, Germany bravely steps forward is proved by numerous particulars of the " Enquete." In any case the cost of labour had only increased a little, in many cases even lessened, although since the "fifties" the weekly income of the operatives had permanently risen, in some instances very considerably, in many cases 60 per cent. This was attained by giving two looms to a weaver, increasing the speed of the looms, and introducing piecework and labour-saving machinery

23. Bein: "Industrie des Voigtlandes," II., 341 ; also "Protokolle der Enquête," p. 105. In Augsburg already in 1839. Compare Grassmann: *loc. cit.*, pp. 22. 23.

23a. Grassmann : *loc. cit.*, p. 96.

24. J. Schoenhof: "Influences Bearing on Production " (1888), a journey-report, out of print.

for the preparation. Whilst in some cases spinning-mill owners complained that the labour capacity became worse as a consequence of increasing wages at the beginning of the " seventies," the continuously increasing capacity of the operatives in power-weaving was, even at that time, according to the evidence of experts, beyond doubt (25). Similar cases since then have been communicated to me, in which, by speeding the machinery, piece-wages were reduced and resulted in an increase of the weekly earnings. In spite of all this it is at the present time less the technically-advanced centralised industry which has made German weaving partly into an export industry than the accommodating itself to changing daily demands, to taste in the patterns, etc. Thus the merchants of London and the manufacturers of Lancashire order, in many cases, German novelties and produce them in large masses if they take (26). The lack of technically perfected productive systems has in many instances resulted in the fruits of the admirable technical and art skill and training which Germany gives to her sons being plucked by other nations.

WEAVING PRICES IN LANCASHIRE.

I.—PLAIN COTTON GOODS.—BLACKBURN.

Width of goods.	Reed (27).	Picks per ¼ in.	Length of pieces.	Twist.	Weft.	Wages per piece.	Weekly production per loom.
Inches. 39	62	.14·6	Yards. 37	30's	30's	Pence. 8·92	Ells. 222
39	62	14·9	37	30's	30's	9·47	215
39	62	16·5	37	30's	30's	10·08	215
40	50	14·6	37	30's	30's	8·72	222

25. Compare " Protokolle zur Reichsenquête," pp. 105, 183, 188, 192, 247.

26. Compare the Second Report of the Commission on Depression of Trade, part I., 4,945, 4,949, 4,977, 4,982, 5,815.

27. The method of counting reeds usual in Lancashire is the Stockport method—the number of dents in two inches, i.e., since generally two warp threads are drawn through one dent, the number of ends per inch.

II.—Four-Shaft Twills.—Radcliffe.

Width of goods.	Reed.	Picks per ¼ inch.	Length of pieces.	Twist.	Weft.	Wages per piece.	Weekly production per loom.
Inches. 34	66	12·2	Short ells. 80	32's	40's	Pence. 15·65	Pieces. 3¾
34	66	13·25	80	32's	40's	16·95	3½
34	66	14·45	80	32's	40's	18·48	3
34	66	1·55	80	32's	40's	19·84	2¾

III.—Burnley Printers.

Width of goods.	Reed.	Picks per ½ inch.	Length of pieces.	Twist.	Weft.	Wages per piece.	Weekly production per loom.
Inches. 34	68	18·75	Yards. 135	Medium (28)		Pence. 40·03	Yards. 200
20	67	18·63	116	..		31·92	215
26	53	12·47	125	..		21·07	352
31¼	56	14·25	130	..		24·42	316

The above figures show extremely low prices per piece, which give the weaver a weekly wage of 22s. to 24s. A comparison with Germany in figures would be impossible in detail, but still the foregoing particulars should not be withheld from practical men .

III.—Labour.

A.—Further Proofs of the Statement advanced from Other Countries.

We can condense our result up to this point in the sentence: Technical progress, in connection with an increase of labour capacity, accomplishes a permanent lowering of piece-wages, at the same time raising the weekly earnings of the operatives and gradually shortening the hours of labour. If we further supported this statement by comparing the present condition of the English cotton industry with its condition in the "thirties" and that of the contemporary German, the cotton industry in its

28. Medium = 28's-45's twist, 30's-60's weft

remaining phases also affords a plethora of proofs. Where the standard of living and the wages are the lowest, there the production is the dearest.

The Russian cotton industry has its seat in two centres—one in the centrally-situated provinces of Wladimir and Moscow, and the other in the North, near St. Petersburg and in Esthland. In the latter district the standard of living of the operative is the higher; but his greater intelligence and cleverness amply counterbalance the lower wages of the middle provinces, as the following table shows (1):—

YEARLY PRODUCTION PER OPERATIVE.

	In spinning.	In weaving.	Daily hours of labour.
	Roubles.	Roubles.	
Wladimir and Moscow.	937	456	14 and over
St. Petersburg	1,928	1,102	12
Esthland	1,513	1,327	

The tremendous waste in labour-power is the chain which, in spite of English machinery and English managers, keeps back the industry of Russia—conditions which link themselves to the days of serfdom and heathenism, when the labourer cost just as little as he accomplished.

An American Consular report speaks similarly respecting Italy: Power-looms in Italy produce far less than elsewhere because the female operatives are very slow in piecing ends, and thereby lose almost 40 per cent. of the time worked. Certainly the wages here are very low in comparison with the United States, but the production in the same time is lower in the same proportion. The Italian spinners pay their operatives 6 to 8 lire per week; but they require 10, 15, and even 20 operatives per 1,000 spindles. The same applies to weaving. An English weaver minds 3 to 4 looms, and has from every one (!) a larger production than the Italian, who seldom minds more than one loom (2).

1. Compare "Commercial Relations of the United States," No. 12 (Oct., 1881); "Report on the Conditions of Labour in Russia" (Lond., 1892).

2. "Commercial Relations of the United States," No. 23 (Sept., 1882, p. 285.

A similar antithesis is found within the United States. Here the South, which produces cotton, appears to be specially adapted also for further manipulation; the technical aids and capital are at hand as in the North; and water-power is also not lacking in the South. In spite of these facts the North is the seat of the cotton industry, although it has to bear the carriage of the raw materials. There, however, is the seat of an old race of operatives of extraordinary productive capacity. The South, which depended up to a short time ago on slave labour, has nothing to set against this race. It is true that the weekly wages in the South are far lower, but the cost of labour is dearer. " I have," says Atkinson, " made a very accurate calculation of the proportion of operatives to the number of spindles, the number of looms, etc., and therein conceded very much for the variation of yarns, the capability of the mills, etc., and still found that in the South there are two operatives for one in New England. This calculation was confirmed by observations on the spot " (3).

The most remarkable confirmation of our contention of reversed proportional conditions between weekly wages of the operative and piece-wages is given by the reports of Mr. James Thornley, who travelled in the American cotton districts in the interests of the " Textile Manufacturer," an English journal devoted to the textile trade (they were printed in the journal mentioned). Their general purport was, that the cost of producing plain calicoes was higher in the United States than in England. On the other hand, the cost of labour for the same production was less in America. In comparison with these facts it is known that the weekly earnings of the operatives in America and England are about as three to two (4). But it is especially remarkable that the cost of labour in America, particularly in weaving, stands very considerably below that of England, but on the other hand that spinning is cheaper in England. Although this is the case the English weaver earns far less than the American; the spinner, who is still superior to his American contemporary, is, however, the highest-paid English operative. For the production of a pound of ordinary printing calico, of a sort which the expert mentioned deems specially suitable for comparison, the following figures are

---

3. Edward Atkinson: *Popular Science Monthly* (Jan.. 1890), p. 371. Compare further: " Address of Edward Atkinson. given in Atlanta, Georgia. Oct., 1890," p. 5.

4. Compare, for this, Atkinson: " Distribution of Products," p. 133.

of value. I, on my side, add the weekly earnings, and tender my thanks to Mr. E. Atkinson for the friendly information concerning the conditions of American wages (5) : —

COST OF PRODUCTION PER POUND (EXCLUDING RAW COTTON).

		New England.		Lancashire.
Total cost of production	..	6·32d.	..	6·08d.
„ labour	.. ..	3·33d.	..	3·48d.
Cost of spinning	.. ..	0·66d.	..	0·47d.
„ weaving	.. ..	1·6d.	..	2·03d.
Weekly earnings of spinner	..	33/- to 35/-	..	35/- to 40/-
„ .. weaver	..	25/- to 37/6 (6) ..		20/- to 24/-

These particulars agree with those of Schoenhof in his " Economy of High Wages," according to which the costs of spinning in England, and of weaving in America are the lower.

In Germany the standard of living of the working classes has without doubt considerably advanced during the last decade; wages have risen and the hours of labour become shorter, without needing an increase in the rate of piece-prices (7). As an instance, in a Bavarian mill for which particulars were repeatedly made, the average wage, in spinning, in 1886 was 2 marks, in 1890 2·12 marks; in weaving, 1886, 2 marks; in 1890, 2·22 marks; in addition to which a lowering of piece-prices was possible in the weaving-shed. In any case the piece-wages were in no instance increased. The average yearly earnings per operative in the Alsatian textile industry amounted, according to information for which I have to thank the " Bernfsgenossenschaft," to : —

1887. Marks.	1888. Marks.	1889. Marks.	1890. Marks.
589·13	589·95	601·85	606·3

A gradual shortening of the hours of labour is without doubt extending in Germany. In 1868, according to the Enquete, the hours of labour in Chemnitz were still 14. Yet the production

5. The particulars for America are, in order to give a wider scope, averaged from the particulars for Fall River, Lowell. and Rhode Island, given separately in the report. Compare " Commercial Relations of the United States," No. 23 (Sept.. 1882), pp. 43, 44.

6. The wages for a capable six-loom weaver in Massachusetts is given as 37s. 2d. The figures for England correspond to the above particulars. They are, as well, confirmed by the evidence of the secretaries of the English spinners and weavers before the Labour Commission at the sittings on 28th June and 10th July, 1891. The English spinners often earn, as the above figures show, 45s. and more per week.

7. Compare Report of the "Reichsenquête,"· pp. 30, 82 ; " Stat. Supplement," part II., 76. 80; special "Protokolle" for Alsace, pp. 291, 296, 337, 376, etc. ; further, for Saxony, the same, p. 98.

has been in most cases no less than formerly with longer hours. Especially known, already quoted by Brassey, is the instance of Dollfus, whose spinning-mill produced in an 11 hours day just as much as formerly in 12 hours. This experience was repeated in other spinning-mills of Alsace (8).

Karl Grad, before the " Enquetekommission," laid great stress on the difference between Mulhouse and the smaller factory districts of the Vosges. The average wage in the Vosges in cotton-spinning mills amounted to 1·77 fr. per day ; in Mulhouse, on the other hand, with shorter hours of labour, to 2·31 fr. But this was balanced by the town operatives producing more. As August Dollfus has proved, the production costs of the same articles are less in Mulhouse than in the remainder of Alsace. They amount there to 0·37 fr. for a kilogramme of yarn of average counts, against 0·40 fr. in the Vosges (9).

Between Germany and England the comparison between Mulhouse and the valley of the Vosges is forcibly repeated (10).

The Swiss inspector of factories informs us of interesting experiences regarding the hours of labour (11). In 1878 a normal working day of 11 hours was introduced into Switzerland, following that already introduced in 1872 into the Canton Glarus. It can already be proved with certainty that the cotton industry of Switzerland, one of the chief industries of the country, has not suffered in the least by these regulations. By calling into service a corresponding speeding of the machinery, the experience of increasing the productive capacity of labour—which in many cases

8. Compare Protokolle of the " Reichsenquête," p. 375. Brassey: " Work and Wages," 2nd ed., pp. 121 and 143.

9. Compare "Protokolle der Reichsenquête," p. 376.

10. The same relation applies to knitting. A firm I am personally acquainted with produces curtains in Nottingham. Silesia. and Austria. The mills in the latter places make ordinary goods for home consumption. Goods for export can only be successfully produced in England. The same difference exists in England. The lace trade has at the present day. in many cases, left Nottingham in order to obtain the advantages of lower wages in the country districts. But the finest articles. which require the most expensive machinery. are exclusively made within the Nottingham " trade-ring," because only there is sufficiently capable labour to be found.

11. Compare " Archiv für sociale Gesetzgebung." vol. IV.. part I.. p. 88. On page 89 particulars are given respecting the weekly wages of the operatives. They are in England twice as high as in Switzerland, in spite of which labour in the English cotton industry is cheaper. Detailed reasons for this are to be seen above.

has led to an increased production—has been gone through. These facts are based upon communications from Swiss millowners accompanied by detailed figures. Numerous manufacturers and spinners expressly acknowledge the favourable influence of shortening the hours of labour. This opinion is certainly limited in one direction. Mills with out-of-date machinery, which at the same time employ the worse, poorer-paid class of labour, have not been able to participate in this development, by which the same production was crowded into a shorter time. Such mills have without doubt been prejudiced by the shortening of the hours of labour, inasmuch as the quantity of their production has experienced in some cases a considerable falling-off. Poor machinery and poor operatives became impossible. The loss with hand-looms was still more complete—it was in exact proportion to the lessening of the time for labour. But these disadvantages for the few show a decided progress for national economy on the whole.

But cannot the flourishing state of Indian spinning be used as an instance against the opinion expressed here? Does not this strongest living competitor of England depend upon the lower wages which are paid in India? Against this view the researches of the Manchester Chamber of Commerce have shown that cheap labour is by no means the advantage of India. According to the view of the Chamber of Commerce, it lies much rather in the constantly falling silver-prices. In India the buying power of silver falls but slowly and incompletely in comparison with the lowering silver prices in the international market, but in every case the Indian spinner always produces under a higher price condition of silver than that which obtains at the time when English yarn is sold in India (12).

That cheaper labour does not create the strength of Indian spinning is shown already by the fact that in India only the coarsest yarns are produced successfully; therefore those in which raw material outweighs capital as well as labour. Twist No. 40's requires about double as much labour and spinning wages as No. 20's. If cheap labour was the advantage of the Indian spinner he would therefore rather spin 40's than 20's. Just the opposite is

---

12. Compare "Bombay and Lancashire" (Manchester Chamber of Commerce, 1888), p. 111. Further, pp. 2, 4, 29, 33, 75. With 20's the cost of labour is the same in Bombay and Oldham. 0·62d. to 0·64d. per pound of yarn; bundling costs, on the other hand, 0·44d. in Oldham, against only 0·35d. in Bombay, taking 1s. 5d. as the value of the rupee.

tho case, as he cannot compete with the Englishman in counts above 36's, although the latter fetches the raw material and must take back the yarn.   The difficulty for the Indian spinner increases in proportion as labour preponderates in the costs of production— a confirmation of the statement by Tucker already given.

On the other hand, the hours of labour in England are 9, with free Sundays and Saturday afternoons.   In India the hours of labour cannot be exactly determined; in Bombay they appear to be 12 to 13 hours (13), in the interior, more.   Added to this, a cessation of labour on Sunday does not exist, but the mill only stops every third Sunday for cleaning purposes.   The religious holidays of the operatives are observed by those who are affected receiving leave, the mill working on with the large number of reserve operatives.   Wages fluctuate in India between 15 and 8 rupees monthly for adults, and 3 and 4 rupees for young operatives.   The spinner proper receives 15 rupees (14)—i.e., with the value of the rupee taken at 1s. 5d., 21s. 3d. per month, the English mule-spinner 35s. to 40s. weekly.   This difference is explained by the fact that in India 3½ to 5 times as many operatives are necessary as in England; that the more unskilled hands lead to a more considerable wear and tear of machinery (7½ per cent. against 5 per cent.); even that the single spindle itself in Bombay produces less in 12 hours than in Oldham in 9 (with No. 20's in Oldham 5½ hanks, in India 5¼ hanks daily).   Schoenhof even calculates that in Lowell 35,000 spindles spin daily just as many lb. of 38's as are spun in Bombay of 20's (15).

In the face of these facts the English cotton industry does not need to fear India in its finer productions.   But Blue-Books already contain facts which point out that peculiar progress of labour in India which is produced everywhere by a vital centralised industry.   In Bombay the wages in the spinning-mills have increased in the 5 years from 1883 to 1888 by 30 to 40 per cent., in spite of which it is asserted that the productive capacity of the Indian operatives has increased so much that the cost of

---

13. East Indian Factories Report (1891). p. 23.   Hours of labour in a spinning-mill in Bombay. without reckoning stoppages. are 13: also another instance on page 24: but on page 25 only 11 to 12 hours; p. 74, 13 hours. The queries as to hours of labour frequently remain unanswered, because "witness has no definite ideas about time."   Thus on page 23.

14. Page 45 of Report just quoted.

15. Schönhof: " Influences bearing upon Production " (1888), p. 8.

labour to-day is rather lower than higher. The number of operatives, up to this time 5 to 6 times as many as the English, is to-day in the best spinning-mill of Bombay only $3\frac{1}{2}$ times as high (16)—i.e., does not stand far behind the German. Add to this that the prices of food have not increased to the same extent as the fall of exchange, but that they will rather remain for a long time to come extremely cheap owing to the increasing opening out of the interior by railways (17). This also acts like a rise in wages, and increases the labour capacity.

We dare not for a moment think that in India it is a question of the introduction of industrial labour into what has been up to now a non-industrial country, as, say, into Russia. On the other hand, India, as an industrial country, was up to the beginning of this century superior to Western countries; it is the mother-country of the textile industry, and up to the time of Arkwright possessed the monopoly of fine yarns. There is now no doubt that under the attack of the factory system Indian industry launched out into the course which everywhere leads, under similar conditions, to progress. To begin with, cottage industry devoted itself to specialties, which, indeed, were dearer than European goods, but were still preferred by the rich of the country as articles of luxury. On the other hand, India plunged quickly and energetically into the factory system, under the protection of the falling exchange. As everywhere in Europe the hand-weaving districts have become seats of the modern textile industry, India also appears destined for the same future.

Mr. James Platt and Mr. Henry Lee, two authorities on the cotton industry, agree with each other by reason of many-sided practical experiences in India, that in no country on the earth, except in Lancashire, do the operatives possess such a natural leaning to the textile industry as in India. "We have not to deal here with a class of savages, but with a people that takes to everything extremely quickly, and which, as experience shows, can be taught with extraordinary rapidity as new spinning-mills continually require new hands" (18). If centralised industrial progress, there-

---

16. Compare " Bombay and Lancashire," pp. 34, 191.

17. Tax-collectors in the interior prefer bad harvests to good ones, because with good harvests the people have no money; wheat being unsaleable.

18. " Bombay and Lancashire," p. 295.

fore, also brings in its train the uplifting of the labour serving it, the latest Factory Act would certainly be an advantage for India, but scarcely for Lancashire.

As in the cotton industry, the argument advanced applies also to other modern centralised industries, as far as their productions are measurable and are comparable all over the world. In this respect the iron trade comes before all others. From the German Iron "Enquete," in 1878, we find that the cost of labour for a ton of pig-iron amounted to less in Cleveland than in Germany, whilst the English shift-wages were far higher than the German (19). The same quantity of pig-iron produced in a day at the German furnaces would cost in Cleveland only 115·77 marks, instead of 145·77 marks in Germany, for labour. The greater capacity of the English and Belgian ironworkers is expressly acknowledged in the Report of the Inquiring Commission (p. 36). The English ironmaster, Lowthian Bell, confirms this relation. "None of these figures," he says, speaking of the production of pig-iron per man in Germany, "reach by far the capacity of a worker at the furnaces of Cleveland, and proves that well-nourished and highly-paid labour is by no means always dearer than less well-nourished and lower-paid labour. As a fact, I have scarcely found that the cost of labour is anywhere lower than in Cleveland" (20). Similarly, according to Schoenhof, the cost of labour per ton of pig-iron is less in North America than in Germany ($1·20 against $1·66) (21), whereas the American wages are known to be double as high and ever higher than the German.

It is true the Iron "Enquete" mentions expressly that in Germany also the capacity of the worker has been increased, "in itself as well as by changes in technical appliances." "It is clear from the particulars brought to light that the number of workers engaged in the iron industry proper has been reduced, and, indeed, in a higher degree than could be expected, by the almost similar

19. Compare "Protokolle." p. 259, Question 8 : p. 698. Question 9 ; p. 789, Table 11. Respecting these latter tables, they can be turned to account by combining the average shift wages per worker paid by the "Bochumer Verein" with those of the Clarence Works in Cleveland (columns 7 and 8). and by the consideration that the production of a furnace at the Clarence Works amounted to seven-ninths of what a furnace at Bochum produced per shift.

20. Quoted by Schönhof : "Industrial Situation" (New York. 1885), p. 77.

21. Quoted by Schönhof. pp. 77, 78. Compare also E. Atkinson : "Distribution of Products," p. 355.

remaining production in respect to quantity since 1871. It is unanimously considered that a further lowering of wages for lessening the cost of production is inadmissible if the labour-power shall not be lessened and the bodily as well as spiritual welfare of the workers endangered " (22).

If we now search for some foundation of the tenet advanced, the proofs—in agreement with the present method of science—can only be historical and psychological. With regard to the historical element we refer the reader to Chapter I., and to the uplifting development of certain working classes from a socially deeply submerged mill proletarianism which is there depicted. In the psychological aspect the following appears to be noticeable.

We have to start from the fact that the enormous increase of production which we observed depends in the first degree upon the machine. Labour has not become more burdensome in the same proportion as the production has increased; much rather is the real bodily exertion less. The mule-spinner does not work 2,000 times as intensely as the active hand-spinner, nor the weaver on the power-loom 40 times as hard as the untiring hand-weaver, and still his production outweighs that of the latter in the proportion given (23). "In the year 1840," said E. Atkinson, in a lecture before the female cotton-weavers at Providence, "the work was hard and continuous—13 hours per day; to-day you can comb and smooth your hair whilst the loom runs almost by itself; the hours of labour amount to 10" (24). Alongside of the operative there now stands a powerful companion in labour—the labour-genius of generations which is embodied in the machinery.

Formerly that operative had the greatest result who moved his hands most continuously. With perfected mechanical arrangements that operative produces the most who has to interfere the least with his hands, and knows how to curtail these interferences to the shortest space of time. For the machine changes in continuous process the raw material into the finished article. The interference of the operative means the eliminating of disturbing elements, and an attendant less production. The chief thing to

---

22. Report of the " Kommission," p. 36.
23. A refutation of the well-known teaching of so-called "more value."
24. " Addresses upon the Labour Question " (Boston, 1886), pp. 11, 12.

be watched is to limit the loss arising from this cause, to make the work of the machine ever more automatic.

The machine has therefore replaced hand-labour. A condition for this was the interleaving of the principle of division with the world's market, which, with the object of cheapening the cost of production, divided the old hand-work into a large number of single functions. That division of labour, as already recommended by Petty (25), as described by Adam Smith in the well-known instance of pin-making, was the first step thereto, that, as the single functions became simpler they could be undertaken by the machine. The machine thereby freed the worker from that far-reaching division of labour which threatened to make man himself into a mere tool. Division of labour has transferred itself from the operative to the machine. The more automatic the machine becomes, the more automatic becomes the labour of tending.

Skilled finger proficiency disappears therewith in an increasing degree, which shows itself, amongst other results, in the advance of the average wages, and, on the other hand, extremes counteract themselves more and more. Even the difference between the sexes is lessened by the machine. During the time of Ure female labour in the cotton industry accomplished still less and was paid lower than that of the male, as at the present time in Germany (26). In the industry of Lancashire this difference is now in many cases neutralised. Especially in weaving do male and female operatives earn the same piecework wages, just as those six and eight loom weavers in Lowell are young women (27).

In spite of this, it would be a mistake if we imagined that labour has become easier compared with former times. As far as a comparison can be made, the opposite is the case. A hand-weaver can work 13 hours per day; to let a six-loom weaver work 13 hours is a physical impossibility. The nature of the work has entirely

---

25. Sir William Petty: " Essays in Political Arithmetic " (Lond., 1699), pp. 35, 179, 180.

26. " Protokolle zur deutschen Enquête," p. 372.

27. Compare Sidney Webb: *Economic Journal*, vol. I.. No. 4.   Also herein the English cotton industry stands in advance of other trades, especially such as are less controlled by modern machinery.   In this industry the equalisation of the difference between male and female labour is the farthest advanced, especially when we remember that in it mostly young unmarried female operatives come into consideration.

changed. In place of muscular exertion there is now the minding of the machine—i.e., mental strain. Those who have observed the mule-spinner in Oldham, in the midst of the whirling of 2,500 spindles, or the female worker in Burnley environed by four or six shuttles, working at the speed of 200 picks per minute, know what a higher degree of mental application is here demanded.

Besides this, the machines, which are always becoming more complicated, require a certain humouring, a treatment full of understanding of those technical thoughts embodied in them, on the part of the operative. Just as the English thorough-bred horse will be led by reason and love, and rebels against the rough treatment of an inexperienced stable lad, so that highly-developed type of factory labour itself demands treatment full of knowledge of its peculiarities, and gives the best results where a certain sympathy for its class striving is vouchsafed on the part of the employer—by which, for instance, the Secretary of the Master Spinners at Oldham (Mr. Andrew) won in a great degree his esteem in operative circles. So also the ever more ingenious machinery does not stand unwilling and unreasonable treatment. Even the wondrous achievements of human skill realise the best result where the workers engaged upon them rise to the height of intelligent labour.

A third reason comes into consideration. The machines are always growing more costly; the production per operative is increased enormously. Therewith the responsibility of the individual worker increases. Compare, for instance, that puddler, upon whose skill solely depends the result of his furnace, with the man who is answerable for the whole contents of a Siemens converter. But in the branch we are dealing with, the same thing also applies. How much greater, indeed, is the responsibility of that operative who minds 2,500 spindles, compared with the old hand-mule spinner whose machine had only a few hundred spindles, and who with laborious toil accomplished, even per spindle, far less than his successor.

Physical dexterity, clever understanding, and the bearing of responsibility are, however, not to be expected from that poorly nourished factory proletarianism which centralised industry overthrew on coming into being. These require a higher standard of living of the operative, and the restriction of the hours of labour

within suitable bounds. By what means are both attained
without causing therewith an economical disadvantage, nay, in
fact, helping onward economical progress ?

We saw that the result of technical progress is a vast increase in
production. Therewith a corresponding lowering of piece-wages
is made possible. But the piece-wages are not reduced in the
same proportion that the production increases, or the operative
would remain in the same position. But the reduction in piece-
wages is somewhat less, so that the weekly earnings increase. A
four-loom weaver receives per loom considerably less than a one-
loom weaver ; but he receives per loom more than a quarter of the
earnings of the latter. He must receive more ; because otherwise
his standard of living could not be higher than that of the one-
loom weaver. With such a standard of living the four-loom
weaver himself would not be possible.

A similar state of affairs is seen regarding the hours of labour.
By the quicker speed, the lengthening of the machines, etc., a
larger production per day is achieved ; a larger production which,
on the one hand, allows a curtailment of the hours of labour,
without which, on the other hand, it would not be possible, since
the labour capacity of the operative is fettered to the fixed limits
of organism. By producing in a shorter time just as much as,
or more than, was produced formerly in a longer time, an array
of fixed charges is cut down. "It is cheaper to exhaust labour-
power in 9 than in 11 hours," said an intelligent employer to me.

After having already written down the above observations, I
find to my joy a thorough similar grasp of the question examined
in the latest work of Marshall : "Elements of Economics" (London,
1892). Marshall also accepts the fact that by machinery a reverse
development results in regard to division of labour. "Machinery
weakens the boundaries between the single branches of trade"
(28). Machinery tends towards a complete automatic discharging
of the work to be done, to the condition which limits the energy of
men to the feeding with raw material, taking away the produced
articles, and minding the machine. "That portion of the labour
which repeats itself is done by the machine, which becomes more

---

28. From the above-mentioned work, p. 163. But when the action has
been reduced to routine it has nearly arrived at the stage at which it can be
taken over by machinery. . . . This machinery constantly supplants that
purely manual skill, the attainment of which was, even up to A. Smith's time,
the chief advantage of division of labour.

and more automatical until, at length, the human hand has nothing to do except put in materials at certain periods of time and to take away the results when they are ready ". (p. 167).

But if thus the demands which the older system of division of labour required from the hand-skill of men become less, the perfection of machinery requires other essentials from the operatives. "The finer the accomplishments of the machine become, the greater the understanding and the more the care which is demanded from those who look after it. Let us think, for instance, of that beautiful machine which on one side feeds itself with steel wire, and gives forth, on the other, fine screws of remarkable finish. It displaced a large number of workers who had reached a high stage of skilled hand proficiency, but who led a sedentary life, straining their eyes with the microscope, and who found at their work little room for any ability except the mere regulation of their fingers. But the machine is complicated and expensive, and the person who attends to it must have reasoning power and a lively sense of responsibility, which form a good share of character-discipline, and which, although more frequent than formerly, is still sufficiently scarce to command a high payment." This instance may certainly show in an unusual degree the influence of the machine on labour, but the same is the case everywhere, in a less degree, wherever machinery replaces hand-labour.

It is certain that if industrial progress depends at the present day on the machine, therewith is the necessity formed for a gradual raising of the standard of living of the working classes. We can herewith justify the apparently paradoxical assertion that the extent of the standard of living of the working classes is a measuring scale of the industrial power of a nation, because it at the same time shows the degree of technical progress. But in the field of social, as in general of organic occurrences, everything is action and re-action. The possession of high standing and capable labour is action, so on the other side an essential for the application and development of technical inventions and therewith the foundation for the building-up of the great industrial power position of a nation.

Not the countries which employ the lowest-paid hand-labour, but those which use the best and most machinery, prove themselves at the present day the strongest in the industrial contests of nations.

It shall now be shown by English factory labour, especially that of Lancashire, in which directions it at once comes into account as a result of centralised industrial progress, and, at the same time, as a demander of its further development.

B.—THE FACTORY LABOUR OF LANCASHIRE'S COTTON INDUSTRY.

That Lancashire to-day possesses the most capable labour in the cotton industry all expert observers agree. Thus J. C. Fielden, a well-known member of the business world of Manchester, sees in the superiority of the labour the chief strength of Lancashire (1). A similar view was expressed by the American Consul in Manchester (Mr. B. Shaw), an acknowledged capable judge, in agreement with German employers before the Enquete-Commission (2). "An English operative," says Mr. Shaw, "is satisfied if he has abundant work and abundant wages ; only a few think of changing to another calling (3). This fixity of labour is of great value to the industry, because long experience creates a dexterity in always minding the same machines, which guarantees the most complete regularity, as well as superiority of the results." Samuel Andrew, the Secretary of the large Employers' Association of Oldham, condenses the advantages of English labour into the following words : "We have at this moment the most capable labour in the world. It is born and brought up well suited and disciplined to its work ; under its wage lists, with the present improved machinery we can depend upon it fulfilling its duty with the accuracy of clockwork."

Upon what do the advantages of North English factory labour depend ? The following points of view can be shown to be valuable : —(a) a high vitality, which finds its expression in greater speed, dexterity, and strength ; (b) the presence of certain mental qualifications which specially suit machine labour ; (c) the peculiar arrangement of labour contracts; (d) the consumption power of the working classes.

(a) The physical superiority of the English factory operative when compared with the Continental is recognised by German

1. Compare a series of articles on Foreign Competition in the *Manchester Examiner*, 1882, especially the articles of 28th November and 5th December.

2. "Protokolle," pp. 14, 81, 227. "Commercial Relations of the United States," No 12 (Oct. 1881), p. 129.

3. On the other hand in America, according to Sartorius von Wattershausen ("Die nordamerikanischen Gewerkschaften," p. 108), the facility for changing a calling still discloses a certain colonial character in the people.

observers, just as the operatives of the great English industries themselves boast of a physical superiority. Nowhere in England, says the organ of the cotton operatives (the "Cotton Factory Times"), are there so many strong and healthy children as in the seats of the cotton industry. The quickness of the "doffers" (young workers who look after taking off the full and putting on the empty bobbins in the throstle-room) is in Lancashire proverbial (4). Regarding the adult worker a German manufacturer says:—"One must see them at a self-actor, with what quickness they doff the full bobbins, or observe the dexterity of the female flyer operatives. Everything is accomplished like a flash of lightning" (5).

When machinery was first coming into use physicians and Blue-Books made mention of specific mill diseases; at the present time the new spinning-mills of Oldham are model hygienic institutions. Phthisis was in the "thirties" a frequent illness of the spinners. To-day, as Dr. Niven, the Medical Officer of Health at Oldham, full of sympathy for the operatives, informs me, it occurs more seldom with spinners than any other class of people in Oldham. The borough of Oldham contains two classes of skilled workpeople—the cotton operatives and machine workers. Statistics show that both classes are far less liable to consumption than the remaining population (unskilled workmen, shopkeepers, etc.). The duration of the sickness is more severe with the machine workers than with the cotton operatives (6).

The progress which the English operative has made in health as well as capacity compared with his forefathers, depends chiefly on an improved standard of living. The enormous progress in the nourishment of the people which England has seen during this century is a most important element favourable to the capacity for competition of English industry as opposed to the competition of Continental industry.

---

4. " Lancashire Characters and Incidents," by T. Newbigging (Manchester: Brook and Chrystal, 1891). Compare the chapter about the " Lancashire Factory Doffers."

5. " Protokolle der deutschen Enquête," p. 81.

6. Compare " Report of Health, Borough of Oldham," 1890. " From the details given in connection with the experience of former years I conclude that the influences which materially affect the health of the population, as far as lung complaints come into consideration, are to be sought for without the factory gates " (pp. 56-9). Compare, also, Atkinson: " Popular Science Monthly " January, 1890), pp. 317-8

The better food of the operatives engaged in England's great industry at the present day, compared with that of English operatives in the "thirties" and the Continental operatives of the present, depends upon two circumstances: one being the higher wages in money, and the other the greater buying power of this money.

We have seen above how the development of technical skill made possible an enormously increased production per operative, and therewith a permanent lowering of piece-wages. We have at the same time given an array of figures to prove that the weekly income of the operatives has risen in the same proportion as piece-wages fell, because the progressive technical development demanded more capable operatives.

The weekly income of the operative at the present time in England is higher than in the "thirties," and also than at present on the Continent. Since this high income depends upon lower piece-work prices, it is nothing but a source of strength to English industry.

Regarding the general increase of the weekly earnings of the operatives during the last half-century, R. Giffen, the well-known statistician, says:—"In all cases where in consequence of repetition labour it has been possible to set up a comparison, an extraordinary increase of wages of from 20 to 50 and 100 per cent., and even more is shown. This statement rather underestimates the real extent of the change" (7).

In the Appendix to the First Report of the Royal Commission on Textile Depression, the Secretary of the Manchester Chamber of Commerce gives similar statistics. According to these, the income of the operatives from 1850 to 1883 has increased for:—

Cotton spinning and weaving, medium counts, by 74·72 per cent.
          ., "   fine   ,.   35·16   ,,
Bleaching and printing "   ..   ..   ,, 50·00   .,   (8)

7. Compare R. Giffen: "Progress of the Working Classes" (London, 1884), p. 6.

8. Compare p. 99; further, the Appendix to the Second Report, pp. 376-7. These statistics are, as a fact, not unchallenged; they are corrected by the author himself in the Second Report, but without materially giving other results.   On the other hand, D. Chadwick ("The Expenditure of Wages," paper read before the British Association. Manchester. 1887) declares that the percentages given are too high.   Since 1860 the earnings of cotton operatives had, however, certainly increased by 10 per cent. (p. 8).   R. Giffen, the leading statistician in England, accepts the figures of G. Lord.   Compare R. Giffen: "Recent Changes in Prices and Incomes" (Royal Stat. Society, 1888, p. 20).

The same thing is shown if we compare the weekly rate of wages given by Baines with those contained in the official statistics (9). From these facts we have the picture of a formidable rise in wages which has taken place in Lancashire during the last century. The official figures are, however, not quite free from criticism. General statistics of wages which can be depended upon are unfortunately not at hand, because no census of the wages conditions of all the operatives employed is available in the cases given.

A comparison which referred to the wages paid to the same classes of operatives in the same mill appeared to me, therefore, to be the most free from criticism. I was fortunate in receiving the following figures from the wage-books of one of the largest and most renowned spinning firms in Lancashire. Since the firm chiefly spins fine yarns, the wages are partly higher than the average wages of official statistics mentioned alongside. But whilst the latter claim only an approximate accuracy, the first are authentic.

| | WEEKLY WAGES. | | | Official average figures. |
	1834.	1850.	1883.	1886.
	s. d.	s. d.	s. d.	s. d. s. d.
Labourers	15 0	15 0	20 0	—
Mechanics..	27 0	27 0	33 0	—
Carders :—				
1st class	30 0	27 0	32 0	37 11
2nd class	15 0	13 6	21 0	28 10
3rd class	—	—	—	24 10
Drawing-frames (girls)	9 0	8 3	14 0	12 5 to 15 4
Preparation	9 0	8 3	14 0	14 0 ,, 14 3
Combing (women)	—	8 6	15 6	—
Jack tenters	—	8 0	16 6	—
Spinners ..	35 0	40 0	42 0	35 6
Helpers ..	14 0	13 0	16 0	14 2

A similar state of affairs results from the wages of a firm, just as old and important, in the neighbourhood of Manchester, which combines spinning and weaving.

| | WEEKLY WAGES. | |
	1832.	1891.
	s. d.	s. d.
Spinner—1st class	35 0	39 0
,, 2nd ,,	28 2	36 0
,, 3rd ,,	28 2	30 0
Dresser	30 6	36 0
Weaver	12 0	18 0

9. Report of the Board of Trade : " Return of Rates of Wages in the Principal Textile Trades," 1889. Baines, pp. 444-5.

These are the wage conditions of two of the most respectable firms in Lancashire, which were already quoted by Ure and Baines for the first decades of the century as instances applicable to the industry of the county.

If the raising of wages depends upon technical alterations, and, therewith, growing demands on the working capacity of the operative, it was the development of centralised industry, of the factory system, which also raised the income of the operative in another direction. The cheapening of food, moving parallel with the increase of wages, is not an accidental occurrence, but is the result of the economical development delineated. This appeared the most effectively in the productions of centralised industry themselves; the striving after cheapening the costs of production and, therewith, of the goods, forms certainly the motive for the technical progress. For instance, in the cotton industry the prices since the "thirties" have gone down by at least one-half.

Cotton yarn, per lb.	(10)		Cotton woven goods, per yard.			
No. 40's.	No. 100's.					
s. d.	s. d.					s. d.
1830 ... 1 2½	... 3 4½		1839	...	... ...	0 5¾
1882 ... 0 10½	... 1 10		1882	...	... ...	0 3¼

Such a development also took place with other productions of industry.

But the cheapening of food was also, as mentioned above, the immediate result of industrial development. The corn duties fell, as soon as the export interest had become predominant, because every burden on the chief imports represented a burden on export. If the economical development on the one side made the English operative the highest paid in Europe, it made England at the same time one of the cheapest industrial countries. The price of wheat in the decade before the repeal of the Corn Laws was 58s. 7d. per quarter; in the decade 1872 to 1882 only 48s. 9d. (11).

But just as important for the operative was the equalisation of prices, since formerly famine prices alternated periodically with extremely cheap prices. In 1836 the price was 36s.; 1838, 1839, 1840, and 1841, it was 78s. 4d., 81s. 6d., 72s. 10d., 76s. 1d. In 1812 we find even an average price of 126s. 6d.; in 1813 109s. 9d., and

---

10. Compare Ellison: " Cotton Trade," p. 61; Giffen: " Progress of the Working Classes," p. 11. Merttens: Paper read before the Manchester Statistical Society, April 18th, 1894, p. 129.

11. Compare Giffen, pp. 8, 9.

1817 96s. 11d. Such variations in prices represented a complete uncertainty of existence for the operative. Regularity of living conditions is the first essential for a regulated standard of living. According to Chadwick's estimates, which refer to retail intercourse, prices for food fell from the "thirties" in the following proportion (12).

An operative's family, consisting of man, wife, and three children from two to seven years of age, requires weekly for food:—

	Prices for similar quantities in							
	1887.		1859.		1849.		1839.	
	s.	d.	s.	d.	s.	d.	s.	d.
I.—BREAD, ETC.:— Eight 4 lb. loaves .. 6 lb. of flour .. Half-peck of oatmeal	4	8¾	5	4	5	8	7	6
II.—MEAT:— 5 lb. beef .. .. 2 lb. bacon	3	11½	4	0½	4	5	4	0½
III.—ACCESSORIES:— 40 lb. potatoes .. 7 qts. milk .. Vegetables, etc. ..	4	6¼	4	3	4	3	4	3
IV.—COLONIAL PRODUCTS, ETC., including:— 3 lb. sugar .. .. ½ lb. coffee .. .. ½ lb. tea .. .. 1 lb. butter	5	3	6	11	7	1½	8	9½
Totals	18	5½	20	6½	21	5½	24	9

The following were the prices of the most important necessaries:—

	1887. Pence.	1859. Pence	1849. Pence.	1839. Pence.
Flour, per lb.	1·41	1·66	1·83	2
Fresh meat, do. ..	6¾	6½	7	6½
Bacon, do.	6¾	8	9	8
Tea, do.	2/2	4/-	4/4	6/-
Sugar, do.	2	5	5	7
Soap, do.	3	4	5	5

At present, however, there is a reduction of from 5 to 10 per cent. on these prices for articles which are supplied by co-operative stores, which is the usual mode as regards the better-situated operatives of centralised industries. House-rent has risen little,

12. D. Chadwick: "Expenditure of Wages," read at the British Association, Manchester, 5th Sept., 1887.

but in this respect the demands are also higher, the operatives requiring better accommodation.

Taken generally, the operative only succeeded by co-operation in benefiting by the lowering of prices. The majority of the cotton operatives of Lancashire are members of the co-operative stores. What a small advance on wholesale prices the operative in buying retail has to pay I determined in the summer of 1891 for the chief seats of the English textile industry.   Since the co-operative societies mostly pay back 10 per cent. dividend, their selling prices to-day are not lower than those of the retail shopkeepers, whose profits have been considerably cut down by the flourishing of co-operative societies.   Let us follow a pound of wheat on its way from the merchant in Liverpool to the operative's home.   The sole intermediaries are the co-operative corn mills and local societies.   The prices of these latter societies are fairly equal throughout the whole of the North of England.   In order, however, not to err on the side of cheapness, I expressly choose a society which is a considerable distance from the corn mill, so that the cost of carriage is included in the price : —

		STAR CORN MILLS, OLDHAM.		DARWEN CO-OP. SOCIETY.
		Wholesale average price of the wheat bought, per lb. Pence.	Selling price of flour at the corn-mill, per lb. Pence.	Consumers' respective average price per lb. flour. Pence.
1883	...	1 09	...	1·42	...	1·47
1884	...	0·94	...	1·27	...	1·32
1885	...	0·85	...	1·13	...	1·18
1886	...	0·82	...	1·09	...	1·14
1887	...	0·87	...	1·10	...	1·15
1888	...	0·86	...	1·07	...	1·12
1889	...	0·83	...	1·08	...	1·13

The prices of a pound of flour were very little higher in Bradford, the seat of the woollen industry.   Thus in 1889 and 1890 a pound of flour cost, on the average, 1·31d.   The lowness of these prices comes so much the more into account since the operatives receive 7½ to 10 per cent. on the amount of their buyings from the co-operative societies.   But wheat flour is at present the most important food of the English operative.   In the North of England it is baked at home by the wife.   The price of bread, which is seldom bought in Lancashire, amounts to ½d. per lb more than the price of the flour.

Prices of meat in the shops of the Co-operative Society at Darwen were the following, and are approximately the same in the whole of Lancashire:—

	Beef, per lb. Pence.	Mutton, per lb. Pence.
1883	8¼	9½
1884	8	9
1885	8½	9½
1886	7½	9¾
1887	7	8
1888	7¾	8½
1889	8	9½
1890	8	11
1891	8	10½

These figures are, however, average values, in which very different prices are included. For instance, in England, even in the co-operative stores, extremely variable prices are paid, according to the quality of the piece. Thus, during the last few years, legs of mutton and beefsteaks cost 1s. per lb., against which the prices of ordinary but good pieces of beef and mutton and pork were as follows (all in the same Co-operative Stores at Darwen):—

	Beef. Pence.	Mutton. Pence.	Pork. Pence.
1888	6½	7½	7
1889	7	8½	8
1890	5¾	8¾	8
1891	5¾	8¾	8

Pieces of lower quality were sold at 4d. On the average 1d. per lb. is paid back as dividend.

I also add, as well, the following retail prices, also co operative society's average figures:—

	Sugar, per lb. Pence.	Butter, per lb. s.	d.
1870	6·34	—	—
1889	3·74	1	1
1890	3·51	1	2
1891	2·99	1	3

What has been said shows an extraordinary cheapening of the most important necessaries during the course of the century (13).

Just as favourably stands the English operative to-day compared with his Continental brother. The following comparison refers to the same week in February, 1892; it concerns the prices of food in Chemnitz and in Hyde (near Manchester, occupied exclusively in

13. Compare Porter: "Progress of the Nation," p. 543, and Giffen.

textile industries), and is given in German weights and measures:—

	Hyde. Pfennige.		Chemnitz. Pfennige.
Flour (1 German lb.)	... 16	......	22
Bread ,, ,,	... 18 (wheat)	......	15 (rye)
Beef (14),, ,,	... 75 to 80	......	80
Beef ,, ,,	... ——	......	66 to 70 (with adjuncts)
Bacon ,, ,,	... 63 to 73	......	80 to 90
Sugar ,, ,,	... 27 to 28	......	30 to 34
Potatoes ,, ,,	... 5·2	......	5·2
Milk (1 litre) ...	... 15 to 22	......	20

In Hyde a dividend of 14 per cent. is paid on the sales; in Chemnitz, in shops, 6⅔ per cent., in co-operative store, 8·3 per cent. (25 pfennige per 3 marks).

The higher wages, in connection with the lower food prices, make possible an extraordinarily good nourishment of the English operative. The English workman lives on meat and wheat-flour bread, whilst potatoes mostly form the chief sustenance of the German factory-worker. If the English operative, as shown above, minds two to three times as much machinery as the German, he also certainly eats two to three times as much—not in quantity, but in nourishing value from a physiological point of view.

(b) In the second consideration there are certain mental qualifications which make the English operative specially capable for working on the machine, the achieved results of a development now almost a hundred years old. In Lancashire, not only were the fathers, but even the grandfathers of the present race machine spinners and weavers.

It is thereby shown how untrue the assertion was that machine labour pressed down the mental level of the operative. The English cotton operative, as well as the North of England factory worker in general, is to-day a son of the generation of technical skill. Technical problems awaken his most lively interest. The fact stands alone of its kind, that the organ of the cotton operatives in Lancashire, the "Cotton Factory Times," always has a

---

14. In England the single piece of meat is sold, according to quality, at various prices; so-called adjuncts (bones, etc.) are not to be found. These latter are generally sold separately.

considerable amount of technical discussions. The contributions of operatives are said to be often, from a practical point of view, so admirable that the paper has subscribers among English fore-men and managers in spinning-mills in India, Japan, and Russia. Interesting for the Continental observer in a similar direction is a visit to some machinery exhibitions in the industrial districts. The operatives here crowd around the exhibited objects and discuss their advantages and failings. It is also a remarkable fact that the trade society of the spinners lets the capability for its secre-taryship of the Amalgamated Societies depend upon a purely technical examination; the answering of questions in writing under control is specified. The "Cotton Factory Times" also urges the greatest possible use of the aid of technical training on the part of the operatives (15). This advice is followed so much the more frequently because the "limited" principle of the cotton industry in England, as in India, grants to young people with technical knowledge from the operative classes at the present time manifold opportunities for bettering their position.

A mark of the technical inclination of the English operative is the Mutual Technical School (16) at Oldham, founded solely by operatives. In it there are lectures, in which the members mutually teach one another about the particular branches in which they are specially at home. Business managers and similar practical people also give lectures here. The school has gradually acquired the possession of all the various machines of the cotton industry. It is exclusively under the control of the operatives.

What has been said shows how the opposition, even hatred, against machinery which permeated the operative in the first period of centralised industry, and is often acquiesced in by phil-anthropic observers, has in Lancashire at the present day been put on one side. If the operative still hopes as hitherto for social progress, he knows that the means lie in the extension of machinery.

But how essential a control full of understanding is for the machine to be worked, and this latter's suitability to the nature

15. Compare also, for instance, Commission on Depression of Trade, Second Report, part I., 5,055, 5,170, where the Secretary of the Spinners' Association expresses himself in favour of every possible advance of technical instruction.

16. Denton-street, off Clegg-street, Oldham.

of the raw material for a qualitative as well as quantitative good result, every practical man is aware (17).

This is not the place to speak in detail about the way in which technical education is being energetically pressed forward at the present time in England. In that it affects the working classes in a high degree, it differs from the acknowledged splendid efforts in the same direction in Germany. The latter produces distinguished trained technical men, not only for Germany—whose demand has not kept pace with the supply—but also for competing countries, especially England, whose laboratories, mills, and technical educational institutions are filled with German experts. As opposed to this over-production on the one hand, technical instruction in Germany has up to now drawn the operative very little within its folds. But how important for the industrial prosperity of a country is a technical training as extensive as possible is acknowledged in general by the great English industrial employers. Thus, one of the greatest of these, Sir William Armstrong, says :— The ignorance of the great mass of persons engaged in industry as regards natural science and technical knowledge is a bar to the progress of the individual, as well as a loss for the nation. Almost every branch of skilled labour could be developed if the persons engaged in it were trained in the elements of natural science, which come into account in the labour (18). As a fact, in England

17. Compare Marsden : " Cotton Spinning " (London, 1888), p. 130. " It requires the closest attention of the carder in order to prevent the cotton being delivered before it is sufficiently carded, by which bad work would result ; and, on the other hand, to prevent it remaining in the card a moment longer than necessary, as this diminishes the product. Cottons differ in the amount of carding they require— some needing more, some less ; others, again, contain a larger proportion of short fibre, and fill the cards sooner, rendering it necessary to strip oftener. On changes being made in these respects the carder should give the closest attention to his cards, in order that he may make any alteration that may be needed in time," etc., etc. In a similar way the nature of the raw material determines the changeable distance of the drawing rollers in the mule, which the spinner has to regulate. The adaptation of the raw material as a variable natural product to the regular working machine is more and more the task of the operative engaged upon it. Compare also " Prot. der Reichsenquête," p. 9. " A clever operative makes less waste than a new beginner. In this respect I believe that we have rather more waste in Germany than in England."

18. Compare " Technical Education " (London, 1889, National Association for the Promotion of Technical and Secondary Education), p. 30. This book gives a glance at the valuable efforts and the extensive literature of this society. In his essay, " Ueber das Wesen und die Verfassung der grossen Unternehmung," Schmoller has drawn attention to the importance of the possession of " skilled labour," and compared it correctly with a state of instability and frequent change of calling. Compare " Zur Social und Gewerbepolitik " (1890), pp. 402, 404, 411.

during the last decade there has entered into existence an extraordinarily strong movement for technical instruction. Not only
does the State by its system of examination by the Science and
Art Department look after the extension of technical-scientific
knowledge to an extent that is probably nowhere else attained in
Europe, but everywhere societies and voluntary undertakings
advance the same thing. Thus at the present time the Corpora-
tions of the City of London devote a considerable portion of their
riches to the extension of technical knowledge (City and Guilds of
London Institute, People's Palace). But especially has the movement its seat in the industrial North, prominently in Lancashire,
Yorkshire, and Northumberland. In the book mentioned the
attendance at technical schools is denoted by maps; the central
points of the attendance agree with those of industry in every
instance.

Everywhere to-day have the long-existing "Mechanics' Insti-
tutes," formerly without technical objects, developed into technical
schools which are to a great extent attended by operatives. Operatives are mostly represented on the managing committees; for
instance, the Trades Council of Manchester on the committee of
the large technical school there. In a similar direction tend the
objects of the Recreative Evening School Association, founded in
Manchester, and extending to-day over the whole country. Its
object is to fill the training education of the trade operatives
taking place in the evening with a technical scientific spirit—to
put in the place of mental work the training of the eye and hand.
On the committee of this society the cotton operatives are represented by the Secretary of the Amalgamated Spinners; the Trades
Council of Manchester has as well its representatives. Just from
their side does technical instruction find its most eager support.

With what importance these efforts are viewed can be seen from
the fact that Government has granted a very considerable sum
(£750,000) to be applied by the County Councils for the support
of technical instruction.

In connection with the movement for technical education stand
the endeavours which stimulate in elementary instruction the
training of hand and eye of the infant. Mr. William Mather, a
well-known industrial employer and member of Parliament, has
succeeded in bringing in a law for the introduction of manual

work into National Schools.   Since then the Department of Science and Art (Circular 44, Manual Instruction) has issued propositions for this kind of instruction.

The movement for technical education is in general an accompanying result of centralised industrial development.   It means nothing else than that the English nation applies also, for the education of the people, the consequences of a national economical law, which depends upon the machine.   The North English operative is born and educated for the machine.   With Continental hand-labour he could not compete; on the other hand he is the cheapest operative in the world wherever he tends the most improved machinery.

(c)   Social relations also grant England a certain start in the competition of nations.   Two conditions come into account.   If Ure had at one time to complain that nowhere in the world was the relation between labour and employer worse than in England, it is to-day more peaceful than in the principal competing industrial countries.   Whilst in Germany, certainly, the turning point of those differences has not yet been reached—we are thinking about the operatives' press-organs only now making their appearance in the valleys of decentralised industry—in England the personal hatred of the connection has disappeared.   Employee and employer stand opposite to one another as business men, at least in the great industry of the North of England.

But especially in the cotton industry has that principle of antagonism between Capital and Labour disappeared.   The operative knows that his chief interest is bound up with that of his employer in keeping the markets for his industry.   Only by their loss could he lose his high standard of living.   Therefore he does not look with envy at the riches of his employer.   Practically enough he argues: " An employer who is doing well can pay good wages" (19).   The chief proof for the feeling of this common interest is the position of the trade unions of Lancashire on the eight-hours question.   As a matter of principle the warmest adherents of the eight-hours day believe they would injure themselves by its introduction at the present juncture, because they are afraid of driving a portion of the cotton industry away to foreign

19. Compare, for further particulars, my book " On Social Peace," II., p. 306.

countries. Therefore they passed a resolution at the last Trade-Unions Congress whereby the demanded introduction of the eight-hours day could be declined by individual industries. The movement for technical education for the opening of India and Africa (20), the bimetallic movement (21), etc., are looked at to-day by operatives and employers as political allies.

But in another respect do the social conditions come into account. Centralised industry is liable to crises as a result of the world's market. They cause loss to the employers alone as long as wages do not exceed the bare-existence minimum; on the other hand they partly affect wages prejudicially as soon as, in consequence of technically advanced conditions, in spite of lower piece-wages the weekly earnings of the operatives are high. The English operatives accept reductions in wages in consequence of bad trade just as frequently as they demand as a right to participate in the increased profits of the industry by increased wages.

In the German "Enquete" many German employers point out this elasticity of wages as a great advantage of England. They complain that they have not the same possibility, because a lessening of wages is simply impossible in the interest of labour capacity (22). But besides this, the principle of this adaptability of wages to crises is also accepted by both parties to the large societies comprising the whole industry, which are not yet developed in Germany. For only thereby is a uniform fixing of wages made possible for the whole of an industry.

In Lancashire, as I have shown in my book "On Social Peace," the normal wages are regulated by lists conjointly agreed upon; on the other hand, the actual wages vary from the normal wages in various percentages according to the state of trade. Lotz declares this, and rightly so, a suitable condition for centralised industry (23).

---

20. Compare Second Report of the Commission on Depression of Trade. part I., 5,103. Further. concerning the .importance of Africa, whose consumption is capable of tremendous expansion and rapidly increases, Ellison " Cotton Trade," p. 155

21. Compare the Bimetallic Manifesto of the United Textile Operatives (125,000 operatives), Nov. 30th, 1891.

22. Report of the ''Enquêtekommission," p. 168. " Protokolle," pp. 86, 296, 299, 344, 375.

23. Compare Lotz: "Ideen zur deutschen Handelspolitik " (Leipzig, 892), pp. 135, 208, and 209

Add to this, that in consequence of the operatives' organisations the employer can more readily stop hands, because the trade unions in cases of scarcity of work mostly help their members, whilst in Germany an efflux of labour has to be feared, or the operative has to depend upon poor-relief. Whilst the English employer possesses, through the trade unions, the advantage of easily obtaining labour and just as easily dispensing with it, the German employer still seeks to attach the workman by money clubs, etc. This patriarchal social policy, also once customary in England, has to-day made room for a purely contracting relation.

(d) The operative comes into account in the industry, not only as producer, but also as consumer. Whilst centralised industrial development increases the quantity produced, it evolves, on the other hand, an extensive population capable of buying. This is the condition of its own existence. Without it the centralised industrial development would only be an episode, and would come to a standstill as soon as the as yet non-industrial nations had established their own industries. But thus every industrial nation extends permanently the home market to the lower classes, and obtains selling markets in the same proportion that other nations become industrial, and, therewith, capable of consumption; as, for instance, the two industrial countries, England and Germany, are to-day the most important markets for each other (24).

Before the modern economical development set in, only limited portions of the population were customers of the industry. The countryman especially, in general scarcely drawn into the world's market, made his own clothing, as is still done in portions of the European Continent (25), and even in certain districts of what were formerly the purely agrarian Southern States of North America (26).

The arising of the world's market brings forward with centralised industry the new class of industrial operatives, who for the satisfying of their wants are forced to buy from the commencement. This consuming power, at first slight, rises hand-in-hand with technical progress and cheapening of food—both results of cen-

24. Compare Ellison : " Cotton Trade," p. 152, and Lotz, p. 202.

25. If, for instance, Viebahn (III., 952) still gives, together with 394,865 hand-looms in cottage industry, 387,969 as partially used, this refers to the very frequent, even to-day not quite stopped, home production, in peasant circles, of clothing at the end of the "sixties."

26. Compare Atkinson : "Distribution of Products," p. 121.

tralised industrial development. But more and more does the interweaving of isolated industries seize upon the circles which up to now kept aloof. The countryman also produces more to sell than to use.

English centralised industry, still in the "thirties" depending upon an under-nourished factory proletariat, stands to-day upon the wide basis of an operative population with high capacity for consumption. Still in the "thirties" were the wages in Lancashire not sufficient to cover even the needs of ordinary food; products of industry were not bought. To-day the raising of the weekly earnings and the cheapening of foodstuffs grants a considerable surplus above living necessities. This is the reason for that astonishing use of industrial productions, especially the results of the textile industry, as the operatives' budgets to follow will show. But it is to be mentioned that the class of industrial workers capable of consumption is by no means limited to Lancashire. It extends as far as the English centralised industries reach. Machine workers, shipbuilders, miners, and partly, also, workers at iron furnaces, enjoy a somewhat still higher standard of living than cotton operatives.

Also the farmer and agricultural labourer are to-day completely drawn into the market; the Scotch "Jack of all trades," of Eden, has also disappeared from isolated districts. Far remote, only to exchange the surplus of his farm, the countryman produces to-day, solely for the wants of society, productions which he perhaps does not need for himself. This so much the more because since the repeal of the Corn Laws he threw himself upon specialties; for instance, meat of good quality, pedigree-horses, garden products, etc., for which the industrial development, on the other hand, pushed forward customers capable of paying. The more legislation, as it has already done in Ireland, favours small landed proprietors, the more does a new home market for English centralised industry extend (27).

27. Compare, concerning the influence of exchange between centralised industry and spade culture, what Atkinson ("Distribution of Products," p. 77) relates about the farmers once producing wheat in the State of New York. By going over to spadework, for which the industrial centres were close customers, they removed themselves successfully from the competition of the large centralised corn producers of the West. Wheat, unlike rye, requires the addition of vegetable food. Wheat contains not only more nourishment, but is easier to assimilate; therefore vegetables are necessary in order to bring the digestive organs into play.

Especially important for the textile industry is the consuming power of the masses. The development of the use of cotton goods is given by the following figures:—

CONSUMPTION OF COTTON GOODS IN ENGLAND.

		In £1,000.		In 1,000 lb.		Per head.		
1820	...	13,044	...	35,620	...	1·5 lb.	...	1s.
1885		25,960 (including imports, 28,217)		201,800	...	5·3 lb.	...	1·55s.

These figures show a considerable increase of the consumption, and give at the same time an idea of the cheapening of cotton goods. The estimating of the use of other textile stuffs is met by certain difficulties (for instance, the uncertainty of the quantity of raw wool produced in England itself). We must therefore look to the operatives' budgets communicated below, by which an extraordinary capacity of consumption is shown. We shall in these, in the case of some families of the cotton operatives of Lancashire, which by no means form exceptional cases, meet with yearly outlays for clothing which reach the total earnings of an adult operative of the German textile industry—indeed, even exceed them.

German industrial employers before the examining "Enquetekommission" are right in looking upon the smaller consumption of the German operative as a disadvantage as compared with England. Indeed numerous examinations of later years give the result that in general only the outermost fringe of the industrial workers of Germany buy new articles of clothing (28). The proofs of this statement have been collected by Herkner. Especially important, as well, are the published workers' budgets from the German Freie Hochstift of Frankfurt a/M. Indeed these researches show, like those which I undertook in Saxony, that not only in the case of operatives of the German cottage industries, but also in those of an important portion of centralised occupations, the wages must be exclusively applied for food.

If the masses in Germany possessed the same consuming power as in the United States or in England, Germany could dispose of more than double the amount of its whole export in textile goods

---

28. "The Social Position of the Operatives in Mannheim" (Karlsruhe, 1891), pp. 245, 250.   Herkner: "Social Reform a Law of Economical Progress" (Leipzig, 1891), p. 55.

in its own country (29).   Germany stands also in this respect on
the step of the economical development which England had
attained in the "thirties."   The replacement of labour by
machinery is still comparatively slight, and therewith Germany
also still lacks that operative, just as capable for labour as for
consumption, which forms to-day the strength of England.   In
consequence of this the farmer has also not yet the market for the
products of his garden and spade which make him himself a good
customer, capable of paying for the productions of centralised
industry.

IV.—Comparison of the Costs of Production in England and Germany.

The rising markets of the world have evolved the modern method
of production on a large scale, and in the first instance in the
cotton industry.   But other trades have rapidly followed in this
latter's footsteps, especially the iron industry, machine making,
and shipbuilding, so that at the present time English national
economy bears a centralised industrial character.   This progress
was a consequence of certain historical conditions arising from
certain natural advantages of England.   But the latter as permanent elements must give way to the continuous cheapening of
the costs of production.   The industrial strength of England depends no longer in the first instance on those natural advantages,
but rather on the fact that English national economy has farthest
advanced the technical, commercial, and social results of modern
centralised industry; and that therewith, both by employers and
employed, that psychological change has been most developed—
that psychological change which, we noted above, occurred with
the departure from the customary foundations of the old methods
of trade.   The onward-driving wheel of the advancement was the
pressure or demands of the world's market.   Seen from this point
of view, the fact will be easily understood that at the present
moment the costs of building and running mills, and of raw materials
and finished articles in the greatest staple industry, are the
cheapest in England.

---

29. Compare Schönhof: "Industrial Situation" (New York, 1885), pp.
54-6.

We will follow this as regards the cotton industry. In spinning as well as weaving the cost of a mill is cheaper in England than anywhere else in the world. This depends on two facts. One is that, in consequence of technical progress and commercial organisation, almost all the requisites for putting up and working a mill are cheaper in England than in the remaining industrial countries. Then remains the fact that the English capitalist, when building or establishing a business, thinks mostly of turning to good account a momentary favourable opportunity rather than of a permanent investment. He therefore saves fixed capital, in order to have as much untied money as possible at his disposal for carrying on the business. The lifetime of a spinning-mill, for instance, is usually assumed to be not longer than 20 years.

Then, besides this principle we have shown, it must be noted that land in England for industrial purposes is in most instances not bought outright, but only taken at a rental for a certain term of years. Under such conditions all luxurious additions which are not essential for the object of the undertaking are more or less eschewed from the mind. Although we cannot assert, as well, that land for industrial buildings is cheaper, England in this respect has also certainly an advantage. German factories are situated either in the midst of traffic communications, where the ground is extraordinarily dear, or are dispersed in the country, where the cheaper price of land is counterbalanced by higher costs of maintenance. In this respect English industry has the advantage of its collectiveness and its division of labour. The factories of Lancashire enjoy all the advantages of extreme centralisation : but as they leave commercial centres and establish themselves in smaller industrial places, and in the vicinity, they enjoy almost agricultural prices of land.

A second consideration is the cost of buildings. Bricks and stone are cheaper in England than on the Continent, a consequence of the technically further advanced and larger proportions of the brick industry which are made possible by the steady demand of an exceedingly great industry (1). But still more important is the difference in price of iron equipments, which in new mills play a continually increasing part. Iron prices differ from those on the Continent by about the amount of duty and carriage added to-

---

1. Compare " Protokolle," p. 80. In England 1,000 bricks cost 14s. to 15s. ; in Stuttgart, 27s.

gether. Building labour in England, in spite of the higher weekly wages of the workmen, is also cheaper than on the Continent. We are reminded in this respect of the particulars given by Lord Brassey (2). According to his experience, English bricklayers and navvies generally work cheaper than Continental or Indian workmen, who receive far less wages.

The greater becomes the advantage of England the more we turn from natural materials, such as land, bricks, and iron, to those in whose production labour and capital take an important position. The advantage of England in this respect is tremendous. The centralisation of the cotton industry in Lancashire has caused the concentration of corresponding machine-making establishments, with thousands of workpeople. Such works as Platt's, of Oldham, Dobson and Barlow's, of Bolton, and others, which furnish for the most part machines for a special branch of trade, can only arise in the centre of a large industry of the foremost rank. The making of machinery also enjoys therewith all the advantages of division of labour in producing on a large scale. The same progress which we have observed in the cotton industry led also in the making of machinery, in spite of a continual advancement of the weekly wages of the workmen, to a progressive cheapening of the production. What importance in this respect the displacement of hand-work by machines has had is shown, for instance, by the remark of Sir Joseph Whitworth, according to which the planing of a square foot of cast iron in 1826 cost 12s. by hand, against which, to day it costs by machinery only 1s.

Machine works have also arisen in Germany wherever a textile centre has been formed—thus, in Alsace. German machine-making is, however, still behind the specialisation attained in England. Just as the German textile industry is wanting in concentration, so does the corresponding machine-making also lack the advantages of that division of labour attendant upon concentrated industry. To make machinery for the cotton industry now and then alongside with other machinery is unprofitable. At the time of the German Enquête machinery for spinning was still mostly, that for weaving almost generally, obtained from England, although the charges for packing, duty, carriage, etc., amounted to from 30 to 50 per cent. (3). Even into Alsace itself was English

2. Brassey: "Work and Wages" (London, 1872), pp. 68, 78, 198.
3. Compare "Protokolle," pp. 18, 403, etc.

machinery imported. It also appears, according to statements before the Enquête Commission, that the prices of machinery in the recent decades had by no means gone down as in England. In a similar direction tended the changing of the tariff in 1878, since English prices plus duty and charges are looked upon, even to-day, as the basis for the machinery required by the cotton industry in Germany.

I am indebted to a celebrated expert for the following particulars in this respect, whereby it may be noted that the difference in freight to Leipzig and to South Germany is only slight:—

	Price at Oldham. Marks.	Price on quay at Hull. Marks.	Price at Leipzig. Marks.
Bale-opener—gross 76, net 53 cwts. ..	1,275	1,500	1,766
Exhaust opener and lap machine, with lattice apparatus and regulator— gross 185, net 138 cwt.	6,426	7,180	7,845
Scutcher and lap machine, with regulator —gross 81, net 64 cwt.	2,699	3,140	3,434
Carding engine, with 106 flats, without clothing—gross 68, net 50 cwt. ..	1,752	2,120	2,365
Drawing-frame, with 3 heads of 7 de- liveries—gross 123, net 107 cwt. ..	3,247	3,820	4,293
Slubbing-frame, 82 spindles—gross 100, net 88 cwt.	2,669	3,140	3,500
Intermediate frame, 128 spindles—gross 110, net 96 cwt.	3,383	3,980	4,375
Roving-frame, 164 spindles—gross 106, net 91 cwt.	3,315	3,900	4,281
Ring-spinning frame, 400 spindles— gross 120, net 100 cwt.	3,519	4,140	4,574
Self-actor, 880 spindles, 1¼ in. gauge— gross 163, net 125 cwt.	4,641	5,460	5,950

What has been said is sufficient to show that English machine-making bears in a high degree the same character as that which we have proved as peculiar to the centralised industrial develop-ment of the cotton industry; the same organisation and division of labour; the same continuous advance in the cheapening of the costs of production, brought about by the replacement of labour by capital; the same cheapening of the costs of labour, accompanied at the same time by an increase in the weekly earnings of the workers. English machine fitters, with whose productions in many cases competition on the Continent seems impossible, stand, how-ever, on the average above the highest class of cotton operatives— the mule-spinners—and are really the aristocracy of England's labour, as well as, in general, of that of Europe. Already at the beginning of the "seventies" they obtained a nine-hours day, and at the present moment stand in the midst of the practical introduction of the eight-hours day (3a).

With the greater development of machine-making England possesses the leading technical position in the cotton industry; for to-day it is almost always from machine works that the technical advances emanate; for instance, the introduction of the self-actor by Roberts and the recent perfection of the ring-spindle by Brooks.

But the cost of founding a business, for main power as well as working machinery, becomes less with the extension of the whole establishment, which means, by the greater average size of mills in English spinning, a further advantage for England.

The cost per spindle is therefore lower in England than in Germany. The following figures for England were obtained by me in making inquiries in the summer of 1891.

	Oldham.	Alsace.	Germany.
			According to the minutes of the Enquête Commission.
No. 20's	24s. ..	60s.	Average cost
Oldham medium (32's to 40's)	20s. ..	50s.	per spindle,
No. 60's	26s. 6d. ..	?	45s. to 55s.

In the 71 limited spinning concerns of Oldham, which were founded in the middle and end of the "seventies," and had then passed through a business crisis, in which therefore the depreciation could only amount to very little, there stood in 1883 in the books 4,217,008 spindles, valued at £4,402,291. According to this the cost per spindle would amount on the average to about 21s.—a result which agrees with the above particulars. In exceptional cases there are, however, in England spinning mills which are built far cheaper—for 18s. or 19s. (4). Apart from these exceptions there is a slow but continuous cheapening of the establishment costs perceivable in Lancashire, whilst according to the German Enquete the same thing does not apply to Germany, or at all events only in a far slighter degree. In France, since the war, the price of the spindle has even risen about 18 per cent., and still remains above that in Germany (5).

3a. Fifty-three hours per week is the present standard.—Translator.

4. Andrew: "Fifty Years' Cotton Trade," p 6.

5. Compare Jannasch: "Europäische Baumwollindustrie," pp. 28, 29.

In the same manner the cost of English looms is also less than those of the Continent; though comparisons are here more difficult than in spinning, because the width and the variation of the goods to be produced have a great influence on the cost of the weaving as well as main-power machinery. Thus, for instance, before the Enquête Commission the particulars regarding the cost of a shed per loom varied between 666 marks (printers' calico) and 1,500 marks (plain twill and fancy calico). In England the establishment costs per power-loom go down to 350 marks and less. In Burnley the average cost per power-loom for buildings and engine amounts to £13; for the other machinery from £5 to £6; together, therefore, £18 to £19.

Advantages similar to those in the establishment costs are possessed by England in the matter of the working costs of the cotton industry. The same applies, according to the usual division, to interest, cost of raw materials, wages, and the so-called general expenses. To these the profits are to be added, which must be included in the selling prices quite as much as the amounts just mentioned. Here also the same thing applies as above for the establishment costs. Also the expenses of working have been reduced, for the whole of the heads mentioned, in the course of the century, not however to the same extent, but rather more in the degree that, the moment Nature retreats from Labour and Capital, in the same degree grows the superiority of England above its competitors.

In the first instance the so-called general expenses of working come into consideration. England has also here an advantage as far as it concerns products of centralised industry, which are produced dearer on the Continent and are subject in many cases to duties—oil, tallow, sizing ingredients, cards, bobbins, paper tubes, shuttles, tying-up cord, etc. On the whole, however, the advantage of England in this respect is comparatively the least; for instance, the cheaper price of coal is connected with a much greater waste in burning materials (6).

With respect to the raw material there is also a permanent cheapening to be observed—one reason being in consequence of the increased planting of cotton and the growing competition of the producing countries. But chiefly is it to be ascribed to the

---

6. Compare Jannasch, p. 86.

constantly further perfecting of the cotton market at Liverpool. According to a detailed estimate in the German Enquete (7), middling Louisiana, in 1878, cost in the English mill 113·55 marks per 100 kilos.; in the Alsatian mill 123·84 marks. This difference will be apparently further increased in favour of England by the completion of the Ship Canal to Manchester—a cheapening of carriage which will be as advantageous to the import of food-stuffs as to the export of manufactured articles, and should cause the long-planned canalisation of the Upper Rhine to be postponed no longer (8).

If German spinners in many cases at the present time buy in the producing country, this certainly means an advantage in so far that they free themselves from the extra expenses in Liverpool. But by no means does this method replace a home cotton-market. German spinners must buy on stock 4 to 5 months ahead. They have therefore to determine their wants long before the time when they know the future demand, and therewith run the risk of a fall in the price of cotton. They can also draw upon Germany at an exchange disadvantage. The English spinner buys, as we have seen, from week to week, at the prices ruling in Liverpool, so far as he does not seize favourable opportunities of covering (9).

And so with the weaver. The cheapening of the yarn manipulated by him has made itself felt far more than the cheapening of cotton, since the fall of prices is more pronounced in proportion as the element Nature is overcome by Capital and Labour.

The progressive cheapening of the raw material has also to be regarded as a general result of centralised industrial development, in any case so far as it depends upon improved methods of production and improved trading organisation. Indeed this development can be blocked by the nature of the raw material, as a product of nature limited in supply. But then technical progress produces

---

7. Compare " Protokolle," p. 358.

8. The importance of waterways is shown, for instance, by the " Protokolle," p. 19, regarding cost of carriage to Alsace :—

	COTTON PER KILO. In Summer, up the Rhine.	In Winter, per rail.
East Indian	4·02 pf.	5·42 pf.
American	4·60 ,, ...	6·29 ,,

9. Compare, for Germany, " Report of the Enquêtekommission," p. 85.

mostly equivalents, as cotton itself has largely become an equivalent for the dearer wool (10).

As we have already spoken of the continuous lowering of the costs of labour within the century, and of the advantages of English producers in this direction as against the German, there remain here only interest and profit still to be touched upon. As long as the profits do not depend upon a monopoly, as was generally the case in the first stage of centralised industry, already referred to, they resolve themselves into two elements; one in an insurance premium, which is paid to the capitalist for venturing his fortune in a more or less risky undertaking; then the employer's wage, which, again, is retained for two reasons; one for the putting to work at a favourable juncture, then for the technical and commercial management of the existing business. It is now clear that, first, the insurance premium falls with the falling rate of interest. This will be so much the more the case as the risk is partly thrust upon wages, which, according to the state of trade, rise or fall.

But the real wage of the employer also falls, and certainly, in proportion as technical and business training become general, its special value therewith falls; and, on the other hand, the growing division of labour simplifies the dangers to be overcome. For both reasons the degree of profit in England has gone down more than on the Continent, and even capital and intelligence is applied to the industry when both have been long frightened back on the Continent. Centralised industry, called into being by individually highly-gifted pioneers, after it has been founded, needs no longer the genius of an Arkwright. The capacities which it now demands are especially to be found frequently in the seats of a high-standing working population. Hence the remarkably lower salaries of directors of limited spinning-mills in Oldham.

And there is another consideration: the social standing of the millowning class always forms an even more considerable portion of its payment. Where bourgeoise society is the first in the State, where industrial callings are highly valued in society, the best powers turn to them even without the enticement of exceptionally high profits, which otherwise seek honour and position in official situations, and partly place their capabilities at the disposal of

10. We think on the quantity of substitutes which are formed from coal, without seeing a limit in the future. in the replacement of iron by aluminium, the attempts to produce starch (food) from celluloid (wood).

the industry of other countries. In the German Enquete it was correctly perceived that the social standing of trade callings in England formed a strong point of the industry there (11). This is a circumstance of economical importance, upon which for the greatest part depends the strength of private initiative in all branches of undertakings in England.

But still something else has to be taken into consideration. In the first stage of centralised industrial development class differences are unavoidable, which are mostly filled with extreme bitterness and hatred. These conditions will also influence in an increasing degree the profits, because they cause many capable powers, and perhaps not the worst, to avoid the industry, or withdraw from it earlier than necessary. We certainly see how under such conditions great employers often belong to the most hated men of the nation. Where, on the other hand, social peace is opened out by centralised industrial progress; where the most enlightened operatives, of their own free will, return their employers to Parliament, for instance, as not seldom happens in the North of England, the position of the employer acquires a meaning which certainly comes into account as ideal property. For as such the feeling is certainly to be reckoned, to stand at the head of those who give back to the nation the inner peace.

He who has been fortunate enough to enter the house of a David Dale, which is filled with tokens of remembrances from operative societies, arbitration boards, etc., in a field which was formerly torn by the bitterest class struggles will value the point of view just presented.

If thus profits, as far as a sort of wage is concerned, go down, so also in the last respect the rate of interest.

The continual lowering of the rate of interest is also a result of economical progress. Whilst formerly loans were chiefly taken for consumption purposes, they are in the arena of the economical system of to-day in the first degree devoted to productive objects. Therewith the quantity of capital at hand, and the offer of such, is continuously increased (12). But the lending capitalist, differently

11. "Protokolle of the Enquête," p. 351: "There is here, in Germany, something which has great influence—it is the fact that trade and industrial, pursuits are not honoured. Industry and trade are only taken up as a pursuit frequently, when no other calling can be found. In England it is otherwise."

12. Manchester Chamber of Commerce, "Bombay and Lancashire," p. 40.

from the employer and operative, has not the possibility of a coalition at hand, because every suitable application of his money produces competition—i.e., creates new capital seeking channels for investment. This strengthened supply can certainly also be balanced from time to time by strengthened demand. But, in general, a retarding moment makes itself felt on the side of the demand—the enormously increased producing power of capital by technical progress. With a sovereign invested in machinery I can to-day produce four to five times as much yarn of the same quality as I could 50 years ago. The joint influence of this speeding with this retarding movement produced for the English industry an important lowering of the rate of interest during the course of the century.

In a similar way England has herein to-day an advantage compared with the European Continent. Ordinary loan capital stands at the disposal of the English cotton industry for $3\frac{1}{2}$ to 4 per cent.; alongside exists, however, the possibility of receiving at any time capital subject to notice at $2\frac{1}{2}$ to 3 per cent.—a system which is used in many cases by spinning-mills in Oldham. On the other hand, the German employer works with an average rate of interest of 5 per cent.

An industrial establishment does not represent a permanent capacity, but rather one which is consumed. Most certainly, as above shown, the tendency of development is from a change of fixed capital to a floating one. Therewith, along with the interest, the creation of a depreciation rate becomes a necessity. According to the rules laid down by Platt, machinery for manipulating cotton should be depreciated by $7\frac{1}{2}$ per cent., buildings and steam engines by $2\frac{1}{2}$ per cent. This amounts to about as much as a total depreciation of 5 per cent. Therefore one can take 20 years as the life of a cotton factory. The introduction of a definite depreciation grants to English spinners and manufacturers great advantages over the Continental ones (13). According to Andrew and Ellison, the English spindle stands on the average in the books at 18s. 6d. per spindle, and the loom at £20.

---

13. Thus according to Andrew: " Fifty Years' Cotton Trade," p. 8.   Compare " Respecting the Depreciation of the Spindles in the Rhine Provinces," Jannasch, p. 44: " The far greater progressed depreciation mostly helped the Alsatians to withstand the revolution in the industry, which was connected with their being taken over by the German State."

But it is easier to introduce a definite depreciation in England than on the Continent; for one reason on account of the costs of establishing, and then on account of the greater producing power of the machinery. The greater dexterity of the operative comes also into account—unskilled hands ruin the machinery, which is the reason, for instance, why the wear and tear in India is far higher—as well as the regularity of the production. Whilst the German textile employer must continually change the machinery to correspond with the great variation of the goods to be produced, the Englishman spins from year to year the same counts, weaves the same goods, and thus escapes from the considerable wear and tear caused by the alteration of the machines.

The following relation of the costs of production approximately result for undepreciated mills:—

COST OF PRODUCTION PER POUND.

	20's.	32's twist.	40's weft.	60's twist.
Wages	$\frac{9}{10}$d.	1d.	$1\frac{1}{10}$d.	$1\frac{3}{8}$d.
Working expenses (strapping, oil tubes, card-clothing, etc., $7\frac{1}{2}$ per cent. deduction)	$1\frac{7}{10}$d.	$1\frac{1}{2}$d.	$1\frac{1}{4}$d.	$1\frac{3}{4}$d.
Depreciation	$\frac{1}{8}$d.	$\frac{1}{4}$d.	$\frac{5}{16}$d.	1d.
Cost of production	$2\frac{8}{10}$d.	$2\frac{3}{8}$d.	$2\frac{7}{8}$d.	4d.
Everything above is interest and profit, in the proportion of	$\frac{1}{8}$d.=5%	$\frac{1}{4}$d. =5%	$\frac{1}{4}$d.=5%	1d.=5%

This relation gives the following reckoning:—

Cost per spindle = a (£1 for 32's twist = 240d.).
Yearly production per spindle = b (50 lb. for 32's twist).
The amount necessary for 5 per cent. in the cost of production of 1 lb. yarn =

$$\frac{5a}{100b} = \frac{24}{100} = \frac{1}{4}\text{d. for 32's twist.}$$

On the basis of these figures a glance at the current prices on the Exchange at Manchester gives the average profits of the spinner. The amounts given certainly cover the costs comfortably; the technically-developed mills produce at a cheaper rate. Thus 32's twist has been sold with a difference in price of the yarn from the cotton of 2d., and still without loss.

For proof I give as an instance the quarterly production relations of a spinning-mill at Oldham with 75,000 spindles.

QUARTERLY PRODUCTION, 582,115 LB. 32's TWIST AND 50's WEFT

		Total cost of production. £ s. d.	Per lb. yarn.
1. Wages		2,767 18 4	1·14d.
2. Working expenses, total		1,273 12 2	0·49d.
Including :—			
Directors' salaries and travelling expenses	£30 5 2		
Coal	323 15 0		
Oil and tallow	70 19 11		
Taxes	74 15 5		
Roller covering (leather and materials)	47 10 0		
Cord, strapping, etc.	91 1 6		
Repairs	214 4 10		
Insurance	78 13 9		
Ground rent	44 14 5		
Employers' Association, etc. ..	18 16 8		
3. Cotton waste as far as not used (sold for £219 10s.)		1,151 0 0	0·57d.
4. Depreciation		750 0 0	0·08d.
Totals		£5,942 10 6	2·28d.

This instance shows how technical skill has already stepped beyond those typical cases; the low depreciation is due to the circumstance that the establishment is no longer in the books at full value.

Similar are the relations in weaving, although here no typical cases can be given. The relations of production in a weaving-shed at Burnley, with 600 looms, in the summer of 1891 were the following: Ordinary Burnley goods—i.e., printers' calicoes, were produced in a width of 30 in. to 34 in. (28's to 45's twist, 30's to 60's weft, 14 to 18 picks per quarter-inch, 56's to 58's reed) :—

HALF-YEARLY PRODUCTION, 3,900,000 YDS.

		Total cost of production. £ s. d.	Per 1,000 yds. s. d.
Wages		5,487 2 0	27 7¼
Working expenses		1,410 7 0	7 3
Including :—			
Directors' salaries, auditors' fees, travelling expenses, etc.	£31 0 0		
Rent for room and power (2¼ per cent. for buildings, and 7¼ per cent. for power) ..	624 3 4		
Cartage	301 15 3¼		
Iron and repairs	127 3 9		
Taxes (mostly paid by the landlord of the building) ..	0 10 9		
Gas and water	38 9 5		
Healds, heald yarn, and reeds	85 7 7		
Shuttles	19 6 5		
Strapping	115 1 5		
Depreciation (7¼ per cent. on the value of the working machinery)		216 16 0	1 7½
Totals		£7,114 5 0	36 6

According to which the cost of production per yard (excluding yarn) was equal to 0·438d.

In this statement, as in the instance given above for spinning, according to custom in England, depreciation but not interest has been added to the costs of production. But in weaving the production may, under favourable conditions, be still cheaper. For instance, the yearly rent for room and power per loom frequently amounts to not more than from 32s. to 36s. (14), whilst they are put down higher in the above instance.

Unfortunately the particulars of the cost of production in the German Enquête (15) are unsuitable for comparison, on account of their great diversity and the uncertainty whether one has to deal with depreciated mills or not, or even whether the employer's wages are reckoned in the costs of production or not. In any case they give, in harmony with Jannasch (pp. 111 and 112), a slighter advantage on lower numbers, and a more considerable advantage on finer counts in favour of England. Not only the higher working expenses, but also the higher costs of establishing, form a disadvantage for Germany. If, with the cost of the spindle at £1, $\frac{1}{4}$d. profit per lb. of yarn means alone 5 per cent. profit, with the double costs of establishment it means only $2\frac{1}{2}$ per cent.

Generally in the branch of cotton industry an international division of labour makes itself felt in the following manner. In spinning it may be taken that lower counts are spun in Germany not much dearer than in England, so that for these a protective tariff is not necessary for all time. Already, with the lower duties before 1879, in which year Germany introduced a system of agrarian as well as industrial protective tariffs, the German spinners of lower counts had driven English yarns more and more from the home market.

In 1877 the import of yarns amounted to only 17 per cent. of those used, as against 47 per cent. in 1858. Since the protective duty at that time was slight, the Germans could (16) even then not have produced coarse counts much more unfavourably than

14. Commission on Depression of Trade, Second Report, part I., 5,766.

15. Report, pp. 36, 37. " Protokolle," pp. 19, 26, 31, 98, 176.

16. For low ordinary yarns No.'s 4 to 12 the duty was 15·8 per cent. of the cost of production ; for all finer yarns, according to the system of weight, duties correspondingly less.

the English (17).   On the other hand, up to 1879 the system of
weight duties was applicable in Germany, according to which a
duty of 12 marks per 100 kilos. yarn was levied, without taking
into consideration the fineness of the yarn.   From 1879 a system
of degree duties came into force, which although far lower than
the protective duties of the highly protectionist States of France,
America, and Russia, still considerably raised the duties on the
finer and finest cotton yarns.   By the new tariff in 1885 the
cotton spinners succeeded in getting further additions to these
duties.   In spite of these facts, Lotz must be said to be correct
when he says that the experiment of Germany to spin its own fine
yarns has to be viewed as a failure (18).   In spite of the alteration in the German duties of 1879, the average of the counts spun
in Germany has been lowered, as shown by the increased requirements per spindle already touched upon.   From the Chamber of
Commerce district of Plauen, which, in consequence of hand and
power knitting, is chiefly dependent upon the use of fine yarns in
doubled form, the following, in this respect, has been communicated to me.   According to these particulars the most important
doubling mills in the district used, in 1891, in cotton yarns over
60's counts : —

> 17 per cent. of German spinnings.
> 7·5   ,,   Swiss   ,,
> 75·5   ,,   English   .,

In addition, it is declared that, for special reasons, comparatively
more German-spun yarn has been used than in other doubling
mills.

The reasons for the superiority of England in this branch are
two.   One is to be found in that tenet of Tucker, that the country
most economically developed, where the weekly earnings of the
operatives are higher, produces just those articles in the production
of which more labour and capital than raw materials come into
account.   This shows itself, for instance, also in a totally different
production, but which, similarly to fine yarns, embodies very much
labour and capital.   As in the spinning of fine yarns, so is England
superior to the Continent in shipbuilding.   But with fine yarns a

    17. " Stat. Erm.," I., p. 5.   But the English were driven out of South
Germany in up to 40's counts and higher ; out of North Germany in up to
30's.   In the 20 years from 1858 to 1877 the percentage of yarns used
which were imported had fallen from 47·7 to 17·3 per cent.
    18. Compare Lotz: " Ideen der deutschen Handelspolitik," Leipzig, 1892,
p. 175

further circumstance comes under notice, which, perhaps, permanently grants an international division of labour in this field in favour of England—the climatic advantages, upon which we have repeatedly dwelt before.

Since Germany possessed many industries which manipulated fine yarns the German Government decided from the 1st February, 1892, on the ground of the Commercial Treaty with Switzerland, but which also stood England in good stead by reason of the most-favoured-nation clause, to materially reduce the duties on yarns above 60's counts. The German Government thus took the standpoint of giving an advantage to pressing interests of certain German export industries over the spinning interests of fine counts unable to make a home in Germany. But the duty reduction pointed out is also in another direction of symptomatic importance. German cotton spinners were always the main centre of Protectionism, and their defeat was nothing else than a sign of the continuously increasing importance of the opposed German export industries, which are interested in Free Trade.

Whilst the real strength of the German export industry lies in other branches, Germany possesses also one in the branch of cotton spinning, a specialty, with which it controls the world's market, and is interested in export. I mean the Saxon vigogne spinning, especially in Crimmitschau, Werdau, as well as Glauchau, Zwickau, and Plauen. Vigogne is a yarn spun on the woollen system from cotton (19). The spinning machinery for vigogne differs from that in ordinary cotton spinning in that the drawing rollers which Arkwright applied to the jenny of Hargreaves are missing. Besides this, the preparation is different, and similar to that used for woollen spinning, because the laying of the fibres parallel, upon which cotton spinning depends, must in this case be avoided. There are solely opener, 3 cards, but no slubbing or intermediate frames. A further difference is that the cotton, before being spun is greased, and mostly manipulated already dyed. Vigogne spinning exists since 1847 in Crimmitschau in that it was mixed with wool and spun according to the system for woollen; at the present time, in 95 per cent. of the vigogne spun in the district mentioned there is no longer a single fibre of wool. Vigogne spinning requires a larger number of operatives per 1,000 spindles—10 to 11—than cotton spinning. The development of

19. Compare the experienced communications of R. Martin. "Der wirthschaftliche Aufschwung der Baumwollspinnerei in Sachsen." Schmöllers Zahrbuch, Band xvii., Heft 3, p. 19 ff.

the machinery for it has not occurred in the same degree, and the mills are materially smaller. There are mills with up to 800 spindles. On the average the vigogne spinning mills of Crimmitschau have 7,015 spindles, of Wardau 4,774; English woollen spinning mills have on the average no more than 2,237 (1890). The vigogne spinning mills in the districts mentioned comprise about 600,000 spindles. Their production is used in the knitting mills of Chemnitz and Berlin and the weaving mills of the Rhine Province and Lansitz. In addition, a fair quantity of vigogne yarn is exported to England, and used by the knitters of Leicester and the weavers of Bradford. The export in 1892 to England was 50,904 cwt. The German export would, according to Martin, amount to six times as much if the vigogne spinners of Saxony were not the largest proprietors of foreign vigogne spinning mills—for instance in Russia, Austria, Sweden, and France. Real vigogne spinning, which greases the cotton, is not included by German statisticians under cotton spinning. In addition, outside of the district mentioned, there are not a few of so-called "two cylinder yarns" produced, i.e., yarns spun without rollers, on the woollen system, even if not greased. Since this class of spinning is not separated from ordinary cotton spinning, the total extent of this industry can scarcely be correctly gauged.

The same thing applies to weaving as to spinning. There, where plain productions are made, and before anything else it depends upon the curtailment of the costs of production by means of centralised industry, England is pre-eminent. On the other hand, everywhere where it depends upon designs, colouring, and finishing, the Germans are capable of competing in the world's market, indeed in many cases are strongly interested in export. Whereas the German spinners are Protectionists, the German weavers have long been Free Traders. Not in a position to compete in prices of ordinary articles for the million with England, they understand, however, how to find customers by adaptations of taste, colour, and design, which in some cases may attain even an artistical completion. In spite of the system of protective tariffs, which at the present juncture obtains in Germany, in spite of the wheat duties, the export of German cotton goods (including yarns) has more than doubled from 1883 to 1893, from £3,600,000 has increased to £7,662,000; whilst, as is well known, American exports in the same period declined.

But especially does the strength of the German industry show itself there, where the textile industries amalgamate with the chemical—thus in printing, dyeing, bleaching, and finishing—in that many productions of foreign textile industries are brought duty free into Germany, to leave the country finished.

In short, Germany has at present dearer labour and dearer capital than England; but it understands how to wedge itself into the world's market, where not so much the advantages of centralised industry nor the skilled machine-labour come into account, but rather where the superior technical, scientific, and art training of its middle classes is decisive.

CHAPTER IV.

THE INFLUENCE OF CENTRALISED INDUSTRIAL DEVELOPMENT ON THE
DIVISION OF THE NATION'S INCOME.

I.—*Generally.*

In what degree are single classes of society sharers in the fruits of that enormous increase of production which centralised industrial methods influence?

A view here looms before us which, at least in Germany, is widely spread, one of the few contemplations in which the operatives and the wealthy classes are to-day opposed—Centralised industry makes proletarians of society, and disperses the middle classes. The poor become poorer, and the rich richer. The tension on both sides is always increasing; a violent contact of the opposite poles will be at last unavoidable.

The bourgeoisie, for this reason, look upon economical progress, therefore, in many cases with an anxious eye. Anxiety about the social consequences sets them even themselves against their own interests. The attainment of an economically great position for Germany—and without this to-day its great political and military power is certainly not permanently tenable—appears to them doubtful on social grounds, because it demands centralised industry and further movement towards machinery. Indeed, the tall chimney appears to such anxious souls as a warning finger—a " Mene Tekel " of the coming day of revolution.

The operatives, on the other hand, greet the economical progress, because it brings them nearer to the moment when the expropriators, ever less in number, will be at length themselves expropriated. Every factory chimney is to them a true sign of the future day of reckoning.

To us it is neither of the two. To us it is a sign, not only of economical but also of social progress, with which the latest trophies in that victorious procession of humanity—extending back to olden times—mean subjugation of the elements of natural power and the freeing of labour.

The opposing opinion is here, as everywhere, to be refuted in the manner that one recognises it as relatively justified as the result of a certain stage of development. Before Centralised Industry grasped trade, the division of a nation's earnings was regulated by custom or by law. As, according to Tacitus, the agricultural lots were divided "secundum dignationem," thus similarly in the whole Middle-Age society were the lots of life. The selling prices of trade productions, and therefore the profits, were fixed by Guilds. Wages and hours of labour were likewise regulated by the Guilds or authorities, or at least fixed by custom. The rent to be paid to the ground landlord for the utilisation of land was also authoritatively fixed. Interest on capital as yet hardly existed, because large outlays of capital for industrial concerns were not necessary; it was originally forbidden by law. In comparison with to-day, the slight total production of labour was divided partly between worker and employer, granting to both a bare existence but no more, and the balance fell to the landed droprietor, who also socially asserted his precedence. Otherwise than prepared by commerce with the interweaving of isolated industries among one another flourished centralised industry. This depended from the commencement on competition, and demanded the removal of the old arrangements of law and custom.

What is, in this stage, when Centralised Industry enters, its influence on the division of national income? Regarding wages we have the so-called minimum standard of life, because the operative physiologically still belongs to the old time. Only by advancing conditions can wages rise a little above it, since the increase of marriages and births serves for the continuation of that reserve army which at once streams to it and presses down wages to the old level. With declining conditions wages can themselves go below the minimum standard of living, in which case the deficit is replaced in many cases by poor-relief, taxes, robberies, etc. Since, on the other hand, the flourishing industry requires capital, but such is still little at command, the rate of interest, as compared with later times, stands remarkably high.

The difference between the price on the one side and interest on capital on the other is received by the employer. He has, in fact, as the predominating teaching generally accepts, labour as well as capital in his service for a fixed remuneration. At such a stage the profits are high, not on account of lower costs of production— these are rather very high compared with later on—but on account of the high prices. The industry still finds itself in a position of monopoly as compared with the home decentralised industry as well as the foreign, just as one produces similar conditions later on by protective tariffs in order to call industries into being. For this reason great fortunes flow quickly together into the hands of the few; everywhere was the genius of the individual pathfinders on the field of centralised industry (Arkwright, Peel).

On that first step of industrial development is that rolling together of wealth in the hands of the few already justified by the reason that, with the meagre possessions among the masses, the necessary capital for the first centralised industries was not otherwise to be brought together. There was still lacking the physiological essentials of enterprise in the form of societies. But those high profits have still a further justification. Political power and honour are still linked with the hands of landed proprietorship, which looks down upon the men with a trade calling as " homines novi." A public walk in life still grants a higher position than even the most successful industrial career. It was still doubtful in England about the turn of the century whether the representatives of centralised industry were to be granted the appellation of "gentlemen." Therefore it needed the stimulus of high profits to win capable heads for industrial callings, whilst they later on streamed to them for the sake of the honour and influence alone which this position assures.

But also for a special reason this collecting of possessions has firstly in the citizen classes its justification. The social progress of a nation presupposes a class which, by its riches, is in the position to apply itself to public affairs without being dependent on the State. On the presence of this class among the country gentry the greatness of the English Parliamentary constitution had once depended. After the foundations of economical life had become industrial, a similar class of citizens with means had to prepare itself for undertaking political as well as social duties. I have pictured in another place how the existence of such independent elements has later on pushed forward the social development of England, after it had become in extensive circles the public opinion that property—as far as it did not serve productive objects—was justified only so far and in the degree as the bearer served the upward movement of those lacking means.

But, in opposition to the former division of national income by custom or law, the new development led firstly, without doubt, to a sharpening of the difference in property possession. Ricardo had such conditions before his eyes when compiling his "Law of Wages"; K. Marx became acquainted with such in the English Blue-Books of the "thirties" and "forties," which he studied. The operative, powerless and hopeless, in such times joins that temporary labour party which places itself without the State, and therefore dispenses with all influence in the State. It is hoped to overpower the State, in order to arrange it in its own interest. As if this happened by a wave of the hand, whilst still the influence in the State depends solely upon the division of economical power between the classes of society. But even this movement is not hopeless. In that it influences the ruling classes, and firstly, in many cases, the agrarian powers, to legislate for the operatives' protection, it drives forward the technical-economical development.

Let us summarise the peculiarities of that first stage of centralised industry. Economically viewed, they are:—High costs of production on the ground of dearer labour (because many hands are required); and dear capital, high prices, and high profits, by reason of a position of monopoly. Socially viewed, they are:— A minimum standard of life on one side, and concentration of riches on the other—class contentions. This stage of the development accompanies the social-political views noted down at the beginning of this chapter.

International competition compels further progress. Continuous cheapening of the costs of production is the leading motive of the development, as was followed more closely above in the case of the English cotton industry. But this coercion for limiting the costs of production regulates the whole centralised industrial development. Without an uninterrupted lessening of its costs of production no industry can hold up its head in the world's market.

We now ask, What are the influences of this development on the division of national income?

The cheapening of the production of a defined article refers to, as we saw, establishing as well as working costs. Included in the latter, again, are all single charges—raw materials, labour, working expenses, interest, profit, etc. Since, however, establishing costs and working costs resolve themselves into cost of labour, interest on capital, and employers' profit of other trades, there remain, in fact, excluding raw materials, only three of the elements named, which are liable to a continuous lowering.

We can here pass by raw materials after what we have said above respecting them. Also in their prices there are solely contained cost of labour, interest on capital, and employer's profit, as far as a priority or ground rent does not exist upon it, the reason for which at present is not to be examined. Apart from the latter, therefore, the whole result of the labour of a nation's, as of every individual's production, is divided between labour and capital, in that the so-called employer's profit, as mentioned above, is of two kinds, and is to be reckoned partly to the one and partly to the other category. In that we shall refer to it later on, we prove firstly, for the centralised industrial development, that within a given product—for instance, one pound of yarn, one yard of cloth, or one ton of iron—the amount falling to labour as well as to capital permanently decreases; the cost of labour because this is continuously replaced by capital; the cost of capital because by technical progress the same capital ever becomes more productive, by the progress of national economy ever becomes cheaper. The operative, the poorer consumer, has the advantage; for him this cheapening of economical commodities has at once the effect of a rise in wages.

But we must further ask,   the amounts falling upon labour and capital decrease in the same ratio? Or does the centralised industrial development alter the ratio so that within a defined product the amounts coming on both items certainly absolutely decrease, but the one compared with the other relatively increases. The answer to this question gives at once the following consideration:—A similar capital produces, by reason of technical progress, more at the present time than 50 years ago; in spite of this, if the interest and profit expected by capital has remained the same, or even gone down, the surplus must therefore have gone to labour.

A view into the reasons of this relation is afforded by that replacement of labour by capital in the cotton industry treated on above.

A capital of 20s. produces an article A; in order that 15 per cent. interest and profit may be realised 3s. must be given from the selling price to capital. In 30 years the same capital produces 6A; in order to pay 15 per cent. on the production costs of 1A, only 6d. has to be appropriated to capital. But in consequence of the increased producing power and quantity the rate of interest, and therewith the premium for risk, contained in the profit has fallen. Seven-and-a-half per cent. is sufficient to make capital seek investment in the industry. There is, therefore, in the production costs of A only 3d. necessary for interest and profit.

A workman produces daily an article B for a wage of 3s., but in 30 years' time 6 B per day. In order to allow him to earn exactly the same weekly wage, only 6d. need now be paid for the production of B. If the workman 30 years ago was a skilled hand-worker, whose skill the machine has made superfluous, a higher weekly wage is not necessary; under certain circumstances a lower is even possible. On the other hand, if the occupation 30 years ago depended already on machinery, and the greater production has been attained by improvement and speeding of the machines, there would be more and more valuable capital applied, the labour replaced by more complicated results of technical skill and natural science, and thus the responsibility of the workman tending the machinery would become greater. A better workman is needed for it, to whom a weekly wage of 24s., instead of 18s., must be paid. In consequence of this, the piece-wages for B could only decline to 8d.

As, with the reduction of the share falling to capital, advancing conditions have come into play, which by the progress of human genius permanently grant increased dominion over nature, and therewith the augmenting production-power of capital, thus with the reduction in the cost of labour, retarding circumstances, the nature of mankind as an organism, by which higher capacity in a definite direction is only possible if the whole condition of the organism is raised. The relation of both, therefore, is reversed, in the course of development, in favour of labour. This means nothing else than that the production costs of a certain article have certainly gone down, whereas, on the other hand, with the lower producing costs relatively more has fallen to labour and less to capital. The following is an instance. It refers to the same mill, combining spinning with weaving, whose capital in 1883 represented the same value as in 1840. In this case the price of an ell of calico of exactly the same quality declined from 1840 to 1883 by 22 per cent., the cost of labour per yard by 41 per cent., the amount falling to interest and profit by 63 per cent., and during the same period the weekly earnings of the operative had risen by 64 per cent. (1).

What applies to a single article may also apply to the whole national production, as far as it depends upon the principle of centralised industry. Labour receives a relatively.higher share. But the centralised industrial system represents such a greater production that, similarly as in the production costs of a single article, the amounts for labour as well as for capital absolutely decrease. Thus with regard to the greatly increased total production, both amounts absolutely increase. On labour as well as on capital falls an absolutely greater amount.

An exception only occurs in so far that extraordinary dexterity becomes replaced by the machine. As the demands on labour become more regular, wages also approach more nearly to a similar level (2). Thus medium wages, according to experience, tend to rise more than the highest, and the latter partially to fall. For instance, the wages of the mule-spinner, at one time, for the finest yarns amounted to double those for ordinary yarns; to-day the wage conditions of both have approached one another.

To those special capacities which were formerly higher paid than later, because they have become partly less necessary, partly more frequent, belong before everything else the portion of the profit which is termed real employer's wage. We have already laid clear the reasons for this.

Extremely influential in this respect operates the "limited" system, which at the present time comprises one-tenth of all business concerns in the United Kingdom. With the largely increased operations of single undertakings, only few large possessors of capital would be in a position to come forward as industrial employers. With them the limited principle puts all those technical and commercial talents into competition which, without consider-

---

1. Compare Atkinson: "Distribution of Profits," pp. 119 and 120; further, "Report on the Statistics of Labour" (Massachusetts, 1890), p. 261.
2. Compare "Protokolle der deutschen Reichsenquête," pp. 291, 376, 337, etc.

able capital, were still in the position to acquire the necessary business qualifications. This circle constantly increases with the growing prosperity of the middle and the elevation of the working classes. It is scarcely possible any longer, owing to the advanced centralised industrial development, for the individual worker to rise up to be an employer on his own account alone, whilst at one time the greatest and most celebrated pioneers of centralised industry emanated directly from the working class. He can, on the other hand, with the necessary talent become a servant of large companies, which, along with talent, require character and honesty; while that first generation of industrial employers, along with their talent, were in many cases indebted for their success to cunning and meanness. Marshall says, with respect to this point: " Perhaps at the present time not so many operatives rise to the position of employers; but more get on to-day far enough to put their children in a position to reach the highest offices. The rise to prosperity is divided over two generations, but the completeness of this movement upwards is to-day perhaps greater than ever. This is better for society. The foreman who still has to obey as well as to order, and sees his children rise up, is in a certain direction more to be envied than the small employer. The children become well educated and make at some time, probably, a better use of their riches " (3).

With this growing competition for industrial leadership in this second period comes the pressure from below, which—as Brentano in his "Arbeitergilden" first pointed out—is exercised by the operative class elevating itself. Both, at this stage of development, force down the profits to a minimum, under which they cannot sink without detriment to the industry. In the first stage of centralised industrial development the employer received the balance after loan capital and operative had been paid; but now labour receives the balance after the payment of interest and management. With an insight into this relation, the leader of the English spinners said to me: One must guarantee the employer, as far as possible, a certain margin of profit, which cannot without loss to the operative be lessened in favour of wages. A high-standing operative class must think about attracting intelligence into industry, and keeping it—if possible, more intelligence than

---

3. " Elements of Economics," p. 195.

the competing industries of foreign countries possess. The operative must pay for finding the most capable employers (4).

As profits thus approach a minimum boundary, wages become more and more dependent on prices, and consequently on the position of the world's market. Whilst in the former stages of development legislative measures could accelerate the alteration mentioned in favour of labour, profit now tends, like interest, to become a permanent power, but wages to rise only by increase of the total production. Legislative measures cannot provide this increase. Since the state of trade partly re-acts upon wages, in the same way the premium on risk, which is contained in the profit, falls (5).

From what has been said we can deduce the following propositions : —

(a) Within a defined product the amounts falling to capital as well as labour absolutely decrease with the development of centralised industry—cheapening of production in favour of the consumer.

(b) The amount within a defined product falling to capital not only decreases absolutely, but also relatively in proportion to that upon labour.

(c) The amount within a defined product falling to labour certainly decreases, but relatively, on the other hand, increases.

(d) The increase of national total production in itself makes possible greater amounts absolutely for labour and capital. On the other hand, the share for capital falls relatively, that for labour increases relatively.

Labour ever receives a greater share of national total production. It receives more and more of the balance which remains after paying the amounts falling to interest and profit.

The social consequence of the economical development here depicted is a levelling-up of extremes of property. So far from the rich becoming richer and the poor poorer, just the reverse is

---

4. Compare a similar view of the well-known E. Atkinson : " Distribution of Profits." p. 70. " Wages are the remainder after profits are paid," pp. 178 and 179.

5 Schmoller " Ueber die Entwicklung des Grossbetriebs und die sociale Klassenbildung." " Share capital, the capital of sleeping partners, also expects really nothing more than payment of interest. This capital retreats more and more from the ruling position." " Preuss. Jahrb., vol. 69, part 4."

the case, which, as to England, has been statistically proved (6).
At the time when the industrial employers socially and politically
conquer the highest positions, new middle classes begin to rise
behind them, which at first gain economically in importance, then
politically. That, indeed, in this later stage of development the
centralised industrial operative has to be counted with the middle
classes is proved simply enough by Atkinson from the fact that
important callings, which hitherto were generally connected with
the middle classes, have gone in income far below the level of the
centralised industrial working class of New England. This is
especially true of large portions of the teaching and religious
classes.

That Germany still by no means stands economically in the
same advanced position is shown by the movement of the people's
income. It can be taken, according to Herkner, that the poor at
present do not become poorer; on the other hand, the rich become
richer, and the middle classes in many cases decrease.

II.—Proofs from Lancashire.

"Prosperous Lancashire!" Under this title the "Spectator"
published the following article, which the organ of the operatives,
the "Cotton Factory Times," of 23rd. Oct., 1891, reproduced :—

" According to the testimony of a late United States Consul at
Manchester, the district of which that city is the centre enjoys a
greater measure of prosperity than any similar community in his
own country, therefore in the world, for in no part of the Continent
are the working classes so well off as in Lancashire ; nowhere are
wages so high, hours of toil so short, and the cost of living so
moderate. None who knew the district in the 'forties' and 'fifties'
can revisit it without being struck by the signs of improvement
and progress which he sees around him. It is not merely that the
population has doubled, and tall chimneys multiplied beyond com-
putation ; these are signs 'of increasing wealth, and wealth may
accumulate while men decay ; the veriest pessimist must acknow-

---

6 R. Giffen: " Increase of Moderate Incomes " (Royal Stat. Society, 16th
Dec., 1887). Compare my book, " On Social Peace," vol. II., p. 491. Atkinson accepts a similar relation for America, which is, indeed, known as the
country where fortunes roll together into a few hands. (" Distribution of
Profits," p. 356.)

ledge that the people are better off, their dwellings more comfortable, their labour less arduous, and their lives altogether pleasanter than those of their fathers and grandfathers. True, the houses are still grimy and smoky, and unsanitary back-to-back cottages too numerous; but these are being gradually superseded by better-constructed dwellings, and there is hardly a considerable borough without its parks and recreation grounds. Poverty and pauperism, the outcome of drink, idleness, accident, and disease, exist in the most prosperous communities; but in Lancashire none who are able and willing to work need to want. Wages were never so high, labour never more in demand. A good weaver, and weavers are mostly young women, can earn 24s. a week. A skilled workman, with two or three children working in the mills, is better off than many a country parson. There are families whose aggregate earnings amount to £400 a year. Day labourers are in demand at 6d. an hour. Nor are high wages limited to the strictly manufacturing districts. In the Fylde country, the garden of Lancashire, farming hands, generally young men, command from 9s. to 11s. a week the year round, with board, lodging, and washing, and farms let without difficulty at £3 an acre. It is satisfactory to find that prosperity has promoted thrift. Every village, almost every hamlet, has its co-operative store, managed by working men, who provide the capital, and neither give nor take credit. The agent of a large assurance company, whose district is partly industrial, partly rural, informed me that it is difficult to find a man whose life is uninsured, and benefit societies number their members by the million.

" All this implies considerable activity. Lancashire people were never slow-witted, and now, thanks to the extension of educational facilities and the multiplication of newspapers, they are become exceptionally intelligent. Fifty years ago, a manufacturer, from whom I had the story, opened a reading room for his hands, and supplied it with suitable literature; but so few of them could read that the others insisted on one of the better-instructed reading aloud to them, and as this led to confusion and bickering the room had to be closed. At that time there was not a single daily paper in the county, and the few local four-page papers sold for as many pence. One can now get a better paper for two farthings. A few days ago I was staying at a country house in the neighbourhood of two contiguous manufacturing villages, containing together some twelve hundred inhabitants. In these two villages are three newsagents, who amongst them sell every day a hundred and fifty halfpenny evening papers, of which latter, however, working people buy but few. I may note as an interesting fact that of the four evening papers vended by the agents in question three run stories; and the proprietor of one of them assured me that without fiction his paper would find few readers. Equally in demand with fiction are accounts of football matches, the Lancashire pastime par excellence. I learnt from a policeman who had been stationed at Coppul (a mining district near Chorley) that it has all but put an end to 'up-and-down fighting'—a method of adjusting quarrels a good deal more deadly than French duelling. Instead of punching each other's heads and kicking each other's shins, the young bloods of the neighbourhood find a vent for their energies in kicking the footballs and fighting for goals."

I try in the following to show clearly the standard of living of the operatives of Lancashire statistically:—

According to the principles of Boehmert, explained in the journal of the Saxon Statistical Office, an examination was undertaken by me, in the summer of 1891, on the standard of living of the artisans of the North of England. The Board of Trade had some years previously made a similar attempt. They had, however, only attained few satisfactory results; first, on account of the partly unsuitable queries asked, then on account of the aversion of the operatives to lay bare the details of their private life to official questionings (1). I was, however, in consequence of an interview with R. Giffen, the celebrated statistician to the Board of Trade, enabled to make use of the experiences of that first examination, while I had, as a private person, more likelihood of getting at the particulars wanted, and of removing difficulties, by a personal exchange of thoughts.

Thus equipped, I repaired to the North of England. But there it immediately became clear to me that only through the organisations of the operatives were the details for my purpose to be attained. This was no disadvantage for the examination, since co-operative societies and trade unions comprise by far the greater portion of the skilled workers in that district. Old acquaintance-ships made my way smooth. Most of the workers' budgets given by me were confirmed by the co-operative societies' organs, which were so much the more suitable for doing this, since the operative

---

1. " Returns of Expenditure by Working Men " (London, 1889).

in Lancashire gets all his necessaries for existence from the society.
I am specially indebted to Mr. J. C. Gray, the general secretary of
the Co-operative Union in Manchester.

I single out pre-eminently the representative of that great industry of Lancashire—the mule-spinner. The two spinners whom
I choose are in the average position of that operative class—an
average from which exceptions are the fewer since in the chief
spinning districts all spinning-mills pay exactly the same wages,
on the basis of the wage list agreed upon with the operatives.

The man is 42 years old, his wife 41 ; they have seven children
—three boys of 9, 16, and 18 years of age; and four girls, aged
respectively 3, 6, 12, and 14.   The family lives in a house in one of
the environs of Oldham.   The house, in which, comparatively
speaking, there is a saving, consists of two rooms downstairs (5 by
4½ yds. and 4 by 4½ yds.), a kitchen joined to the house behind, a
small cellar, and two bedrooms a storey high.   The rent amounts to
4s. per week.   To my question as to what formed the principal
food of the family the man gave the answer applicable for the
operative of the North of England—wheaten bread and meat.
Meat, mostly beef, is eaten daily at least once, potatoes, coffee,
vegetables, etc., performing only the part of accessories.

The man and four of the children work in the factory ; the man
as mule-spinner, the two eldest boys as piecers, and the two eldest
girls in the preparation rooms.   The hours of labour amount to
56½ per week for both father and children.   The weekly earnings
of the man reach 40s. ; but since there are only 49 to 50 weeks in
the year to be reckoned as working ones, the yearly income is put
at £98.   The yearly earnings of the children amount to £92 19s.
3d.   Since the wife and the younger children earn nothing, the
income of the family from wages accordingly amounts to £190
19s. 3d.   The wages of father and children flow together, as is
generally customary in the North of England, into the family
exchequer—a circumstance which ensures so much the more the
high standard of living of this working population, since marriages
do not take place much too early.   In addition to the income mentioned there comes one from savings and co-operative societies'
dividends, amounting to £15 yearly.   The total income, therefore,
amounts to £206.

The man is a member of the Oldham Co-operative Society and of
the trade union of mule-spinners, which extends over the whole of
Lancashire.   In the co-operative shops everything is bought—not

only food, but also clothing, etc. One shilling per week is paid to
the trade union. But since this union grants relief only in case of
want of work (13s. per week, or in case of a strike 15s. weekly),
the man and wife are also insured in a friendly society against
sickness, for which they pay 5d. weekly, and receive in case of
sickness 8s. per week. The children who are working are also
similarly insured. The man takes a trip every year with some of
his children—in August, during the so-called "Oldham wakes," at
which time the mills close for a week. He goes mostly to one of
·the neighbouring watering-places on the coast, and this absorbs a
portion of the savings. The total expenses amount to about
£185 ; therefore about £21 is saved per year.

As a second representative of the spinners I choose one from
Hyde, a place near Manchester well known from its connection
with the history of Chartism. The man is employed in one of the
largest spinning-mills, belonging to the Ashtons. His age is 47
years, that of his wife 42. He has married rather late, and has
only two children—girls of 15 and 17. The family rents a house
consisting of four rooms and a kitchen—two living rooms on the
ground floor, two bedrooms a story high. The measurements of
the front room are 4½ by 4½ yds., of the back room 4½ by 4 yds.
In this case relatively more value is laid out on the dwelling than
in the one mentioned before. The rent is 4s. 6d. per week. In
this case, also, wheaten bread and meat are given as the chief
nourishment. Meat, and indeed beef, is eaten once a day.

The man earns 30s. ; the daughters, one a weaver, the other in
a hat works, each 10s. per week. Here also only 50 working weeks
are reckoned, and 14 days are expressly mentioned for holidays
and relaxation. Thus the yearly income, with £6 8s. in dividends
from the co-operative society, amounts to £131 8s.

The man is a trade-unionist, which costs him 1s. weekly ; for
insurance purposes 1s. weekly is paid to friendly societies. The
insurances are as in the foregoing case. The man is, as well, a
member of a social club, and subscribes to the trade paper, "The
Cotton Factory Times," a non-political paper, and also—as he
belongs to a political party—to a Liberal paper. As long as the
children did not work the family were partly dependent upon the
savings which both partners had made before their marriage. The
wife has, since her first confinement, ceased working. Since the
girls went to work the yearly savings have been considerable, the
object being to secure the parents in old age, and to allow of some-

N

thing for the children when marrying. The man is a zealous member of the Unitarian body, a sect that was introduced into Hyde by the Ashtons, and to which not a few of their operatives belong. Since the yearly expenses only amount to £107, there are savings of £24 to be noted.

The budgets of both families come out in detail as follows. Their interest consists in showing how centralised industry, where it is oldest and most developed, produces far from proletarians. Much rather does there appear to be new middle-classes arising, both as regards standard of living and capability of thrift.

a.   WEEKLY EXPENDITURE FOR HOME USE.

	A.			B.		
	Lb.	oz.	s.	d.	Lb. oz.	s.	d.
Wheat bread (bread is baked at home)	72	0	8	6	17 0	2	0
Oatmeal	1	0	0	2	...	...
Rice	2	0	0	4	...	...
Potatoes	30	0	1	3	15 0	0	9
Tea	1	4	2	3	0 8	0	10
Sugar	14	0	2	11	5 0	1	0½
Milk	3½ qts.		0	10½	5 qts.	1	3
	Lb.	oz.					
Coffee	0	0	0	3½	...	...
Eggs	Six		0	6	Twelve	1	0
	Lb.	oz.			Lb. oz.		
Butter	8	0	8	0	2 8	3	1½
Cheese	1	0	0	8	0 8	0	4½
Meat : Beef	6	0	4	6	6 0	5	0
Mutton	1	0	0	10	...	...
Pork	0	8	0	4	...	...
Bacon and ham	1	8	0	9	1 0	0	10
Vegetables (cabbage, onions, turnips, beans, etc.)	...		0	6	2 0	0	1½
Salt	1	0	0	0¼	1 0	0	0¼
Pickles	...		...		0 8	0	3
Jam	0	8	0	3½	1 0	0	4
A. Herb beer (this drink is non-alcoholic, since both families embrace teetotal principles)	16 qts.		1	0	4 qts.	2	0
B. Ordinary beer	...		...		...	...
	Lb.	oz.			Lb. oz.		
Soap (washing materials)	...		1	1	...	0	4
Light (petroleum , gas, and candles) ..	...		0	3	...	0	6
Tobacco	0	1½	0	4½	0 2	0	8
Coals (yearly average)	...		2	0	...	2	0
Other expenses	...		1	0	...	...
Weekly expenditure for house ...			£1 18	8½		£1 2	10½

b.   OTHER WEEKLY EXPENDITURE.

	A.			B.		
	£	s.	d.	£	s.	d.
Rent	0	4	0	0	4	6
Trade union	0	1	0	0	1	0
Friendly society	0	0	5	0	0	5
Further insurance	0	1	1	0	0	7
Social club		...		0	0	1½
Newspapers	0	0	1	0	0	6
Insurance for paying doctor in case of sickness	0	1	0		...	
School money	0	1	0		...	
Walks, trips, enjoyments (in case A come under the heading of yearly expenses)		...		0	4	0
Various	0	1	0		...	
Total Weekly Expenditure ...	2	8	3½	1	14	0

c.   YEARLY EXPENDITURE.

	A.			B.		
	£	s.	d.	£	s.	d.
Weekly expenses × 52	125	11	0	88	8	0
Clothing	30	0	0	8	0	0
Shoes and boots, etc.	5	0	0	2	10	0
Larger repairs	4	0	0	0	14	0
Thread, etc., for wife for mending ...	0	9	0	0	13	6
Furniture, utensils	3	0	0	1	5	0
Doctor	Paid	week	ly.	0	10	0
Taxes	1	4	0		...	
Other expenses (especially for the trip during the Wakes)	15	0	0	5	0	0
Total expenses	£184	4	0	£107	0	6
Total income	206	0	0	131	8	0
Savings	£21	16	0	£23	12	0

Next to the spinner, the weaver is the chief representative of the
Lancashire cotton industry.   His standard of living is below that
of the spinner.   Men and women are here employed in the same
manner, but seldom married women.   The girls marry compara-

tively late, and mostly only when they have saved something, which makes it possible for them to give up factory labour after the birth of their first child. This is the explanation of the long holding together of adult family members in a common dwelling. If the children grow up and earn money, the time for saving begins anew.

We now give the budget of a weaver at Bacup. The man is 58 years old, the wife 54. They have seven children, who live together in one household; five male, two female—ages, 18 to 31. The father and all the children are cotton weavers, the mother does not work. The total income of the family amounts to £227 yearly, of which the father earns £45 and the children £168, while £14 is the amount of dividends received from the co-operative society.

Wheaten bread is looked upon as the chief nourishment, in addition to which meat is eaten once daily. The expenses for the dwelling-house are comparatively low—3s. 6d. per week. For this amount the family has a house consisting of four rooms, one of which is used as a kitchen and for living purposes. The father is not a trade-unionist, but the sons pay 1s. 2d. weekly to the weavers' society. For educational purposes 6d. per week is paid; to this must be added 25s. yearly for Sunday schools and religious objects. Very considerable are the savings in this case; they amount yearly to about £50. They are invested in the Post Office Savings Bank, in building societies, and in the co-operative society, partly in the names of the parents, partly in those of the children. These savings have the object of assuring to the parents a comfortable old age, of supplying the children with something when married, and also of making it possible for the family to have an outing during the holidays, for which the expenses vary.

A further case refers to a weaver's family at Darwen. Man and wife, 39 and 33 years old, are both cotton weavers. The wife also goes to work for nine months of the year, because she has only three children, whose ages are 7, 9, and 11. In the year which is taken into account, from the summer of 1890 to 1891, the man has only worked 48 weeks. He lost two weeks by sickness, and has had 10 days' holidays. The total income amounted to £101 7s., of which the man earned £52 16s., the wife £43 1s., £4 10s. being the dividend from the co-operative society, and £1 was sick money from the friendly society. The expenses amounted to £94 15s.

6d., so that £6 10s. remained as savings. The living conditions of the family are eminently good; for a rent of 4s. 6d. the family has 4 rooms, two being used as bedrooms. The size of the front room is 14 by 13 ft., of the back room 13 by 9½ ft., the height being 8 ft. In front of the house is a little garden. Wheaten bread and meat are looked upon as the principal food, beef and mutton in equal quantities forming the meat. The man is a trade-unionist, and pays 4d. per week to the weavers' branch society, for which he receives in case of want of work 9s. per week, and, in addition, death money amounting to £6. The same amount is paid to the friendly society, which grants 10s. per week sick money, and £10 in case of death.

As my last representative of the cotton industry I bring forward a fustian-cutter of Hebden Bridge. The husband is 52, the wife 49 years old; there are six children from 14 to 23 years of age—two sons and four daughters. The mother does the work in the house; the children are engaged in the fustian trade. The husband earns 24s. weekly. He has not worked for six or seven weeks of the past year; he has had thereof 20 days' holidays, and lost 19 for other reasons. The children, who had similarly about 14 days' holidays, earned together in the year £172 4s. To this has to be added £12 6s. as dividends from the co-operative society, and £5 interest from other investments. The total income is £244 4s., the total expenditure about £175, and the savings nearly £70. Of these savings, however, only a small proportion was invested, the larger proportion being applied for holiday trips and similar exceptional objects. The co-operative society's dividend was not drawn, but was allowed to remain invested.

The family lives in its own house of five rooms, one of which serves exclusively for living. The dimensions of the rooms are as follows: Front room 15 ft. 3 in. by 12 ft. 3 in., back room 15 ft. 3 in. by 9 ft. 3in., height 8 ft. The kitchen is attached to the house behind. The chief food is wheaten bread, and meat is partaken of five times per week. Under the heading of expenditure there is none for trade unions, because the husband and children are employed in a co-operative undertaking. On the other hand, he pays 4d. per week for insurance against sickness, for which sum 8s. per week in case of illness and £8 in case of death is paid. Very important are the sums applied for clothing—£40 per year. The remainder is shown by the budget given:—

WEEKLY EXPENDITURE.

	A. Weaver at Bacup.				B. Weaver at Darwen.				C. Fustian Cutter at Hebden Bridge.			
	Lb.	oz.	s.	d.	Lb.	oz.	s.	d.	Lb.	oz.	s.	d.
Wheat flour	30	0	3	6	20	0	2	7	48	0	6	9
Oatmeal	5	0	0	10	1	0	0	1¼	4	0	0	7
Rice	2	0	1	0	1	0	0	4	2	0	0	5
Potatoes	16	0	1	0	10	0	0	6	12	0	1	0
Tea	0	8	1	6	0	6	0	10½	0	8	1	4
Sugar	8	0	3	4	6	0	1	3	8	0	1	10
Milk			2	7½			1	10½			3	6
Coffee	0	8	0	9	0	2	0	2½	0	1	1	8
Eggs			1	6			2	0			1	5
Butter	6	8	8	4	2	8	3	3	4	0	5	0
Dripping, lard	2	0	2	0	1	0	0	5				
Cheese	0	8	0	4½	1	0	0	8	1	0	0	9
Meat: Beef	6	0	5	0	2	0	1	6	7	0	5	3
Mutton	3	0	2	6	2	0	1	8			1	0
Pork	2	0	1	4								
Bacon and Ham	1	0	0	7	1	0	0	7	2	0	1	6
Fish	1	0	0	3	2	0	0	8	2	0	0	10
Veget'ble (salad, cabb'ge, etc.)			2	0			0	4			0	8
Salt			0	0½			0	0½			0	1
Mixed pickles			0	4½			0	1			0	6
Jam			0	6	2	0	0	5	4	0	1	2
Beer							0	8				
Spirits			0	6								
Temperance liquors			0	6			0	3			0	6
Soap	5	0	1	3	3	0	0	10½	1	8	0	6
Lighting			0	7			0	6			1	0
Candles			0	1½								
Tobacco			1	0	0	0½	0	1½				
Fuel			1	0			2	3			2	6
Blacking, wash'ng liquor, etc.			0	5			0	2				
Rent (add to C value of house)			3	6			4	6			4	3
Trade union			1	2			0	4				
Friendly society			0	10			0	4			0	4
Other insurance (children)							0	3				
Social and political clubs			0	6							0	4
Newspapers			0	2½			0	2			1	0
School money (case A, evening classes, etc.)			0	6			0	10				
Trips and enjoyments			2	6							2	0
Total weekly expenditure			£2 14	5			£1 10	7½			£2 7	2
Yearly expenditure			£141 9	8			£79 12	6			£122 12	8

YEARLY EXPENDITURE.

	A. Weaver at Bacup.	B. Weaver at Darwen.	C. Fustian Cutter at Hebden Bridge.
Brought forward ..	£141 9 8	£79 12 6	£122 12 8
Clothing	16 10 0	6 0 0	40 0 0
Boots, shoes, and clogs ..	3 12 0	2 0 0	3 10 0
Repairs	1 10 0	..	2 0 0
Thread and sewing materials	0 4 2	0 5 0	0 12 0
Kitchen utensils, furniture ..	1 0 0	0 3 0	2 0 0
Books (in case B from the library of the Co-op Society)	1 0 0	..	0 18 0
Doctor, chemist	4 0 0	0 15 0	1 5 0
Taxes	2 0 0	..	1 18 6
Other expenditure (for A, expenses for Sunday schools and religious purposes; for B, washing)	1 5 0	0 0 0	..
Total yearly expenditure ..	£172 10 10	£94 15 6	£174 16 2
Savings (for A and C, including the expenditure for yearly holidays)	£55 0 0	£6 0 0	£69 8 0

As a proof of the fact that the cotton operatives of Lancashire are by no means in an exceptional position, but rather that their position is merely that of the operatives of English centralised industry generally, the following instances are also quoted:—

The first instance refers to a representative of the miners in Northumberland. The husband is 44, the wife 40 years old, and they live in the neighbourhood of Delaval. There are eight children of the marriage, aged respectively from 2 to 21 years— four boys and four girls. The father and the two eldest sons go to work—all three in the mine. The father earns 36s. per week, the sons 25s. and 14s. The hours of labour amount to 40 per week, and, on the average, 6 hours' overtime. Every fortnight a day's holiday is taken, so that in reality only 11 days are devoted to work. The yearly income of the father amounts—reckoning 50 weeks yearly—to £90, that of the two sons to £97. To these sums a yearly dividend of £19 4s. from the co-operative society has to be added, and from other investments £28 6s. This gives a total yearly income of £234.

WEEKLY EXPENDITURE.

	A. Miner in Northumberland.				B. Machine Fitter in London.			
	Lb.	oz.	s.	d.	Lb.	oz.	s.	d.
Bread (case B bought ready, as usual in London)	...		...		48	0	5	6
Flour (case A baked by wife)... ...	66	0	7	9	4	0	0	6
Oatmeal	...		...		2	0	0	4
Rice	3	0	0	9	0	8	0	1½
Potatoes	28	0	1	4	24	0	1	6
Tea	0	8	1	3	0	12	1	4½
Sugar	9	0	1	10½	6	0	1	0
Milk		...	1	3¾		...	1	3
Coffee	0	4	0	4		...		...
Cocoa	0	4	0	6	0	4	0	3¼
Eggs		...	1	0		...	0	9
Butter	3	8	4	4½	3	0	3	6
Lard, etc.		..			0	8	0	4
Cheese	1	0	0	10	0	12	0	6
Meat : Beef	5	0	3	11½	6	0}	7	1
Mutton	10	0	9	2	4	0}		
Pork	3	0	2	0	1	0	0	8
Ham and bacon...	0	8	0	3				
Vegetables (turnips, cabbage, onions, etc.)		...	0	6	0	8	0	4
Salt		...	0	1		...	0	1
Mixed pickles		...		...		...	0	1
Jam		...	2	4		...	0	3
Beer (A, teetotaller)		..		...		...	1	6
Spirits		...		...		...		...
Temperance cordials		...	0	6		...		...
Soap and washing materials		...	1	0		...	0	9
Lighting...		...	0	6		...	0	5
Candles		...	1	4½		...		...
Tobacco (B, non-smoker)	0	3	0	9		...		...
Fuel (case A, free)		...				...	1	9
Other expenses		...	3	0		...	3	0
Rent (case A, free, value 5/6 per week)		...		...		...	7	0
Total weekly expenditure			2	6	8¾		1	19	10
Yearly expenditure			121	9	11		103	11	4

YEARLY EXPENDITURE.

	B. Miner in Northumberland.			A. Machine Fitter in London.		
Brought forward	£121	9	11	£103	11	4
Trade union	1	19	0	3	5	0
Friendly Society (case A, Foresters)...	3	18	0	2	3	4
Life insurance	1	14	8	2	12	0
Social and political clubs	0	4	4		...	
Doctor (case A pays 3d. per week, B needed none)	0	13	0		...	
Further insurance	1	14	4		...	
Trips and enjoyments	3	10	0	3	18	0
Other expenses (pocket money for children)		...		7	16	0
Clothing	37	4	8	10	10	0
Boots and shoes	7	17	2	3	0	0
Repairs	1	7	0	1	0	0
Thread, etc.	0	7	0	0	3	0
Furniture and utensils...	8	1	3	0	15	0
Newspapers and journals	3	7	3	0	17	4
Books	1	8	6		...	
Yearly expenditure	£194	14	7	£139	11	0
Approximate annual savings ...	£40	0	0	£6	0	0

The other side of the balance-sheet is debited with £229 6s. There is no rent included in this expenditure, because the miners of Northumberland have nothing of any moment to pay for the rent of their houses, which belong to the colliery proprietors. These houses are the ordinary dwellings of the North English workman. They comprise 2 to 4 living rooms, in the foregoing case four, in two storeys, each 28½ by 18 ft. The coal-hewers also receive coals for nothing, delivered for about 6d. per fortnight for carting expenses.

The man is a trade-unionist and co-operator, also a member of a friendly society; and so with the two sons. The trade union pays, in case of stoppage or other intermission of work, 10s. per week for support; the friendly society, for sick support, 10s., and, in addition, £8 funeral money in case of the death of a member, and £2 on the death of a child.

Remarkably high are the expenses for newspapers, books, etc., inasmuch as the miners of Northumberland are noted for active intelligent interest. By this fact, as well as by the high relation in which the single items for clothing, etc., stand to the expenses for food, the budget detailed above appears completely like that of one of the middle classes. The chief nourishment here is also wheaten bread and meat. The wife as well as the daughters, the eldest of whom is 16 years of age, do not go to work.

Side by side with this is given the budget of a machine fitter at London. The husband is 43 years old, and the wife the same age. They have six children—two boys and four girls—from 6 to 17 years old. The husband earns 41s. per week; the children, of whom the eldest son is becoming a machine fitter and the daughter works in a cotton factory, earn together 18s. The man estimates his annual income at £105, to which sum £45 is added by the children; the total income is therefore £150. There are 50 working weeks taken into account, because two weeks have to be reckoned for sickness and holidays (9 days yearly). The man declares he has never lost any time on account of labour disputes or want of work. He is a member of the Amalgamated Engineers, to which society he contributes 1s per week, and for which he is entitled to sick pay, and support in case of want of work and in old age. In addition, he spends 1s. 10d. per week for further insurance objects, partly with the friendly society called the Hearts of Oak, for the object of sick insurance. The house, which comprises five rooms, is comparatively dear, as in general dwelling-houses in London are dearer than those of the North English operatives. Three rooms are applied to sleeping purposes, and two for living in (two rooms 14 by 12 ft., three rooms 10 by 9 ft). In this case, also, meat and wheaten bread form the chief nourishment. The budget shows meagre savings, in connection with which, however, the considerable applications for insurance purposes have to be taken into account.

The figures given reveal the enormous advance of the English operatives when compared with the "thirties" (see page 88). On the other hand, numerous German operatives' budgets that have been published bring us to the conclusion that the standard of living of German operatives at the present time about balances that of the English in the "thirties"—a further proof for the dependence of the position of operatives on the condition of economical development. In the same degree that Germany has advanced less towards centralised industry, and that hand labour still preponderates over machine labour, is the standard of living of the German operative less than that of the workers of the present English centralised industry.

In most of the German workers' published budgets the income scarcely covers the expenditure; very frequently a deficit occurs which is balanced by benevolence and poor relief, in many cases by prostitution—even by misery and want. Excellent service in the cause of determining the conditions of life of German operatives has to be ascribed to the inquiries—published by order of the Ministry of the Grand Duchy of Baden—of Woerishoffer, for the celebrated and well-known Committee on Baden Factory Inspection. Even for the skilled workpeople of well established centralised industries (for instance, of the chemical industry) it appears, according to these, that the most favourable result is the ever scanty attainment of the physiological minimum of living. In spite of which, these communications contain—in connection with the information concerning other German working classes, especially concerning the known conditions of the German cottage industrial workers—proof that sound centralised industries always make possible a relatively higher status of living of the operatives. While for the mass of the workers in German centralised industries the nourishment—mostly potatoes and rye bread—may at least scantily supply the physiological demands, that of the cottage workers shows, in comparison, an apparent want of nourishment (see page 88). I quote, as an instance from one of the textile centres of North Germany, the following operative's budget, which seems to me, after comparison with another, to stand rather above than below the average. The family consists of the husband (49 years old), wife (53 years old), and four children (5 to 17 years old). The husband and the two eldest children are employed in a power weaving-mill. The man earns 15s.; the two children together contribute 7s. per week for food and lodgings to the parents:—

WEEKLY EXPENDITURE FOR FOOD AND HOUSE, etc.

		M. pf.
Rye bread, second quality	42 lb.	5 60
Potatoes	30 litres	1 80
White bread (small rolls, 25 grammes)	2 lb.	2 0
Wheaten flour (2nd quality)	2 ,,	0 40
Meat (Sundays only)	¾ ,, }	0 45
Dripping	½ ,, }	
Vegetables (peas, linseed, rice, etc.)	—	3 40
Coffee	—	0 20
Butter	2½ lb.	3 40
Skimmed milk	6 litres	0 60
Rent		3 20
Sick money and old-age insurance		0 65
School money		0 15
Total		21 85

It results from what is given above, in comparison with the

English operatives' budgets, that the chief food of the English operative—meat and wheat—is with the German a luxury. Especially is this applicable from the item of ¾ lb. meat weekly for a family of four adults (of whom three work) and two children. A comparison in figures between German and English operatives' budgets is impossible in detail, by reason that one certainly knows that wheat is more nourishing than rye. A positive relation of value between both cannot, however, be given, on account of too great variations according to the harvests, conditions of the land, etc. But something further is certainly to be taken as general—the income reaches, in favourable cases, no further than for nourishment. There remains for other purposes, as a rule, little or nothing over.

In addition, German industry lacks consumers of mass articles. Skilled workers, even in the most favourable cases, and if the children or wife work as well, scarcely ever spend above £15 yearly for clothing and other industrial productions, whilst in the English budgets given above this expenditure runs to £50 and over. A Leipzig book-printer's family—therefore belonging to one of the highest classes of operatives—with only two children, has only £9 14s. yearly left over for clothing and shoes. "In order to save boots, the children run about barefooted in the warmer season of the year." The household utensils of the German worker's family are scarcely ever bought new, but, like the clothing also in numerous cases, from the broker, or received through charity. Numerous proofs of this statement are given by the Frankfort workers' budgets (2), which by no means refer to a specially low working class—a disadvantage not to be under-rated for German industry, which, as numerous statements before the "Enquetekommission" show, feels keenly a rise in food prices, reductions in wages, or curtailment of employment in other important branches of trade, especially in mining and iron working.

---

2. " Schriften des Freien deutschen Hochstifts" (Frankfurt a. M., 1890). A worker's family with four children and £57 income spent only £5 for clothing, washing, household goods, and repairs. The head of the family says 'he buys perhaps occasionally a pair of working trousers or some such indispensable article of clothing, but for fifteen years has not bought himself a complete new suit." The furniture is mostly second-hand when forming the household. Even the sofa is missing in most cases. There is never a room used exclusively for living purposes ; living and sleeping are generally combined in the same room. Frequently one room serves the whole family for living and sleeping, and in many cases the same is partially sub-let. Compare pp. 37, 44, 70, 85, 94 ; further, Herkner, pp. 49-64.

If one visits the English operative in his home, its appearance convinces one that there is here more than the bare standard of living, that certain demands for comfort are fulfilled, which has a most favourable influence on the family life. Let us go, for instance, to the spinner in Hyde, whose budget was given above. In front of the house there is a small garden. It was, at the time that the particulars for the budget were got (August, 1891), filled with blooming plants. The house door leads into the living room, the size of which has already been given. In the middle of the side wall there is a large fireplace, with a clear, flaring coal fire. On it is a kettle, in which water for the tea, indispensable at every meal, is boiled. At the side of the fireplace we find an oven for cooking meat and baking bread. In the middle of the room stands a large square table, the meal-table of the family. Against the second wall a long sofa, against the third a large mahogany set of drawers, upon which were some stuffed birds and some books. Against the fourth wall of the room stands a piano, for buying which the operative with pleasure applies his savings, chiefly in Lancashire, the population of which has a special inclination and capacity for music. I have seen one in many operatives' dwellings, even in weavers' houses at Bacup, who did not pay more than 3s. 9d. for rent (3).

Even if the value of the instrument as well as the musical productions on it are meagre—it was related to me that the two daughters had deemed 10 lessons each sufficient for learning the art—in any case, the life of the operative of Lancashire gains a cheerfulness by the practising of music, which is doubly to be wished by the sad commonplaceness of the industrial localities of the North of England. The floor of the room is covered with oil-cloth. Nowhere is there missing an arm-chair for the head of the family. Five further chairs complete the furnishing.

Behind the living room there is a kitchen. The same, however, does not serve for cooking, since this is generally done in the living-room, but for preparing the dishes, and chiefly for washing. We notice particularly the large built-up washing boiler, arranged for heating with a coal fire. At the window there is a slopstone

3. The lack of pianos in similar workers' dwellings in Germany was pointed out by me in a paper partially reprinted in "The Textile Mercury" and the "Manchester Chamber of Commerce Monthly Record" on March 28th, 1891. "Even though Germany is noted for its makes of pianos, I never remember having seen one in the house of a daily-bread toiler."—*Translator.*

with water-tap.   As a chief article of furniture there is not often
missing a wringing machine, which serves for wringing-out the damp
clothes, and which I have seldom missed in any of the houses of
the cotton operatives visited by me.   Behind the kitchen there is
a small yard, with a shed for coals.   A small staircase leads from
the kitchen to the upper storey, whose two rooms are used for
sleeping purposes, and are furnished with beds, drawers, etc.

This is the customary type of the operatives' houses, of which
not a few present more extensive furnishing.   Generally, the first
thing in this respect is a sewing-machine.   The similarity of the
architecture is as astonishing as the furnishing.   The worst type
of operatives' houses, which at the present time is gradually
diminishing, differs from that described in that the yard and the
kitchen disappear from behind, and the houses are built back to
back, and the living-room downstairs takes up the whole area
in front.   The buildings which exist above the average have the
kitchen connected to the house in the yard, so that below there
are   two rooms, one opening to the front, the other to the back,
which mostly means three rooms above.   They also often
possess a special entrance hall.

These types of buildings occur in the factory towns near Manchester, as well as in the seats of weaving in North Lancashire.
The above-described building and furnishing cannot by any
means, after the numerous instances I have seen, be regarded as
a case standing above the average.

Quite especially as notable proof for the high standard of living
of the cotton operatives of Lancashire is the amount of capital
widely distributed in their circles, which results from the balances
of the numerous operatives' budgets.   In this respect there
appears to be a sort of decentralisation of society by an increasing regular division of wealth—a consequence, as we have already
seen, of the centralised industrial development.   As opposed to
this, the view of Karl Marx is certainly wrong, that the working
classes, in consequence of centralised industrial development
economically pressed down, still rise up to political power, until
they at last, holding political power in their hands, cause the
economical reversal which would change them from non-possessors
to mutual possessors of existing capital.   Economical decentralisation—that is, a proportional division of wealth—has, much

rather, always historically preceded a proportional division of political power. Countries with unequal division of possessions were always oligarchal—thus countries of landed estates, of commerce, and of flourishing centralised industries. First, in proportion as the machinery system, developing itself, raises the working classes economically, do they gain real influence, of which the present Labour party lacks the first stage of the development, because it is based upon economical weakness.

Now in what way, we ask, are the widely extended savings of the cotton operatives of Lancashire invested? Into account come insurance societies of every kind, especially the large and rich friendly societies; further, Government as well as private savings banks, building societies, industrial undertakings, etc. (4). Here we only bring to notice two kinds of investments; the co-operative societies and "limited" concerns. Regarding the co-operative societies I refer to what is said in the first volume of my book "On Social Peace," as well as that excellent work by Miss Potter.

As an instance, we only point out here the tremendous business transacted by the Oldham Co-operative Society. This society consisted, in December, 1890, of 11,000 members, belonging exclusively to the working classes, and had in the year 1889 net receipts of £341,195. It possesses a large number of shops for groceries, clothing, bread, and butcher's meat, for boots and shoes, furniture, drapery, etc. It has, further, a branch for building houses, and had up to the time mentioned built 623 operatives' houses for about £100,000, which, for the most part, had already become the private property of individual operatives. In addition, there is a savings bank attached to the society, with deposits amounting to £18,000. The society has invested a part of its property in limited spinning-mills, partly in shares and partly in loans. It paid £50,000 in dividends to its members in 1889—that is, nearly £5 per member, in addition to £5,000 interest to loan owners.

Besides this, the society spent considerable sums on education and recreation. The Educational Committee had arranged, in the year mentioned, a large number of lectures on various subjects, partly in connection with the University Extension Scheme, partly with those institutions which apply themselves, as pointed out

4. Compare Report of the Commission on Depression of Trade, Second Report, part L, p. 136.

above, to the fostering of technical knowledge. Instruction classes were held in cotton industry, shorthand, botany, physiology, hygiene, book-keeping, and dressmaking The society possessed a library of 13,075 volumes, besides several reading-rooms supplied with numerous newspapers and journals. It also arranged tea meetings, balls, entertainments, etc.

Respecting house-building by the societies, I received the following communication from the Bacup Society's committee:—"The average price for which we sell houses to our members amounts to £210. The society gets the houses built on contract by local builders, and sells them by auction, when ready, to its members. These either pay the whole price at once, or must pay interest for the amount left owing, and, in addition, £1 10s. every quarter, until the whole amount is paid off. If they wish to pay more speedily, it is, of course, accepted. The living rooms are 5 ells wide and 4 ells long, the kitchens 2 to 3 ells; behind the house there is a yard 12 ells square. A storey high are 2 to 3 bedrooms. A lobby runs the whole length of the house (from back to front.)"

In another co-operative society the houses were paid for within 19 years, under the following scheme, on the basis of 3 per cent.

Of the £190 borrowed:—

	There falls of £15 12s. paid:— To interest.			To capital payment.			Leaving as balance.		
	£	s.	d.	£	s.	d.	£	s.	d.
At the end of 1 year	9	10	0	6	2	0	183	18	0
" 2 years ...	9	3	10¾	6	8	1¼	177	9	10¾
" 3 " ...	8	17	6	6	14	6	170	15	4¾
" 4 " ...	8	10	9¼	7	1	2¾	163	14	2
" 5 " ...	8	3	8½	7	8	3½	156	5	10
" 6 " ...	7	16	3½	7	15	8½	148	10	2
" 7 " ...	7	8	6	8	3	6	140	6	8
" 8 " ...	7	0	4	8	11	8	131	15	0
" 9 " ...	6	11	9	9	0	3	122	14	9
" 10 " ...	6	2	8¾	9	9	3¼	113	5	5¾
" 11 " ...	5	13	3¼	9	18	8¾	106	6	9
" 12 " ...	5	3	4	10	8	8	92	18	1
" 13 " ...	4	12	10¾	10	19	1¼	81	18	11¾
" 14 " ...	4	1	10¾	11	10	1¼	70	8	10½
" 15 " ...	3	10	5¼	12	1	6¼	58	7	3¾
" 16 " ...	2	18	4¼	12	13	7¾	45	13	8
" 17 " ...	2	5	8¼	13	6	3¼	32	7	4¾
" 18 " ...	1	12	4½	13	19	7½	18	7	8¾
" 19 " ...	0	18	4½	14	13	7½	3	14	1¼

interest. Interest and capital payment amounted to £15 12s. annually.

From what has been said it results that a happy solution of the so-called operatives' house question is to be found in the last degree in a greater participation of the working classes in national possession of capital.

Of special interest is the development of the "limited" principle in spinning at Oldham, and certainly not only from economical, but also from social points of view. It has already been touched upon how the "limited" system helped onward the development of spinning, and made possible concentration of capital, and therewith a considerable lowering of the costs of production.

It is a remarkable fact that those large limited spinning-mills at Oldham, furnished with the most improved machinery, which to-day can generally be looked upon as the leading ones, are also socially interesting pictures, and in fact emanated from a movement of the working classes.

Their origin is ascribable to the co-operative movement, which has always had its chief seat in Lancashire. The banks of the little river Roach, which washes Todmorden and Rochdale, are certainly those of a second Tiber, going out from which the co-operative idea, according to the thought of its supporters, should conquer the whole world (5). As a fact, however, the efforts of the co-operative societies at production have mostly failed, and have proved themselves only possible under the first condition of having morally exceptionally high-standing members. On the other hand, the co-operative stores, to which belong the extensive masses of the cotton and machine operatives of Lancashire, had an increasing success. They educated the operative for the practical management of business. Besides which they collected, as savings, the dividends, which in many cases were not drawn by the members, forming considerable capital which required investment. Both conditions must come together in order to make possible the successful formation of "limited" undertakings by the working classes. A further circumstance favoured this development; numerous Oldham employers had arisen from the ranks of the operatives, as well as that large class of overlookers, technical men, and managers, which stands between employers and operatives. In all

---

5. Compare my book "On Social Peace," I., p. 311.

O

countries of the world Oldham operatives, as managers and over-lookers, have formed spinning-mills and managed them, especially in India and Russia.

As a rule they return to their native town with their savings. They are people who, in general, are the cleverest in the cotton industry, and who still retain a close feeling of kinship with the working class from which they emanated. At political and social meetings the position of the cotton trade has for a long time formed the most interesting theme. Thus a considerable degree of commercial knowledge extended itself into the widest circles, helped forward by the reading-rooms, conversation-rooms, lectures, and educational evenings of the co-operative societies, technical educational institutions, etc. The highest-paid class of operative in Oldham, also, which is engaged in machine works, depends in a similar manner on the condition of the cotton industry, and joins in the interest for the position and technicalities of the trade.

Thus it happened that with the support of the co-operative stores, as early as 1860 a limited spinning-mill was established, which counted numerous operatives, and people who stood socially little above the operatives, amongst its founders. This spinning-mill, the Sun Mill, to-day one of the largest and best establishments in Oldham, has a brilliant record behind it. In the first ten years it was able already to declare dividends of from 10 to 30 per cent. Soon after it a great number of similar undertakings came into life. All these formations emanated from people who could make a claim to special knowledge, and were still by no means separated socially, as it were, from the operative by a gulf. Fitted throughout with the best machinery, these mills were most keenly supervised by their shareholders. Thus they have in the period of trade depression of the " seventies " held up their heads in an acknowledged better degree than numerous private firms (6). Not a single one of these "limiteds" came at that time to grief.

Of course there is also capital from larger capitalists invested in these limited spinning-mills, in spite of which most of them have kept their character as undertakings of the working classes. An infallible proof of this is, that at the general meetings the votes are counted, not according to the number of shares held, but according

6. Thomas Ellison: " Cotton Trade," p. 133.

to the number of shareholders (7), and in this way with ninety per cent. of all companies in Oldham. A minimum number of shares to qualify as directors is not specified, but every shareholder is equally eligible. "Almost the whole population of wage-workers and small trades-people in the town ·of Oldham are connected with spinning" is stated in the annual volume of the Co-operative Society at Manchester. The same thing is confirmed to me by letter by Mr. Samuel Andrew, the Secretary of the great Employers' Association.

Operatives who will not undertake the risk of possessing shares hand over their savings to the undertakings in the form of loans; loans are accepted down to the lowest sums. The shares themselves, also, do not exceed the nominal value of £5. Amongst those who invest their money in spinning-mills are also trade unions, and I know from the mouth of the gentleman himself that one of the most noted trade-union leaders of Lancashire filled at the same time, for a certain period, a post of trust with one of the largest limited spinning concerns of Oldham.

The competition for directors' positions, the publicity of the whole book-keeping, as well as the pride of the shareholders in the possession of the best machinery, has the ultimate result that all such undertakings, without exception, have had commercial success. Mr. Samuel Andrew, the highest authority on the cotton industry, has, before the "Commission on Depression of Trade," extolled the ability of these directors emanating from the working class, and ascribed to these undertakings the salvation of the cotton industry. Also in the time of inflation at the commencement of the "seventies" the commercial foundation of the companies has been completely free from reproach. The best proof for this is the permanence of the undertakings; further, also, that to-day individual employers in many cases would rather invest their capital in these companies.

The wide scope of the English "limited" laws, which leave a large portion of the companies' articles of association to the parties (for instance, the value of the payments on the shares, the value of the shares, voting power in general meetings, etc.) has favoured this speedy development, economically and socially. Far less successful than in spinning are the attempts of similar

7. Compare "Co-operative Wholesale Annual," 1884.

limited undertakings in the weaving branch. There are, however, in this respect, instances enough, for example, the "Self Help" weaving mill, at Burnley. The Edward Rawlinson previously mentioned said before the "Commission on Depression of Trade" that there were six limited weaving concerns in Burnley, with altogether 661 shareholders, of which 213 were workers for wages.

What are the social effects of the development portrayed? The participation of the large masses in the industrial profits tends more than anything else to the softening of that class conflict which was called into existence by the flourishing centralised industry. Even if within the factory the strictest discipline is kept the personal relations of all shareholders are put into operation on the field of equal rights. Are not the directors of these companies mostly drawn from the working class? More important still is a second point. It appears here clear and distinct before the eyes of the operative that he depends in the utmost degree upon the condition of his industry; that everything that concerns it concerns himself. This view is easily attained where a large circle of wage-receivers not only depend upon wages, but at the same time upon industrial profits. They follow eagerly the market reports, which are published every week in the "Cotton Factory Times." The limited principle makes it possible for them to be as well informed about the condition of the industry as private employers. This relation has a double effect. If the adaptation of wages to profit variations of itself already results from the dependence of the great industry on the state of trade, as above stated, so must this adaptation be achieved most rigidly in Lancashire, where the operatives clearly overlook the commercial position of the industry, the possibility of increased wages, and the inevitableness of reduced wages. But the operatives learn, on their side, to understand also the justice of the so-called management wage. They gain the experience that it is essential for an industry as far as possible to possess the most capable managers, and that outlays with this object are well rewarded.

Those shadow sides, which otherwise the form of limited undertakings have attached to them, appear here for the most part overcome. It is the custom to point out, as the chief disadvantage, that the shareholders generally only appear to be employers, that the general meeting shows an appearance of managing, and the board do mostly as they like with the shareholders who are inexperienced in business. Thus, it is said, the members of the board exercise, in fact, the power of employers, without bearing the personal responsibility of the employer. This disadvantage is, however, not unavoidable. It is impossible, where the shareholders, living on the spot, have the working of the business before their eyes, and are even at home in the trade of the limited undertaking, yea, even have people under them who, within the industry, are generally reckoned amongst the cleverest, as, for instance, those veterans of cotton spinning who have earned their spurs in India, Japan, Russia, etc. In such a case the general meeting is a monarch jealous of his rights, who keeps his servants under strict control.

It is specially deserving of mention that these so-called co-operative limited concerns of Oldham, of which there are about 70, are by no means producing societies. They grant even in no wise a profit bonus to the operatives, wherein certainly lies one of the reasons of success. Participation in profits does not pay in cotton spinning, because the system of piece-wages gives to every one sufficient incentive for labour, which would not be increased by sharing in the profits. Besides, the wages are so high that they cannot be increased without reducing the managing salaries and risk premiums of the shareholders in an uneconomical manner. The only way to improve wages is by economy in labour through technical progress. Those limited companies have indeed, on the one hand by extraordinary cutting of production costs and pressing down of yarn prices, brought down the profits to the lowest possible degree; on the other hand they have been typical examples of technical progress.

But in order to judge the condition of the working class, a simple description is not enough—one must seek a glance into their feelings and thoughts. I therefore ask the reader to spend a day with me in Lancashire, which for me will for all time belong to the most interesting reminiscences (8).

---

8. How strange this appears to many Germans is shown by the following extract from a paper given by me and printed in the "Menchester Chamber of Commerce Monthly Record" (March 28th, 1891):—"Here in England, as all readers know, the workers, or at least the majority of them. I am glad to say, get to Blackpool, Southport, the Isle of Man, or some other watering place, once or twice a year. The German workman knows nothing like this. I remember a manufacturer asking me to send him some small articles in a couple of days. It was a holiday time, and I told him it was impossible, because our works

For a great many years it has been customary to have a week's mill holiday in most of the industrial places of Lancashire. This takes place in the months of July to September (the so-called wakes). A large portion of the cotton operatives, as well as machine workers, use a portion of the savings they have made for trips and journeys for their health. Everywhere there exist special savings clubs, in which, for the object we are treating of, payments are made during the whole year (so-called "going-off clubs.") In Oldham alone for the last few years there was at the commencement of the holidays, £65,000 drawn annually from these clubs for trips, of which about £45,000 fell to the cotton operatives and £20,000 to the machine workers at Platt's and other machine works, as confirmed to me by Mr. Andrew.

The operatives then disperse to the neighbouring hilly country of Derbyshire and the districts of the English coasts; many of them go to London in order to visit the sights there worth seeing, and some even extend their travels to the Continent (9). But more popular than anything else is the seaside. Especially crowded in these days by trippers is the Isle of Man and that seaside resort, Blackpool, situated in Lancashire.

Along with a clergyman of my acquaintance, who wished to visit his parishioners on one of these holiday days in Blackpool, I went to the seaside place mentioned. Arriving there by one of the excursion trains, we strode through the over-filled little town, consisting of lodging-houses, and betook ourselves to the beach. As far as the eye could follow, on the sands surged thousands of people, well nourished and well dressed; the men mostly of that strong, rather plump build, as mostly appears to us in Englishmen; the girls and women, in growth, stature, and colour of complexion, in many instances genuine Britons, along with a few Celtic types. "Ninety per cent. of these people," my companion informed me, "are mill-hands," i.e., operatives of the cotton in-

---

were closed for four days. ' Have you no work to do, that you are closed ? What will your workmen do the whole time ?' ' We are obliged to close for annual holidays,' was my reply, ' and our workmen will in most cases go to some watering place or other for three or four days.' The incredulous smile with which this was received left no doubt whatever on my mind that I was risking my reputation for telling the truth. Not on this occasion alone has this phase of the English workman's life been received with suspicion. The average German employer cannot grasp the fact that a workman has the right to a respite from manual toil as well as he a respite from brain work."— *Translator.*

9. Compare " Co-operative Wholesale Annual," 1884, p. 200.

dustry, "the remainder mostly machine workers." His practised eye soon recognised in the crowds the representatives of the chief branches of trade in Lancashire. "That slender, caring-for-himself man, who with his better-half came on the trip, is a mule-spinner who can earn £2 and more weekly. That stronger-looking man next to him is probably a representative of the machine making everywhere planted alongside of the cotton industry, and then certainly a member of the well-known Amalgamated Society. That full-grown girl, who evidently places great value on herself and her outward appearance, may be one of those four-loom weavers so numerous in our town, with weekly wages of 24s. or more, and fair savings. The younger people, more cheaply and gaily attired, come out of the carding and preparation rooms. There may also be, among the younger ones, ring-spinners represented, whom our friend Mullin is now organising." "If you will notice," continued my companion, "the outward appearance will already teach you that the women here marry later than among the miserable proletarians of our capital. It was formerly otherwise. As long as they could not economically worsen their position by marriage, the female cotton operatives also married early, and frequently had children before marriage. To-day they think mostly, instead of this, of entering into marriage with certain savings, which enable them to give up factory labour after the birth of their first child. Thus it happens that families here remain longer together than is the case in other places in operative circles. Fifty per cent. of these people, but certainly a large percentage, may, however, have taken the temperance pledge—a movement which is also specially supported by the younger trades societies."

While we thus wandered chattering on the beach, the life of the people's holiday developed itself about us. Besides fortune-tellers and nigger minstrels, and, on the pier-heads, dancing couples, there were hobby-horses, which, also a sign of the times and place, were driven by steam engines. My companion assured me that the increasing whistling of the engines ministered to the pleasure of the crowd, who also in their holidays would not miss the voice of the once-so-hated King Steam. Alongside of all these we saw preachers surrounded by crowds of listeners, next to which children played unconcernedly in the sand. While the incoming tide washed away the gardens built by them, with their borders, it led my companion into a tirade against private property in land.

In the meantime the hour for dinner had struck, and we accepted the invitation which had been extended to us by an acquaintance and parishioner of my friend. We betook ourselves to one of the lodging-houses, which was occupied by a company of about 50 persons, all cotton operatives from the town where my companion lived. At the head of the table sat a sturdy, fresh-looking old man—a patriarch amongst his fellows. Next to him sat his worthy better-half, to whose care a large proportion of the young folks present was entrusted. The meal placed before us consisted of tea, ham and eggs, and mutton with potatoes and green peas. In addition there was a favourite temperance drink, whilst teetotalism was not expected from the German.

Placed, as a guest, next to the old man, I tried at once to bring him to old times, upon which he commenced most readily. His parents, he related, had been hand-weavers in the North of Lancashire; he had grown up amidst the most bitter poverty. He could scarcely speak and walk before he had to turn the winding-wheel. Then, at 8 years of age, he had entered a spinning-mill, and first went into the carding-room, in which at that time a great number of children were employed. Later on he was promoted to be a piecer; since, however, fortune had not been sufficiently favourable to him to let him become a spinner—on account of the large number of piecers necessary at that time, 4 to 5 per spinner, only few succeeded in attaining this position—he changed to powerloom weaving.

In the "twenties," in which his youth had fallen, not only had his family, but the whole population of his native place, led a life full of privation. The customary nourishment was oat-cakes and potatoes. On the other hand meat was unknown, and he had only seen the first piece of wheaten bread when he had wandered from the North of Lancashire to an environ of Manchester. The old men, when they had become incapable for work, had generally gone into the workhouse, for they had no savings to support them. But the youths of his time had been red-hot Chartists, he himself one of the most eager. He remembered very well the great popular man, Fergus O'Connor. He also remembered well how the police had dispersed their meetings and had put many of the participators into prison. Even blood had now and again flowed, since armed encounters had not been seldom. But especially did there remain, even at this time, in the recollection of the operatives that bath of blood on "Peterloo" Field, where the yeomanry of Cheshire had charged the cotton operatives of Manchester,

To my question—What, then, had been the meaning of Chartism?—the aged man answered: A Labour party in Parliament, State rule by the general vote, in order to evolve from the law against the poor a law for the poor. With Chartism, and after this had stepped above its height as a political movement, there came a time of larger and distressing strikes. He remembered especially the Christmas month of 1842, and the great strike at Preston in 1853, which had lasted 40 weeks, and for which, from Blackburn alone, £700 per week had been contributed. The strikes had brought in their train formidable distress and great bitterness. There were at that time no trade unions, and those strikes had been more eruptions of the heart than the result of thought.

Since then a tremendous reversal had taken place. The young people we saw joined together around us for the joyful holiday—those girls, of which every one spent £3 and more during the holidays, those youths, who let out in football and other sports the surplus of their muscular energy—shook their heads in unbelief if he told them that never a thought of holiday and sport had entered into the imagination of their grandparents. The change to a ten-hours and nine-hours day's labour instead of thirteen hours; subsistence wages, co-operative societies, trade unions, and political freedom, in place of the suppression of the labour movements, marked the progress. "But if you wish to see the true sign of this change," continued the grey-haired veteran, with beaming eye, "it lies before you on the table, the strength of Lancashire," as he raised with triumphant bearing a piece of wheaten bread. Cobden was a sacred being to the old man. "We fought the battle, and we have won." With these words he closed his story.

Very interesting was the opposition which he received on the part of the clergyman in his admiration of Cobden, as well as in his defence of trade unions. This gentleman, like many of his class, described himself as a Socialist, and attacked the trade unions as conservative institutions. They retarded progress and obscured that ideal which mankind, and especially the Christian, has to strive for—to help forward the kingdom of righteousness on earth; to build up on earth a representation of the heavenly Sion;

to work to the end that the will of God shall be done, not only in heaven, but also on earth. But of these ideals there can be no question, he argued, as long as a large mass of bodily as well as spiritually miserable proletarians filled the depths of society, especially in the large towns. By want and social isolation it was excluded from all emotions of the human spirit, and was forced by poverty and uncertainty of existence to crime and prostitution. The elevation of this class was, in his opinion, only possible by a gradual limitation of private enterprise, and extension of public undertakings under the control of the workers. Therewith alone would the disturbing difference between rich and poor be eliminated.

It was interesting to observe how this expression of political feeling found numerous supporters amongst the women. Especially did an intelligent young female weaver defend the position of the clergyman. It was bare selfishness, she said, if the classes of the operatives of centralised industry would be satisfied with what had been attained, without considering other downtrodden working classes.

The men opposed the somewhat obscure Socialism of the parson, especially the younger men, and a mule-spinner, who was present with two daughters—the one whose household budget we have already given. In any case one was in the path, he thought, of practical and permanent progress, which really only allowed itself to be gradually extended to an ever-widening circle of the people. But since their own fathers at one time had emerged out of the unvarying crowd of helpless proletarians, it was to be hoped that new circles would continually loosen themselves from its bonds and rise up. The way thereto was a double one—first by union, and then by legislation. He did not oppose the latter by any means. Much rather was it exactly the cotton operatives of Lancashire who had understood how to put this weapon into operation for themselves—certainly the most of all operatives in the world. But for this they were indebted to the wise do-ut-des policy of leaders, who ever each time only put forward immediate demands, and had often made themselves indispensable to the ruling powers.

Therewith the position of the operatives in society in the last decades had improved extraordinarily. Numerous trade-union leaders filled at the present time the honourable position of Justices of the Peace in their native places. A representative of the cotton operatives of Lancashire had been sent by the Government to the Berlin Conference for the protection of workers, where he and another English member had really been the only operatives. The Home Secretary had lately visited the offices of the Amalgamated Weavers at Accrington on his journey through Lancashire, and had there been introduced to the representatives of the society. On the Board of Trade the excellent Burnett, a former machine-fitter, took a high and in every respect esteemed position. In the present existing Royal Commission for Examining the Conditions of the Working Classes, operatives sat next to employers and aristocrats, with equal rights, and were treated by them as equals. All these things showed how much the operative, who formerly stood without the State, knew to-day how to attain an esteemed position within it.

He doubted, however, whether the operatives would use their influence for helping forward on a large scale the changing of private undertakings into public ones. He would not give his opinion about other branches of trade, because he held this question as one to be decided in each individual instance and according to practical considerations. In numerous cases, especially in London, the Socialists who demanded State undertakings might be right in regard to the municipalisation of water companies, tramways, gas-works, and docks; regarding transport arrange ments it was questionable. All this he only knew from hearsay But regarding the cotton industry, which he knew, he said: "Hands off." A State institution was here impossible, because officials would defend the world's market worse than private employers. A mere fraction of a penny often decided at the present time the battle of nations. In advanced economical and social relations private undertakings guaranteed the cheapest form of payment of the manager, who, at the same time, ensured the most skilled management. If Socialists pointed to the "limited" principle as a proof of the possibility of their ideas, they thought hereby of that unsound form where the shareholders themselves, standing quite aloof, were often—only too often—wrongly led. In Oldham the shareholders were skilled employers.

If, however, the difference of employer and worker could not be given up, extreme differences between rich and poor counterbalanced one another. By the fact that great capitalists frequently withdrew their capital from one undertaking and divided it amongst many, it was proved that the function of great riches was slighter to-day than 50 years ago.   In Oldham those limited concerns which were managed by directors from the operatives' class displaced the older private undertakings.

As opposed to these temperate utterances the clergyman defended that social idealism which demanded the elevation of the poorest of the poor.   This scene made clear to me that peculiar stage of the English labour movement, according to which the Radical wing to a great extent shows the touch of a religious enthusiasm.   As Ben Tillett, the leader of the dockers, said to me, he had to give a speech daily, but on Sundays he preached twice, and as Sidney Webb ascribes the last successful election to the County Council in the first degree to the Dissenters and their preachers, so also here the parson took the side of that helpless and deeply submerged mass of humanity, above which the taught and organised workers of Centralised Industry stand higher than the families comprising the House of Lords stand above him.

A few weeks later my studies led me into a circle of operatives of one of the most important textile centres of Germany.   I met here the same friendly reception, the same willingness to support scientific researches, also a similar social idealism.   But it differed at once from that drawn above in that it did not stand in connection with the traditions of ideal goodness of humanity; the operatives themselves as well, not the priests and women, were here the bearers of that idealism.   On the other hand, there was a lack of manly criticism of the problems on the side of reasoning and understanding.   Why should we tread the laborious path by which the English operative has bettered his position, since assuredly in a few years the great revolution must take place which will of itself bring everything wished for?

As I related this my comparison between German and English operatives to an industrial employer, he declared: German operatives are preferable for me, since their wishes and strivings are placed in a cuckoo's home of clouds, which, when they think it to be near, again disappears in the distance.   I could only reply to this that this weakness of German operatives also comes into expression in their work, and the carnivorous Englishman is, in the utmost degree, still the cheaper worker.

CONCLUSION.

In conclusion, there are two misunderstandings to be avoided. By no means is it to be accepted, in the first place, that the present economical and social conditions of the staple industry of Lancashire are in general those of English industry. Much rather, in the field of English textile industry, are the various stages of the development of centralised industry to be seen at the present time side by side. Accordingly we meet here also social conditions which possess much similarity with those of Lancashire in the "thirties" and of the present German.

If we go, say, for instance, from Manchester to Bradford, the centre of the worsted industry, we enter into another economical as well as social world. Even the raw-material market is here less developed than that for cotton. While the spinner in Lancashire buys from week to week, the wool is sold at half-yearly auctions in Liverpool. Therewith there is a special class of wool-buyers necessary in Bradford, who attend to the mixing and combing of the wool on commission. Both occupations have; throughout, the character of a season business. They are done during one part of the year in day and night shifts, whereby the wages are low, and the conditions of labour are opposed to health. For instance, the wool-combers (one to every two combing machines), who labour, in the night shift, 60 hours per week at 120 deg. F., have no more than £1 per week, and lose 20 weeks in the year for want of work.

In economical development the worsted spinning and weaving of Bradford stands behind, compared with Lancashire ; 10,000 spindles are given me as the average number for the worsted-spinning mills of Yorkshire, and 60 to 100 looms for the average weaving-mills in Bradford. Where there are exceptionally large mills they do not depend upon the "limited" principle, which is in general little developed, but on the monopoly of some specialty or other. Hereto belong, for instance, the weaving-mills in Saltaire.

In the same way the conditions of labour in the worsted-spinning mills of Yorkshire and the "stuff goods" weaving-mills of Bradford are far below those in Lancashire. The female operatives in the spinning-mills do not earn above 10s. per week, and the weavers in Bradford between 7s. and 16s. The operatives' houses which I visited in Bradford, as well as in other places of Yorkshire, are far behind those in Lancashire. Especially frequent are the so-called back-to-back houses, which have no back yard, and often enough have only two rooms, one above the other —the older type of English operatives' houses, which in Lancashire are dying out more and more. But, remarkably enough, these houses are not only relatively, but frequently absolutely, dearer than in Lancashire, since the operative here did not understand, by means of co-operative building societies, to press down rents in general (1).

The operatives are less organised, and remarkably enough Bradford is the only place where, for the coming Parliamentary elections, special Labour candidates are in the field, whilst otherwise, as is well known, the operatives in England attend to their interests within the political parties. The relation between employed and employers is extremely strained, and reminds one of the conditions of those German mill districts in which the labour movement has severed the relations of olden times. But especially hated is the relation, in those gigantic concerns above mentioned, which outwardly kept up the old patriarchal dominion.

A peculiar light flashes upon the state of affairs if we consider that it does not here by any means depend upon a staple industry fostered by export, which, like that of Lancashire, dominates in its branch the world's market.

As is known, there exists between the German and English worsted industries certainly a far-reaching division of labour, which prevents them in many respects from being close and immediate competitors. We shall not, however, be far wrong, looking at everything all round, if we view the German and English industries in this branch as equally important in economical development. Therewith there are similar social conditions between

---

1. Thus the operatives' dwellings in Manningham, near Bradford, are not only far worse, but in fact dearer, than those in Oldham—4s. 6d. to 5s. 6d. per week, against 3s. 6d. to 4s. 6d. A better-class dwelling-house, which in Oldham or Hyde would cost 6s. per week, cannot be got in Bradford under 8s.

both; therewith the difference between Bradford and Lancashire, although both are only separated by an hour's railway journey.

But still further proofs of the dependence of the social on economical conditions are shown by the industry of Yorkshire. In different districts of this county woollen weaving still exists as a cottage industry, as in Oldham, Skelmanthorpe, Clayton West, Scisset, and Darby Dale. The position of the hand-weavers still employed here reminded me in many respects about what has been said regarding the hand-weaving of Lancashire in the "thirties." While at the present time in Lancashire we only discover with difficulty the last examples of this once numerous class, they still form in Yorkshire the main population of the small weaving villages mentioned; and although, indeed, children can scarcely be taught it any longer, the complete dying-out of hand-weaving may still extend to another generation. . The number of hand-weavers in the woollen industry may, however, even to-day, not reach to above a few hundreds.

The woollen spinning and weaving, economically and socially little advanced, which has its seat in and about Leeds, is also, as well, dispersed in small undertakings. The average size of these spinning-mills is only from 2,000 to 3,000 spindles; of the weaving-mills, only 40 to 50 looms. In most cases the mills prepare the yarn, or a portion of it, for their own use. The largest spinning-mill in Batley has, for instance, no more than 7,680 spindles. Differently from worsted yarns, woollen yarns are spun with a machine similar to the self-actor in the cotton industry. I noticed, in visiting several of these woollen-spinning mills, what a large number of operatives were required in comparison with Lancashire. A pair of mules here has no more than 600 to 800 spindles, but there are, however, 3 to 4 operatives for minding them; added to which comes the spinner as well, who looks after two pairs of mules—i.e., 1,200 to 1,600 spindles. In the same ratio the wages are lower than in Lancashire, and the labour conditions, although, on account of the small mills, not so extreme as in Bradford, are just as little desirable. In the same manner, the woollen weaving is by no means involved in the world's market, and solely satisfies a limited and entirely home demand.

On the other hand, there is within the whole English woollen and worsted industry only one branch which, in the same way as the staple industry of Lancashire, maintains the front rank in the world's market—the weaving of those fine worsteds for men's clothing in and about Huddersfield. And, as a peculiar confirmation of our proposition, Huddersfield not only pays the best wages within the whole woollen and worsted industry of England, but its social conditions are the most advanced, and show, as well, much similarity with Lancashire, which, the further one goes into Yorkshire, the more does it disappear.

The weaver in Huddersfield earns double as much as the weaver in Bradford (20s. to 24s.). If he does not also mind more looms than the weaver in Bradford—mostly one, exceptionally two—the machinery to be tended by him is certainly far more complicated and costly.   A loom in Huddersfield represents three times as much capital as a loom in Bradford; therefore here is also the more favourable position of the operatives to be attributed to a further developed replacement of labour by capital. But, on the other hand, Huddersfield is not only a famous centre of the co-operative movement, which early extended thereto from out of Lancashire, but also the seat and outlet of a trade-union organisation for the whole woollen and worsted industry, while the societies of the operatives in Bradford and Leeds still bear that semi-political and Radical character which always denotes the labour organisations in the first stage of centralised industrial development.

But, in order to see the most striking confirmation of our proposition above given, let us go to Macclesfield, that ancient little town in Cheshire, which is the seat of the English silk industry.

The technicalities of the English silk industry are the same as long ago. The principle of the industry is here in its widest extent still of a cottage-industrial character. The position of the hand-weavers is an extremely low one, and reminded me even of the bad cottage-industrial conditions in Germany. The ordinary weaver earns about 10s. per week. From this, however, a great portion is deducted for rent, loom, winding, etc. In any case, I confirmed a great many, and these not exceptional cases, in which not more than 5s. net per week was earned. Still worse is the extraordinary irregularity of work. Some of these silk-weavers assured me that they searched unsuccessfully for work several months, even half the year. The household budgets of these people, of which I made up several, reminded me of those of the Zittau hand-weavers mentioned by Rechenberg (2).

Interesting observations were made in this direction by a hand-weaver from Macclesfield, formerly president of the trade society of the hand-weavers—since dissolved—on a journey to the Continent in company with the President of the Macclesfield Chamber of Commerce (3). His report shows that the position of the hand-weavers in Macclesfield is worse than that of their like at Crefeld. "It is not to be denied," says the report, "that the hand-weavers of Crefeld are far better clothed than the weavers at Macclesfield" (page 24). "We came to the conclusion," continues the report, "that the average wages of the weavers at Crefeld were higher, and the standard of their social comfort was better, than in Macclesfield; that extreme poverty, in which a greater portion of our cottage weavers are involved, does not exist in Crefeld" (p. 26). On the other hand, the report says in regard to Macclesfield: "If lower wages are a means against the dying-out of an industry, Macclesfield ought to-day to be one of the most flourishing communities in the world" (page 38). "No silk weavers on the whole of the Continent have such long hours of labour as our weavers" (page 47).

In spite of all this it is not to be denied that the industry of Macclesfield is being strangled by a continuous decline; that it is beaten, especially by Crefeld, in the English market itself (4). This is due to various reasons. For one, the better accommo-dating of Crefeld to the taste of the market, especially of the London market, thanks to the better technical instruction, the superiority in designs and colours, etc. The consequences of these are that the weavers in Crefeld have far more regular employment, that they also receive longer warps than in Macclesfield (150 ells against 20 to 40 ells). The German industry possesses here, therefore, according to this report, in a peculiar degree that advantage, as far as this is possible in the branch of a hand and luxury industry, which otherwise in general (for instance, also

2. Compare pp. 42 and 43.

3. "A Macclesfield Handloom Silk Weaver at Lyons, Zürich, and Crefeld," 1886. The publication of the report of the journey was refused by the Chamber of Commerce at Macclesfield. For a glance at the report I am indebted to the gentleman who travelled with him.

4. Thus the report of the Travelling Commission closed with the words — "Give back to injured Macclesfield her trade, long lost to Crefeld."

in calico-printing) is in favour of England—the character of a staple industry.

But something else comes here into consideration, continues the report. The weavers at Crefeld are far more industrious and capable than those needy fellow-creatures who, in the streets of Macclesfield, often seek employment for weeks and months unsuccessfully. "One fact specially drew our attention: the Crefeld weavers do not bear that anxious and desponding expression of features of people who are to-day miserable, and are yet afraid of the next day. Just the opposite, they present an intellectual elasticity which, unfortunately, is not general among the weavers of Macclesfield" (p. 24). Respecting drinking, this is on the Rhine a form of sociability, in Macclesfield a vice. The weaver of Crefeld is different from his fellows in Macclesfield, thoughtful about saving time at his work—as a rule in other branches just the advantage of the Englishman compared with German operatives. But the greater capacity of the German silk-weavers comes all the more into consideration since he works on more valuable and better looms.

Therefore, to a certain extent, the advantage of high-standing labour shows itself in more perfected working tools; also on the field of cottage-industry. But in silk weaving, at present, the change to centralised industry has set itself into motion, and changes the cottage industrial conditions we have delineated by going over to the power-loom. Also on this new field the standard of living of the operatives in Germany appears by no means to be lower than in England, as is otherwise generally the case. As at the time of the great strike in the silk-plush weaving-mills of Lister, at Manningham, in 1891, the demand for lowering wages was founded by the directors on the fact that the wages would even still be far higher than in Germany, one of the chief representatives of the Crefeld industry in this branch addressed a letter to the "Bradford Observer," in which he proved that the corresponding weekly earnings of the operatives in Crefeld were not lower, but rather higher than in England (5).

---

5. The letter was as follows:—

"Sir,—In reference to the report of the annual meeting of Lister and Co., Limited, you gave in your paper of the 4th inst., it will perhaps be welcome to receive some rectification with regard to Crefeld weaving wages.

"The Chairman (Mr. S. C. Lister) said that in offering 14s. wages

However this may be, in any case the transition to the power-loom, which has also begun in Macclesfield, contains within it a step forward for the weaving population. The weekly earnings in the power weaving-mills of Macclesfield amount to more than double, even triple, the earnings of the hand-weavers. An ell of plain goods, 22 in. wide, costs therewith for weaving, on the hand-loom, 1s. 4d.; on the power-loom, 8d. On the other hand, a hand-loom represents a value of £8 to £10; a power-loom—i.e., only the working machine, exclusive of building and driving-power—£30 to £35. Therefore also here appears replacement of labour by capital, and therewith a raising of the standard of living of the operative.

This tendency of centralised industry shows itself also in that the aristocracy of labour in Macclesfield, apart from the power-weaving only just rising up, has its seat in the silk-spinning mills, centralised industrial concerns which, far superior, look down upon the surrounding weavers' cots (6).

If we glance back at what has been said, we can extract from it the following· confirmation of our views developed above:—

1. The weekly earnings and the standard of living of the operative in the English cotton industry is about double as high

and 15 per cent.—which was equal to 16s. 3d. per week—the directors of the company were offering just double what the Crefeld manufacturers were paying to their velvet weavers. In stating this Mr. Lister shows himself to be very badly informed. The weavers in our factory can easily earn 20s. to 21s. a week, and those who are rather skilful earn 26s. to 28s. a week (56 to 60 hours' work), some even more. All large Crefeld manufacturers pay about the same wages.—I am, etc.,
" Crefeld, 16th Feb., 1891.   " M. DE GREIFF."

6. Also in another branch, akin to the textile industry, which seemed up to now in a hopeless condition, the appearing centralisation has improved at last the conditions of working. The misery of the female workers in made-up clothing and dressmaking is well known. Centralised industry in the last ten years has seized this branch of industry. and presses hard the cottage industry in articles of general consumption. In Leeds, the centre of this industry, there are to-day about 20 clothing establishments. If we visit the largest we find a tremendous building, reminding us of the largest spinning-mills of Lancashire. One thousand three hundred and fifty girls and 300 men are at work; up to forty folds of cloth are cut through at one operation by the machine; 10,000 to 13,000 suits are made per week. All labour is accomplished by the most improved machinery, of which, for instance, the button-hole machine makes a button-hole and hems it with thick stitches in 25 to 30 seconds. The operatives who mind these machines are not only occupied under better working conditions as to ventilation, etc., but are also paid far higher wages than the tailoresses working without mechanical power.

as in the woollen and worsted industry; in the latter about double as high as in silk-weaving at Macclesfield. Corresponding to this, the cotton industry is the oldest and one of the most developed centralised industries of the world. The English woollen and worsted industry is economically not so far advanced; it stands, as it were, in certain respects on that first step of centralised-industrial development we have so often spoken of. Corresponding to this is the degree of social development; in it to-day preponderates class struggle and class hatred, as opposed to the highly-developed conditions of labour in Lancashire, where the period of class struggles falls back into the "thirties" and "forties." Finally, the silk industry shows, along with the worst position of the operatives, also technical conditions remaining extraordinarily backward.

2. The position of the operatives of the German cotton industry is far lower than that of their contemporaries in Lancashire. In the woollen industry the English stand only a little above the German ; decidedly higher only in the district of Huddersfield.   In the silk industry the German operatives enjoy rather a better standard of living than the English.   On the other hand, the English cotton industry in neutral markets is far ahead of the German. In woollen and worsted both stand about equal ; only the Huddersfield industry is superior in foreign competition.   On the other hand the German silk industry is driving back the English in its own country.

3. England, as the more economically advanced country, has its strength on that field of the textile industry in which labour and capital mean almost everything, and the raw material is of far less value in the articles produced. The younger but upward-striving industrial country has thrown itself first, with the greatest success, on textile productions in which material as compared with labour and capital come largely into consideration, both of which latter production elements are cheaper in England than in Germany.   Therewith England produces more goods for the million, Germany goods for the use of the wealthy classes. The first demand centralised undertakings in the highest degree, the latter, on account of the vagaries of fashion, taste, etc., are identified easiest with smaller undertakings.

The highest standard of living of the working classes, therefore, shows highly developed exporting centralised industries, the reason for which, as above ascertained, lies in the continuous replacement of a church, the prominent features of which are apparent far out of labour by capital. But from this follows the refutation of an objection which has perhaps been met with above by many readers. For instance, readers perhaps ask, Do not some of the operatives have their means of livelihood withdrawn by the continuous replacement of labour by capital? If one operative attends to as many machines as formerly three operatives, the one may well receive a higher wage, but what becomes of the other two? We saw, opposed to this, how that development was just only possible on the ground of economical elevation of the industry concerned. The English silk industry cannot, in consequence, go over to the power-loom, because its market is not stable; the elevation of the cotton industry, on the other hand, in spite of all technical progress, allowed an increase in the number of operatives. There were in 1835, 220,134 operatives, against 504,069 in 1885, engaged in it.

I should like to avoid a further misunderstanding—that is, that I neglect, concerning the economical development, the importance of social moments. When I pictured those social movements by means of which the English operative has attained his present height, especially the change of public opinion accompanying this development, I found already the necessity of proving the economical correctness of this development. If one up to then could not object that the high standard of living of the English operative was built upon certain foundations; that it would become untenable with the rise of competing industries in countries of so-called cheaper labour; that it must become forced back by the pressure of the world's market, I tried, on the contrary, in what has gone before to prove, on the field of the oldest centralised industry of the world, how it was just the pressure of the world's market to which centralised industry and machine-making were indebted for their origin, and how the continual development of both necessitated an elevation of the classes serving them. If the economical correctness of social progress is maintained, this is not to be understood as if the social progress is always or only frequently caused from a known understanding of its economical advantages. In this respect those earlier social movements had, alongside, at least a strong influence.

Allow me to make use of a scene to throw some light on this relation. The height which certain classes of skilled English industrial workers have reached is similar to the towering steeple in the moving sea, showing the discouraged captain the way to the harbour through storm and waves.   That steeple rests upon columns, of which no slight portion has been erected by the benevolence of the citizens.   But these columns would not bear the steeple, and the benevolence of the citizens would avail nothing, if the building, instead of being on sure rocks, was erected on shifting sands.   Similarly, all social movements are fruitless without a powerful economical foundation of strong and technically progressive centralised industries.